Praying For The Darkness

Dr. Christopher Cortman

Blue Ocean Press
Tokyo

Published by:
Blue Ocean Press

Japan Office
6F & 7F TOC Daiichi Bldg.
1-8-3 Shibuya
Shibuya-ku, Tokyo, Japan 150-0002

URL: http://www.blueoceanpublications.com
Email: books@blueoceanpublications.com

ISBN: 978-4-902837-38-4

DEDICATION

This book is dedicated to the numerous survivors of satanic ritual abuse who courageously shared their stories with me in the hope of healing:

K.S., D.L., C.G., B.B., A.K., J.F., B.E., L.F., L.M., T.O., D.C., J.K., C.B., E.R., J.A., B.A., C.H., J.H., H.M., B.H., J.S., P.S., P.A., andD.C.

Your remarkable capacity to survive and even triumph has touched me more than you'll ever know. You are the people I admire most, for you are the bravest individuals I have ever met.

PREFACE

When it comes to the topic of recovered memories, the fields of psychiatry and psychology appear as a house divided against itself.

Many practitioners have stumbled upon at least one credible patient who spontaneously "recovers' long- repressed (forgotten) memories of childhood horror and abuse. The remembering of these incidents, along with expressing the accompanying appropriate emotion, seems to afford the patient the capacity to release toxic feelings and begin a journey of healing.

But along comes a group, the False Memory Society (FMSF), who make a persuasive claim that memory can be altered, tampered with, or even created by people of influence upon suggestible others. The natural by-product of such claims, of course, is the notion that psychotherapists, intentionally or not, may be guilty of creating "false memories" for their clients. Perhaps worse still, these false memories contribute to serious allegations against parents and other innocent adults of abuse of all sorts, especially sexual.

Granted, some less competent practitioners have encouraged the creation and/or embellishment of accountsof childhood abuse and attracted media attention. The resulting skepticism casts doubt over all recovered memories, genuine or not. Likewise, therapists who have facilitated a client's recovery of legitimately repressed memory have also come under fire.

While resolving this issue is beyond the scope of this book, my intention is to illustrate that the mind, for reasons of self-protection, has the capacity to repress traumatic material, create discrete storage compartments (alter personalities), and tuck away memories forever or until stimulated later in life.

This book also explores other controversial issues within (and without) the mental health field: the concept of true multiple personality disorder (dissociative identity disorder); the existence of devil-worshipping cults comprised of people of money, power, andinfluence; the spiritual reality of God, Satan, and demonic forces, and the impact of such upon human beings.

My purpose is not to settle controversies but to describe what happened to me and around me--a psychologist--in the course of treating several similarly afflicted patients.

This book is not for the faint of heart. Yet woven throughout the material is hope, courage, andinspiration.

Although I have changed all names and identifying details of my patients for purposes of confidentiality, the book is based *entirely* on actual events.

I would like to thank these individuals for their permission to share the compelling events of their lives. Here are their stories.

ACKNOWLEDGMENTS

With deep appreciation and thanksgiving, I recognize the following people for aiding me in the development of this book: my now-retired office manager, June Frega, for countless hours of typing, retyping, and re-retyping this manuscript from a notebook full of illegible cursive.

Through it all you provided helpful critique, generous doses of excitement, praise, friendship, and love. And, oh yes, you still managed to get all the office work done and keep the practice afloat. May God bless you with great health and longevity until the day He brings you home to run His office.

To my editor, Laurie Rosin, a special thank-you for believing in me and this project from the beginning. I presented myself initially as a little boy on a new Schwinn with training wheels, afraid to ride and even more afraid to fall. You comforted me with your soothing words of confidence, for after all, you are an expert rider. And although I hit a few potholes and dead ends along the way, your gentle guidance and kind leadership always led me back on track. So, thanks to you I'm now riding while gleefully exclaiming, "Look, Laurie, no hands!" Kudos also to your staff, especially the "TroodleMeister," who became someone fun to call and E-mail as the project progressed.

To my clients who read chapters and contributed helpful feedback, again I thank you for your pearls of insight. You know my subject matter far better than I do, and I appreciate the donation of your time, effort, and knowledge. Thank you, P.A., J. A. B., K. C. M., J. H., J.K., and J.F.

A thank-you to all my friends, especially Marc, Glenn,

Bob, Neil and Sally, Mu, Eddie, Losty, Perryhead, Fred, Cathy, Tony, Paul, Kenny, David, Michael, and others for your tireless questions of "How's the book coming?" and "Am I in it?" as well as encouragement and support from the outset. I'd also like to request that each of you buya copy, so my mother won't be the only one.

To my family members, including in-laws and out-laws, I thank God always for the privilege of having you in my life. Now I thank you for the love and devotion that only a family can give. Thank you, Dad, for allowing me to say less than flattering things about our relationship. Youare more important to me now than ever before, Mom, sorry about the choice of topics. I know you would have preferred a "Venus and Mars" bestseller to a book on satanic cults. Please understand that this was a story I had to tell. Maybe you can pick the next one.

What do I say about my sweet Laura, the person who not only tolerated my living this story, but then re-living it through the written word? Thanks for listeningtomy chapters over and over, until admitting that you had committed them to memory. Thank you for the many weekends that you afforded me hours of freedom to write while you.

Say, what didyou do during those hours? Seriously, Iamforeverindebtedtoyouforall you do and all you are. I love you!

And finally, I tearfully acknowledge my late brother, Vinny, who passed away on February 7, 2000, of congestive heart failure. For those of us who knewyou, your disease was a misnomer: your body may have failed you, but your heart remained true. God bless you in your new life!

TABLE OF CONTENTS

Chapter 1

The Body Follows the Mind

"Just let yourself relax and drop deeper, deeper into a hypnotic trance ... still deeper, more relaxed. You're safe here. It's okay. Just let yourself go."

I didn't know what to expect as I watched Shirley McIntyre's head loll against the recliner's high back. Her hands rested comfortably on the mauve leather arms, and the well-worn soles of her sandals--angled heels in, toes out-- on the footrest indicated total relaxation.

She left no clue as to where she might take me this session. In the eleven months since Shirley had first walked into my office for psychotherapy, her case had become progressively more disturbing. She had begun with memories of incestuous relations perpetrated by amonstrous father and before long had introduced me to the bizarre world of Multiple Personality Disorder (now called Dissociative Identity Disorder or DID). Once thought to be one of the rarest of psychiatric disorders, DID is now frequently discovered in cases of severe childhood trauma. And from what I was learning about Shirley, she certainly qualified to be described as a survivor of severeabuse.

My gaze moved up from her sandals and along herpetite frame to her protruding belly. She looked as if she were at least seven months pregnant. I couldn't take my eyes off her stomach. *How could this happen?* I asked myself. Shirley was well beyond the normal childbearing years and had a hysterectomy many years before. Today was Friday, and when I had seen her on Tuesday, her abdomen was perfectly flat.

This was no trick. She had brought me a Polaroid photograph of her distended belly, without clothes, as proof. Where was I when they taught about this in graduate school?

As Shirley descended into a deep trance, her eyes rolled back into her head, suggesting her apparent cooperation with the induction. Like other DID patients waging similar horrific battles with their past, she was easy to hypnotize. The relaxed, deep state of concentration known as hypnosis seemed to come naturally. As she fell into trance, I found myself also drifting, back to the time last March when first we met...

I was treating a disproportionately large number of survivors of childhood sexual abuse in my practice in Sarasota, Florida. A sophisticated small town between the Gulf of Mexico and Sarasota Bay, it was called the Athens of Florida. The resort community boasted its own ballet, world-class opera, and live theater galore. Possibly people gravitated to this county of sun, sand, and exotic flowers because their inner life was so bleak. Some of my clients had no conscious knowledge of abuse upon entering therapy but began "recovering horrific memories only after forming a safe alliance with me.

I began lecturing on this topic--"Healing from Childhood Sexual Abuse"--for the community at large. One evening after presenting at a local hospital, I saw Shirley waiting patiently off to the side of the foyer until the last of the crowd had expressed their appreciation and had filed out. A prematurely gray-haired woman in faded jeans and a clean but well-worn T-shirt, she handed me a note featuring one line of scribble, reading: "Please help me."

Admittedly I took pity on this woman who had neither the capacity to express her plea aloud nor the wherewithal to hold eye contact. Instead, she stared down at her Ked's as if they might run off without her. I exchanged a business card for her note and instructed her to call the office and make an appointment. I promised I'd do my best. At that time, I was completely unaware that I was vowing to scale the Mount Everest of therapy cases.

Shortly afterwards, Shirley confessed that she had known intuitively during the lecture that I would nothurt her. During our third session together she announced, "I remember what you look like."

"What does it suggest--that you can remember how I look?"

"It means I don't have to look past you. I can look at you. For the first time in my life, I'm willing to trust someone. Don't let me down." Shirley lifted her dark brown eyes from the floor to meet mine--the longest period she had sustained eye contact to this point.

Shirley was a no-nonsense lady, hardened by many years of abuse so severe I found it almost incomprehensible. Her recovery, it seemed, meant everything to her. Thirteen years of sobriety from alcohol and drug addiction preceded our initial meeting. These facts convinced me very early in our relationship that she truly wanted help.

Shirley did not phone me between sessions except for emergencies. Her Wednesday call, however, had seemed entirely unnecessary. Her naturally deep voice ascended an octave as she blurted, "Did you notice if I was fat yesterday?"

"No, you didn't look fat yesterday," I replied evenly. If Shirley weighed 110 pounds on her five-foot-two frame, I'd be surprised.

"Well, I look seven months pregnant!"

"You look seven months pregnant, or you *feel* like you are?" I wanted to give her an out.

"No, I *look* seven months pregnant."

"Okay, Why don't you take some Polaroids and try to hang in for two more days? You have an appointment on Friday, and we can have a double session if you like.

I wanted to laugh. It had been a long time since anyone other than the tabloids had boasted of an immaculate conception. And even they never claimed that the gestation period could be compacted into one day. But I had learned never to doubt Shirley. Her yea was yea, and her nay was nay. If Shirley said she looked pregnant, I knew I had better brace myself.

That Friday, I greeted Shirley with anticipatory anxiety, feelings I normally reserve for sporting events. It was hard to remain anxious, as the sight of her lumbering toward me with her swollen belly in one ofthose maternity dresses, with her gray hair, proved to be too entertaining for me to contain a smile.

"Oh, my God, Shirley, *could* you be pregnant?" Iasked, my IQ temporarily reduced to the level of potatosalad.

She quickly forgave my gaffe, and even managed an awkward laugh. Now, we journeyed into Shirley's unconscious mind. "Take me where you need to," I requested, convinced that she was prepared to access whatever information we needed to release her pain and resume control over her body.

"Okay, I think I'm there." "How old are you, Shirley?" "It's not Shirley. I'm Linda."

"Oh, hi, Linda." Linda was a twelve-year-old alter personality whom I had met only a week before. She'd mentioned that she helped Shirley deal with life whenever she was "fat--especially when she was pregnant." Linda was protective of Shirley, as are all alter personalities.

"Where are you, Linda?"

"She's on the table." Linda spoke in the third person, as alter personalities frequently do. This would increase the likelihood that Shirley could later recall whatever she needed to without falling apart emotionally. Simply put, "if the horror happened to someone else and not me, then it's not so bad."

"Are you alone?"

"No, the cult ladies are there: Myra, Ellen, and Shirley. They're all there. Shirley hated Myra. She's so mean to us. *Cult ladies?* I wondered. "What's happening, Linda?" "They got her tied down to the table in the kitchen at Myra's house. They're mad at her 'cause she's pregnant. It's a joke, you know what I mean?"

"No, what do you mean?"

"I mean they're the ones who *got* her pregnant. The guys in the group."

What group?

"They have sex with anyone they want to," Linda continued. "But it's our fault 'cause we're pregnant."

This time Linda/Shirley was referring to herself in the first-person plural, also common among multiple personalities.

"How are they blaming you?"

"The name calling. Myra is the worst." Linda winced in pain as she recreated the onslaught of verbal assaults from Myra. "Hurry up, you little whore, we haven't got all day.

Spread your ugly pussy, bitch. The Master awaits the little one."

"Be brave," I said, hoping to offer Shirley and her alters a word of encouragement. "I'm still here. Thiswill be over soon."

Although Shirley's face had been etched by a hard life, I still felt as if I were addressing the child onthe cold metal table.

"What now, Linda?"

"Myra is still at it. 'Maybe next time you'll learn to keep your fucking legs together, you little slut!'"

"What about your mother?"

"Oh, she's right there with the others. Not as mean as Myra, though." Although this was not Shirley's first uncovering of a repressed horror story, I was still unnerved to hear that a mother, any mother, could allow this type of abuse. But one thing was evident: Shirley believed what she was telling me.

"What's happening now?" I really didn't want to know. I would have preferred to stop, bring Shirley back to the present, and tell her to forget the whole thing. But my experiences in treating the Shirleys of this world had taught me that *they* would dictate what they needed to share in order to heal. My job was to provide a safe environment for them to accomplish that. If I brought her back for my comfort, she would walk out with a swollen belly and little in the way of relief. We pressed onward.

"They're giving her something… a shot. Ellen is a nurse. Oh, they're trying to induce labor. 'You're an embarrassment to all of us, you fucking tramp.' I can't believe what they're doing. They're beating on her with kitchen utensils. I mean, like Shirley's mom has an eggbeater and they're pushing on her stomach and trying to get the baby out."

My stomach waged a war with nausea. "And what about you? How are you feeling, Linda?"

"Completely numb. I am there to absorb all the pain, so Shirley feels nothing."

As she relived the event, Shirley's breathing became so intense, I half expected to deliver my first child. Sweat poured down her pale white cheeks as she exhaled shallow, rapid breaths, the way actresses do when their movie role has them about to give birth.

But there was no live baby in the office. Andthere was no live baby born to Shirley.

"It's not breathing," Linda continued in a detached narration. "Myra's complaining that the fuckin' cord is wrapped around his damn neck. 'He's dead, for chrissakes. Your daughter can't do a fuckin' thing right, now canshe?'

"Shirley's mom never defended her, Linda said tightly. "Never said a thing. Then the ladies took a sharp knife and began to chop the dead baby into pieces while they taunted Shirley. Myra was the loudest. 'You're not only a useless little slut, you're also a fuckin'murderer, Shirley. You killed your own boy. Now how 'bout that?'

"Then the ladies placed the parts of the dismembered little boy on Shirley's naked body." Linda paused. "She could feel the blood pour down her sides and onto the floor."

Somewhere in the telling she suggested that Linda was now gone, and Shirley--the adult Shirley in myoffice--was now capable of owning the memory for herself. Linda had completed the task of carrying the memory and storing the feelings for more than thirty years. Her work was done. Myra, though, was not. She scored with one moresarcastic comment to share with Shirley as she led the ladies from the room. "Why don't we give the mother some time alone with her new baby, eh, girls?"

The snickering women filed out, leaving Shirley alone to cry.

And cry she did in the office, sobbing and pouring out tears as I handed her tissues one after another until she was ready to return to the present, the reclining chair, and the office.

I was relieved to see the tears flow. I always am. Tears typically convey that we have located the source of our emotional pain, and the expression of that pain contains the promise of the beginning of healing.

After a while, Shirley blew her nose and calmed down. She knew her assignment even without my suggesting it-- saying good-bye to the baby. I reinforced the need to express her sorrow and attempt to make peace with the tragedy. She hugged me and thanked me for the help. Her stomach seemed somewhat smaller, but Shirley still looked pregnant when she left. Rarely had I given anyone a tougher assignment.

Shirley said good-bye to her infant in a letter. She seemed to find solace in the notion that her child now belonged to God and that she would someday be reunited with the newborn. She gave him a name, Mark--an identity to validate his brief existence and the profound way he touched her life. The sincerity of her letter and Shirley's simple belief in a reunion touches me to this day.

When she appeared the following Tuesday with her stomach flattened and back to normal, we were both relieved. And I must admit I was excited to share the account with my colleagues, none of whom had ever heard of such a thing. Fortunately for me, no one scoffed at my account.

But one psychiatrist seemed to say it best when she offered me her explanation for Shirley's pseudo-pregnancy: "The body follows the mind."

And Shirley? Seven years later, she still shows no indication of any protruding stomach or problems related to this incident.

But she was far from finished with remembering the bizarre and the horrific.

Chapter 2

The Tell and the Denier

I find it difficult to spend a fifty-minute session with a client without experiencing some change in my energy level. The more exciting and challenging cases, characterized by a significant investment from the individual, tend to energize me. Conversely, non-motivated patients--people who prefer the world to change so they won't have to--can deplete my energy.

On this day, the fourth time I would see Shirley after the pseudopregnancy, I opened the morning with an evaluation of a new client. An underachieving late adolescent, she had dropped out of high school the day she turned sixteen. Depressed and addicted to virtually everything from alcohol to nicotine to cocaine, she proved to be a highly motivated patient. We seemed to hit it off, and the girl apparently left our initial session with an inkling of hope, which in turn produced in me a powerful adrenaline surge and a confirmation as to why I had wanted to be a therapist in the first place.

And then came Shirley.

Small talk passed faster than a Florida winter and left both of us seemingly eager to get to work.

"I'm thinking about moving away," she opened, with a casual delivery that belied the significance of her words.
I provided the animation. "You mean out of the state?

What led to that idea?"

"My dad is here, that's why."

"And?" Sometimes there is no more effective question. "As long as he's here, there's always danger."

"What kind of danger, Shirley? How is he a threat to you currently?"

"You don't understand, do you?" She bore a pathetic look, her eyes fallen, her deeply creased forehead heldup by her trembling left hand.

"I suppose I don't. I do understand that your father severely abused you as a child. I know he wounded you physically, sexually, and emotionally--to the point that you were incapable of handling the trauma yourself. I also understand that you managed to survive by creating other people to help you bear the horror of it. And I'm learning that you are remembering many of those experiences lately. But why is your dad a threat now? You're an adult and can set boundaries. You have the right to restrict his visits or eliminate them altogether. You are not a helpless child anymore, Shirley."

My well-intentioned pep talk, designed to empower Shirley to assume some control over her family relations, was a wasted effort. I might as well have been reciting the Gettysburg address in Japanese for all the impact it had on Shirley.

She turned her head toward the door, away from me and my floundering attempt to help her. We lost eye contact for what felt like two full minutes. I didn't know how to respond to the body language, so I elected to do nothing.
At least I wouldn't be doing any harm, I told myself. I could feel some of my energy draining into an almost visible puddle of helplessness.

At last, she returned her gaze to meet mine. But she wasn't Shirley any longer. The troubled, insecure expression that labored to maintain eye contact had been replaced by a confident, purposeful expression. She spoke easily, as if she were the rising star in a public- relations firm.

"Chris, it's time for us to meet. The people inside call me the Teller because I am capable of providing information on the inner workings of Shirley's mind. You will need to consult often with me if she is to continueto share her life with you."

"Okay, I appreciate that," said I, excited that I had stumbled upon the jackpot--Shirley's alter personality that could serve as a compass, ensuring that I never veered too far off-course. (This aspect of self is not unusual among multiples; called the Inner Self Helper [ISH], the phenomenon is commonly reported in the literature on multiples.)

"Teller, may I ask you a question then? What's going on now that she feels a need to move?"

"Do you remember when she came in here looking pregnant?"

I nodded while fending off a powerful urge to respond sarcastically. I knew I would forever carry the memory of her incredible swelling and story of horror.

"Well, her father was a participant in that group Linda spoke of. For all we know, he may still beinvolved.
He still visits Shirley when he likes. And merely by looking in her eyes and speaking sternly well, she becomes that helpless child again. There is no fight, no 'boundaries,' as you say. He merely imposes his will upon her. Try to understand."

"Back up a minute. I don't understand anything about this group. Linda mentioned a cult. What kind of organization is this?" I kicked off my loafers and leaned back in my chair, almost bracing myself for whatever response she might deliver. I had waited two weeks now to find an appropriate moment to follow up on her flashback about the delivery and mutilation of the baby.

"She's not ready to hear any of this, Chris, so I need you to keep it a secret from her."

Again, I nodded, despite my complete awareness of being asked to keep a secret from the same human being who was sharing it with me.

"Shirley was born into a family of people who worship the devil. The group extends beyond her family, to a lot of powerful and influential people in New England. Like the other children, she was subjected to cruelty and torture. Only the survivors are considered worthy of devotion to the Master. The weak are weeded out and destroyed."

Master? I thought. There's that word again. Linda mentioned it in regard to preparing the baby for something, but the child never drew a breath. I gathered their idea of a master is Satan, the Prince of Darkness whom I first learned of in Sunday school. I shuddered at the implication that people of power and influence--anyone, for that matter--would bend a knee toward the devil in worship.

The Teller continued. "Shirley was a quick study and managed to survive virtually anything that the group members conjured up as a test. But she had a great deal of support. There are many of us she knows nothing of. We all helped her to excel within the group. This proved to be a good thing for her father, who was promoted consistently within the order."

"You're saying that this is a formal group with rules and positions and roles for the members?" I preferred to believe that if any such group did exist, it was comprised of disorganized, uneducated misfits on the fringes of society.

"Oh, yes," she responded matter-of-factly, "this is a formal association not only in New England but throughout the country. The group is entirely secretive, with severe penalties delivered to anyone who betrays the code of silence. Please understand that I am taking Shirley's life in my hands by sharing this information with you. And yours, too. You must tell no one about this."

"I am obligated, as you know, to maintain confidentiality on all the information you share with me, from the trivial to the most personal. But in what way is your life in jeopardy by telling me? And what about mine?"

"Chris, I can't tell you any more about it right now. Just please take this very seriously." Without another word, the Teller closed her eyes and bowed her head as if conveying a moment of reverence.

Seconds later, her eyes flew open, then darted nervously about the room. Apparently, my client was momentarily disoriented as to her location. I watched as she gathered herself and gradually regained eye contact with her ever-amazed therapist.

But she still didn't seem like Shirley. This time she presented with a hardness, a school-girl defiance that afforded me little respect. "You're not gonna buy any of that bullshit, are you?" she challenged, an uncharacteristic smirk accompanying her aggressive speech. She placed her left hand upon my desk as she leaned forward in her chair.

Her intimidating stare captured my attention. "And to whom am I speaking?"

Her eyes shifted nervously. "Why is that always important to you? What does it matter who I am?"

I realized immediately that this part of Shirley had something to hide. I had no idea what.

"I don't know," I responded. "I guess I just prefer to know your name. Then I'll know how to greet you if we meet again."

"Well, I'd rather not say.

"That's fine," I replied mildly. "What brings you here to speak to me?"

"Nothing brings me here. I bring myself here." Defiance flashed from her eyes.

"And you probably want to accomplish somethingwhile you are here?"

"No, I don't want to accomplish anything. You need to realize that the Teller don't know shit. We don't know anything about any cult. She's just dumping a load of *crap* on you." She seemed to be gaining momentum as she continued, and her words spilled out in a rush."Teller does that to get attention, that's all."

"So, Teller's job is to make up tall tales to get attention, is that right?"

"Yeah, you got it." She relaxed a bit in the recliner, apparently confident in her resolve to extinguish any flames ignited by the Teller.

"So, you must have a role, also." without waiting for a response, I added, "I'd say by the sounds of things that you might be a Denier."

I was fishing. I'd read very little about multiples but remembered that many times such a role was not uncommon for at least one of the alters. But I did not anticipate her response to my conjecture.

Once again, the eyes darted anxiously about the room,

never approaching mine, before rolling back into her head and then snapping closed. They reopened seconds later, and the familiar, kind-but-defeated face that Shirley wore had returned. She shrugged as if to say, "So?"

"Shirley, is that you?" I inquired, feeling foolish to ask what sounded like such a silly question. She nodded.

"Do you remember... anything?"

She shook her head as her eyes welled up with tears. "What's the use?" she began as she reached for the tissues. "I don't even remember our sessions half the time! How is this supposed to be helping me if I don't even know what's going on in session?" She angrily tossed a tissue into the wastebasket near my desk.

A good question--one I didn't have an answer to. I would not dare tell her what had happened, not after the warning I'd received from the Teller. So, I muttered something about understanding how difficult and frustrating this had to be for her. I also promised her that when she was ready to know the information she had shared, she would.

I took her cash payment almost apologetically, wondering if I really deserved any compensation after turning Shirley away more confused than she had arrived.

And she wasn't the only one. I sat and pondered what I'd just observed: an alter preparing me for a personal Armageddon through revelations of organized cults, populated by high-powered Satan worshippers, andtop-secret information that jeopardized my life. Then another alter saying it wasn't so.

Whom to believe? I didn't know for sure, though the Teller seemed far more sincere than the Denier. But could any of that be true? Nah, I wanted to believe theDenier. But what about that pregnant belly? I was back to square one, not knowing where to take my stand.

But was it even my job to make up my mind about her truth? No, I decided quickly. My job was to facilitate Shirley's coming to her own resolution, finding her own truth. My purpose was to make it safe for her to quell the inner storm that was now raging after years of quiet.

But did I know what I was doing? I had no formal training in dissociative disorders and no other cases to fall back on.

Should I refer her elsewhere? I thought. There's a guy in Sarasota who… no, wait a minute. She unveiled this info to me for a reason. She thinks she's safe here. I won't hurt her, but can I really help her?

I had no time to ponder further. A young man of fifteen waited outside. He'd walked in on his father's suicide and needed some answers.

But today, all I seemed to have were questions.

Chapter 3

The Gynecologist

That week I had been challenged with more than my share of unusual cases. First there was Joseph, a budding gynecologist. Polite and gracious with a gentle bedside manner, Joseph had difficulty understanding all the panic that his examinations had generated. A small but growing caseload of young females sought his services. Most lived in his immediate neighborhood; all were word-of-mouth referrals. There was just one problem with Dr. Joseph's practice--he was five years old.

A brief history of Joseph and his family, detailed by his mother, Carla, yielded nothing unusual--no reported abuse of any kind.

"It is normal for boys of Joseph's age to play doctor," I told his gum-chewing mother. "But few kindergartners operate walk-in clinics. He must be very good."

Carla allowed herself what might have been her first genuine smile since walking in on her son's latest examination.

Carla confessed, "I was horrified, walking in on them and seeing Joey with his toy stethoscope on Ginny's chest. She was just sitting on the bed, as naked as a jaybird, with her legs spread wide. I don't know where he was going next." The tension returned to her face, and her eyes filled with tears.

"How did you react?"

"Pretty well, I think. I tried not to shame either one of them. I told Joey it was time to eat lunch and suggested to

Ginny that she put her clothes back on. I walked her home, and when I returned, I asked Joey what he was up to.

He said, 'I'm gonna be a doctor like Uncle Mike'--his father's brother. He couldn't tell me how many patients he has, but he named five of the neighborhood girls."

"Does he see them all in his bedroom?" As I took notes, I wondered if he was the rare doctor who made house calls.

"I don't know. I can't imagine he's done all of this right under my nose. We have a lot of children in the neighborhood--not just girls--and many come over to play at my house. I know one thing--they won't be playing in there with the door closed anymore!"

"I'm sure that's a fine idea. You've done well to not humiliate Joey. Don't allow this to create a perception of yourself as a neglectful parent. These things happen because kids are curious, not because parents areteaching the wrong things, you know?" I decided to cap off my lecture with one more shot at humor to encourage Carla to relax. "'What's he charge anyway?"

Carla snickered. "I don't know, but I haven't seen a dime of it. I should charge him a rental fee, shouldn't I?" Now she was cracking the jokes ... a good sign.

I ushered Carla to the waiting area to meet Joey. A perfect little gentleman in a plaid shirt and little boy blue shorts, Joey peered up from his *Highlights* magazine, where he was trying to circle as many kitchen appliances "hidden in a tree as he could. I noted that Joey was better dressed than Carla, another clear indicator that neglect was not an obvious issue here. Joey sparkled at our introduction, and when I escorted him into to my office, he plopped down on the couch as if he had done it a thousand times before. The boy was adorable, with his mom's dark eyes, and little nostrils that grew larger when he spoke.

"I hear you're quite a doctor," I began.

"Yup, I eszamin people with my stettascope," he offered proudly.

"What else do you do with your patients, Joey?"

"Nothin'. That's it."

"Where do you put your stethoscope, Joey?"

"On their tummies." Joey pointed to his entire torso. "Anywhere else?" I was as gentle and nonthreatening as I knew how to be.

Joey swallowed hard and exhaled. This was going to be tough. "Sometimes I eszamin their privates, but you know what?"

"What, Joey?" I couldn't imagine what.

"Girls don't have pee-pees," he said earnestly. "Boys have pee-pees. Girls don't."

I dared to go further. "What do girls have, Joey?"

He frowned to think. "Nothing. There's nothing there."

Admittedly, I was speechless for a moment. "So, do you touch the patients in their private areas?"

"Only with the stettascope." He was assuring me that all his procedures were medically sound and of the highest ethical standards.

"Do they ever touch you, Joey?"

"No."

"How come?"

Joey thought a minute and shrugged "Cause I'm the doctor." This was conveyed proudly.

"I see. Well, do you have a medical license, Joey?"

Joey looked at me as if I'd just asked him to spell

stethoscope.

"Uh… what's that?"

I knew I had him. "You know, a medical license. Every doctor has to have a license, you know." I continued to lay it on thick because he stared wide-eyed at me with this new revelation. "See mine on the wall there? Let's go read it." I read the license word for word to him, so he knew that I, unlike him, was the Real McCoy.

I continued with a very concerned look on my mug. "You see, Joey, you can't do examinations if you don't have a medical license. Do you drive a car?" I went for the analogy.

"No."

"Why not?"

"Cause, I can't see over the wheel yet, and Mom won't let me."

Not really what I was hoping for. "You need a license to drive a car," I said, "and you have to be sixteen years old to get your license. You also need a license to be a doctor. If you don't have a license, Joey, you can't do examinations. You would be breaking the law, and you'd get into a lot of trouble!"

I could see concern, if not fear, on Joey's precious face, which I believed was necessary only to make my point. Now it was time to bring him down.

"You and I are friends, right?" He nodded.

"Well, I'm not gonna tell anybody about the examinations that you've done, but I need your promise not to examine any more people until you get your medical license.

Do you understand?"

"Uh-huh."

"Do you promise?" "Yes."

"No more examinations, okay?" "Okay."

I explained to Carla in Joey's presence what Joey and I had concluded together for two reasons: to reiterate to Joey the agreement made and to explain to Carla what had transpired.

As Carla and Joey left, I sensed their relief. I smiled at the fun I had just had and laughed to myself at this little guy who could get girls to come into his room and take off their clothes with the old, "Trust me, I'm a doctor" routine. I considered his wisdom in treating *young* patients, so he wouldn't have to deal withMedicare.

And then there was Shirley. We had been seeing each other twice a week for a total of three fifty-minute hours, and almost without exception the content of our sessions were becoming increasingly gruesome. She shared reported memories of repeated rapes by her father and his best friend, Jim; horrific infanticides in rituals to appease their "master" and the emergence of several alter personalities previously unknown to Shirley and me. One more alter activity marked this eventful week ofsessions.

Only a few months after Shirley's pseudopregnancy,she dealt herself another difficult hand.

"Look at this," she moaned in a self-defeated tone. "Can you believe this thing?" She opened her shirt to reveal a huge butterfly tattoo, with a wingspan of several inches, multi-hued and superbly crafted. I half expected it to fly.

Perched above the left breast and spreading across her breastbone, the butterfly appeared as if struggling to emerge from Shirley's bra.

"That's some tattoo, Shirley. But why do I get the idea that you're not happy withit?"

"Happy with it?" Shirley fumed. "Are you kidding? I

hate it!"

"Is it different from what you wanted?" I inquired.

Shirley frowned at my obvious misinterpretation of her disgust. "I didn't want the tattoo. I didn't want this one, either" she said, and rolled up the right pant leg of her well-worn beige shorts. Out poked the head of an angelic creature in the same green-red color pattern. "I lost time this past weekend. I don't remember getting these. I'm embarrassed by them. Most of us are. I just hate them, Chris."

Shirley yanked a couple of tissues from the box and yielded to powerful emotions. Her face caved in as she faced yet another betrayal in her life. This one was different, though; rather than being a helpless child at the mercy of a powerful adult, this was self-betrayal. Her paradox read like this: "Some force did this to mewithout my permission. That force is also me."

Her tears poured out onto an ever-increasing pile of tissues. As I handed her the wastebasket, Shirley excused herself to the ladies' room.

Shirley's short absence provided me the opportunity to reflect on the time some six months before, before I realized she had a dissociative disorder. She had complained of bad headaches and lost periods of time. She had become so "forgetful" (or what clinicians label *amnesiac),* she had to leave little Post-It notes as reminders for even the most basic of behaviors, like whether or not the dishes in the dishwasher were clean.

When money was reportedly "missing" for the second time, I suggested that she make an appointment with a local neurologist.

Neurological testing yielded negative results. Shirley

did not have a cyst, brain tumor, or aneurysm. The physician suggested the possibility of stress-related symptoms. The inference, of course, was that the problems were all in Shirley's head. While I resented the insulting suggestion, before long she proved the doctor to be a wise man.

A Thursday-afternoon phone call from Shirley provided the next clue. I returned her call in between my two and three o'clock sessions. "Yeah, Shirley, how are you?"

"Shirley's not here," she said in Shirley's unmistakably husky voice.

"C'mon, don't play games. I only have a minute. What's going on?"

"I'm not playing games. Shirley's not here."

The speaker was clearly serious, as I knew Shirley to be. I removed the foot from my mouth and continued, "Okay, sorry. So, who am I talking to?"

"Julie." Same voice. Same inflection. New name. "Hi, Julie. What can I do for you?"

"For me? Nothing. I didn't call you."

"Well, I'm Dr. Cor----"

"Yeah, I know who you are."

"Well, will you let Shirley know I called?" I felt strange leaving a message for the person I was talking to.

"I'll tell her."

I swallowed hard and dropped my right arm to my side, a death grip on the telephone receiver, staring straight ahead at a poster on the office wall, seeing nothing.

Robotically, the arm ascended, then stopped inches from my face, permitting me to inspect the handset as if the secrets to our strange conversation lay within. Immediately, I was aware of the implications--Shirley communicated from an alter personality, as if she hadthe condition known then as *multiple personality disorder.*

Nothing else struck me as obvious: What challenges would this disorder present? How would this revelation influence the course of treatment? Why would Shirleyfirst display this condition over the telephone? I needed to be content with the notion that these questions, though reasonable, would take time to answer satisfactorily.

That was the first of many conversations with Julie, the highest functioning of Shirley's alters. Apparently, time had come for Shirley's various parts to surface,given that she was now in a therapeutic relationship, featuring safety and a newfound decision to trust.

Shirley returned from the ladies' room wearing a determined look.

"You okay?" I knew she had survived worse. She'd survive the tattoos.

"I'm all right. So, what do we do now?" Shirley looked at me intently.

"Why don't we find out who's behind the tattoos?Might as well get to the bottom of it, all right?"

Although she leaned upon me for direction, Shirley was ultimately the boss and could veto my recommendations.

"Do we have to do hypnosis? Is there another way we can do this? I mean, I prefer to remain as close by as possible so I won't lose any more time."

"No, not necessarily hypnosis. I think our objective here is to find out what happened. Do you have any ideas?"

Shirley kicked her shoes off, pulled her legs up on the chair, and sat Indian-style. She shut her eyes, tucked her chin, and shut down. Silence overcame the office. I didn't know where Shirley was taking me, but I knew she was going inside, and something was about to happen.

Minutes passed with Shirley frozen in the same position, barely breathing. All at once her eyes opened and peeked around the room as if waking up from a slumber in a strange place. She looked at my feet--my shoes were also kicked off--and worked her way up slowly until she found my face. Shirley, or whoever the emerging alter was, made eye contact for only a moment. She shuddered, and her eyes darted away, then roamed the room again before bravely locating my glance once more. My natural inclination was to reassure her not to be afraid. But then it became unnecessary.

A smile engulfed her face, shy, flirtatious, with an element of invitation. Without a word, her facial expressions conveyed an awkward youthfulpresentation.

I spoke first. "Hi."

Another enormous smile erupted, clearly atypical for Shirley's serious manner. "You asked for me?"

"Who are you?"

"I'm Beth." She laughed nervously.

"Who are you?" "I'm Dr. Cortman, or Chris, if you prefer. I'm glad you're here, Beth. Do you know anything about the tattoos?"

"The tattoos? Yeah! Aren't they great?"

This was not a rhetorical question. She awaited my approval before continuing. "They're beautiful. Why don't you tell me the whole story of the tattoos, okay?"

"I went to Tampa, 'cause I heard of this tattoo parlor. I wanted a real nice one, you know?"

"Uh-huh. What made you want a tattoo? And why a butterfly and an angel?" I asked, always searching forsome deeper meaning or symbolism.

"Well, I just think they're really cool, and I wanted everybody to like it."

"Who's 'everybody,' Beth?" "All the other ones, you know."

"The others inside?"

"Yeah. I thought they'd really like 'em."

"So, you wanted to impress everyone with the tattoos. For what reason?"

"So, they'd like me. No one inside ever considers what I want important."

"Did it work? Do they like you more after the tattoos?"

"No. No one likes it. Now everyone is mad at me. It's like they hate me because I went and did it without permission."

"Wow. That backfired, huh? I'll bet that's hard." "Yeah."

"Listen, Beth. I have a question. Do you know when you came to be? Do you know what I'masking?"

"Yeah, I know. Why do you wanna know, anyway?" Defensiveness lent an edge to her voice.

"Well, I'm just trying to help Shirley. And I need to get to know all the people inside and what they've been through. It's okay if you don't know me well enough to trust me yet."

"No, I kinda remember when it was." All the flirtatious gestures had vanished. Beth's tone reflected a somber mood. "I can tell you about it. We were at a meeting. It was in a wooded area, and candles were everywhere. People were dressed in like these black robes and standing in a circle. It's like they're singing or something, but it's not happy singing, and it's not in English. It was more like chanting, you know?" Beth'stone frosted the room.

"Uh-huh. Where are you, Beth?"

"I'm off to the side now with other little kids.I feel like I'm waiting for something to happen." Beth stopped and stared at the pattern in the carpeting.

"What's the matter?" I asked.

"It's nothing. I'm okay. Can we talk about something else?"

"Sure, what would you prefer to talk about?" "Um ... I don't know. Are you married?" "No, are you?"

Beth laughed heartily, a reminder that she didn't possess Shirley's battle-hardened demeanor. "No, I'm only thirteen."

"Thirteen, huh? Are there a lot of teens inside Shirley?" While off the subject of the ceremony, I figured, why not extract a little more information about Shirley's system of alter personalities?

"No. I'm the only one. Most are children. The rest are adults."

"How many in all do you figure there are?"

"I don't know." Her eyes closed. Her head dropped again. Something was going on inside Shirley. Again, I was fascinated. Again, I was helpless to do anything but wait.

She brought her legs up and hugged them, seemingly for protection. All was quiet. Suddenly the eyes reopened and looked directly at me with a menacing stare.

I sighed, exhaled, and dug deep for what appeared to be the next challenge. "Welcome," I began. "Who's here?"

The new alter glared my way with a look that could only be interpreted as hateful or worse yet--evil. No words. Just a penetrating stare. A chill crept down my spine. "You don't seem like Shirley or Beth, "I said. "I'd love to meet you if you'd like to talk."

"You don't want any part of me." The mystery woman sneered in a successful attempt to intimidate me.

"Well, I assume you're here 'cause you want to talk to me, right?"

A mocking smile ran across her face, followed closely by a look of disgust.

"I'm not here to talk to you, no. I'm here to warn you. You'd better leave all of us alone. Shirley is mine anyway, and your so-called therapy doesn't stand a chance. You're only hurting Shirley. You don't know what you're doing."

To a point, she was right. I didn't know exactly what I needed to be doing. But I wasn't willing to accept that I was hurting Shirley. That accusation offended me. I knew I was accomplishing something with her.

"If that's what you're here to tell me, you are wasting your time. I won't leave Shirley alone as long as she wants to be here."

My voice contained an element of defiance. I was unaccustomed to dealing with angry, evil alters, and my first decision had been to fight fire with fire. Seconds later, I concluded it was not therapeutic to become defensive with the nasty alter.

"You sure you don't want to tell me your name?" I challenged.

"Look, leave us alone, understand?" One more venomous look pierced my armor, and then in a flash, the angry lady was gone. Again, the eyes closed, signaling me that another change was imminent. As Shirley returned, the helplesslook of despair accompanied her.

I felt partly relieved, partly disappointed. I had wanted

to confront the angry alter. Instead, I attempted to reorient Shirley to the session.

"Hey, you okay, Shirley?"

"Yeah." She emitted a heavy sigh. "I'm fine."

"What do you know about what just happened?'-' I wondered if she was capable of breaking through the amnesiac barrier.

"Well, I guess everything. At least I know how these stupid tattoos got here. It doesn't make me feel a whole helluva lot better, though."

"Yeah, I understand. You heard her say it was a place in Tampa, right?"

"Well, I already knew that. I didn't tell you, but we have the receipt from the parlor. It was paid in cash. That's how we pay everything. We learned from the group never to put our name on paper if we don't have to. That's why we don't have a checking account."

"Shirley, listen, we're about out of time. But before we stop, who was the second alter here? You know, the angry one?"

Shirley's blank look said it all; she had no knowledge of the defiant alter personality. She merely shrugged.

"Well, it's all right for now. Just know that someone else was here who isn't happy about our work together. Let me ask you to try to get in touch with this part of yourself by journaling. Bring in whatever you write. Nice job today. See yousoon."

"Thanks, Chris." As always, Shirley paid cash for her session at a very reduced rate. She exhaled one moretime. "Are we gonna make it?"

"Yeah. Hang tough."

I was admittedly shaken after my first encounterwith a

part of Shirley that was downright evil in her presentation. If she were an alter of Shirley's, didn't that mean she was basically a good person? Could she act entirely on her own without Shirley's consent, like Beth did? If so, what was she capable of? Ruining Shirley's sobriety with a drinking binge? Returning to the cult? Hurting me? I shuddered at the possibilities running amok in my mind. As bizarre as my imaginings could be, I still had no real understanding of what Shirley was capable of doing in altered states of mind.

Chapter 4

The Mentor

Dr. Richard Levine is a friend of mine. After years as a psychology professor at a prestigious Atlantic Coast Conference university in North Carolina, Richard brought his family to south Florida in quest of a better life. He settled into a pricey home near the Atlantic Ocean outside Ft. Lauderdale, then opened a private practice and established a lucrative consulting position for himself. Less than two years after his migration to the Land of Sunshine, his wife of fifteen years ran off with a local attorney and promptly served Richard with divorce papers.

Richard and I had met at a Florida Psychological Association (FPA) convention in Key West. He sat behind me at an early morning meeting on psychological ethics and couldn't help but notice my Yankee baseball cap (an accessory used to hide my unwashed mop). Born and raisedon the Lower East Side of Manhattan, Richard had grown up a Yankee and New York Giants fan. For us, the prerequisites for lifetime friendship had been met.

We went out for dinner and filled each other in on our lives and hit it off extraordinarily well, poignantly illustrated by the fact that when I asked him to loan me a supportive, objective ear on the phone one night months later, he offered to drive to Sarasota to see me. I hoped he would offer to provide me with the gift of his clinical knowledge and experience in exchange for my friendship and some beach time.

"What the hell," he said sadly, "my weekends are my own. She won't let me see the kids. It'll be a pleasant escape for me."

Having recently landed a once-in-a-lifetime "steal" on a beachfront townhouse condominium on Siesta Key, abarrier island off Sarasota, I prepared for the visit of another single man by buying a bag of pretzels and placing the Pizza Hut delivery menu under the refrigeratormagnet.

Richard arrived early on Saturday afternoon, dropped his overnight bag in the guest bedroom, then caught me up on his heartbreaking family life. As his features twisted with pain, he abruptly rose and disappeared into the guest bedroom. In short order he returned dry eyed and smiling, sporting swim trunks, a bare chest, and a new attitude.

Ever the academician, Richard grabbed a ballpoint pen and an oversized loose-leaf notebook from a pile on one of the dusty bureaus.

"All right, tell me about your multiple." He had officially declared an end to small talk.

"Okay. I don't know what you already know about dissociative disorders, but--"

"Not a bloody thing, truthfully, other than the basic diagnostic criteria. I've never treated a multiple. But fear not, I'm a pretty quick study," he bragged, sprawling out on the newly laid gray carpet in the living room. From his new vantage point, Richard could admire the Gulf view through the double sliding glass doors that separated the room from a screened-in lanai. Beyond stretched some seventy-five yards of beach before the sparkling waters of the great sea. I plopped down next to him and watched him take notes.

"Well, let me ask a question," I began. "How does one become multiple? Apparently, the mind has an amazing escape hatch to turn to whenever a person is traumatized."

"Dissociation."

"Right. As you know, one can learn to 'go somewhere else' during frightening or painful episodes. So, the more a child is exposed to trauma, the more adept she is at mastering the art of leaving the ugliness behind. Soon it becomes possible to create a separate part of self--a fragment--that emerges and takes the place of the child during a horrible scene. When the episode is finally over, the child and the fragment switch places, and--bingo!--it's as if the whole thing never happened to the child. The horror show happened to someone else, who has now been shipped away to the far regions of her mind."

"That's brilliant," Richard marveled. "Thank you."

"No, asshole, what the child does."

We laughed. "Yes, it is," I agreed, "but there's more. Let's say every few nights my father sneaks into my room to molest me."

I stood to make my way around the corner and into the kitchen, where I fetched two glasses of bottled waterfrom the rented cooler. I raised my voice to ensure that my friend could still hear me.

As soon as I hear his footsteps, I disappear into the darkness and leave Dad with 'Jennifer,' the one who is terrified and frozen stiff. Maybe later I develop 'Cindy,' who performs any sexual trick Daddy would like, just for his approval. As Cindy, I may even tell myself that I like sex and become promiscuous throughout my life. Then, having learned how easy it is to switch into others, I begin doing it almost routinely to cope with any difficulty or challenge. Little by little, I form an elaborate system of alter personalities. Some even mimic the abusers and punish me for doing wrong or telling someone about the abuse.

Shirley, the woman I'm treating, has an alter who self-mutilates with a razor, just like she was taught to do in the cult."

Richard studied my face in complete concentration as I continued. I explained the protective role of deniers and the creation of inner self-helpers. I described the alters' different roles, and how the ISH mainly reports what's going on inside when asked.

"But a big part of the problem is a lack of any controlling faction," I went on, "so different alters jockey for position to have their needs met. Multiples suffer from the inner competition and turmoil. Voices are going back and forth, and poor Shirley has arguments going on inside her head."

"Well, that's normal to an extent," Richard pointed out. "For example, one part of me wants to save every penny and become rich, and another part wants to spend and enjoy. So does that make me multiple?"

"No, you're undoubtedly psychotic, Richard, but not multiple. And yeah, that's an accurate analogy. But with multiples, one alter can take over and act on something without the knowledge of the others. One of the alters can buy something or sleep with someone without Shirley's being aware of it. These amnesiac periods are one of the defining characteristics of multiplicity."

Richard didn't seem to mind my lecturing him, presumably because treating multiples is such a specialized field within clinical psychology.

"Now let me give you the scoop on my patient: She's in her mid-forties, divorced, with an eight-year-old who lives at home. Shirley works her butt off doing the graveyard shift at an all-night restaurant. She's serious, determined, very honest, and open. I've never seen anyone want to get better as much as she does. She has no insurance and barely makes ends meet."

"So how does she afford you?" cracked Richard. "Look who's talking!" I responded playfully. My friend's professional credentials entitled him to charge more per hour than anyone in practice in my little town.

"Actually, she confessed after three sessions that she couldn't afford me. But she said, 'I trust you and really want your help!' I couldn't say no. She pays whatever she can, always in cash."

"Does her family help her out?"

I would have laughed if his question hadn't been so ridiculous. "Her parents live across town, but she doesn't want any part of them. She's terrified of her father. Claims he comes over whenever he wants and does what he wants. She's really..."

"He's screwing her?" Richard interrupted.

"Yeah. Throughout her life. Not much anymore. He's an old man, but the sight of him paralyzes her--he literally owns her. She detests him, as if he were the devil himself." I shrugged. "And who knows, he may be."

"They should fuckin' exterminate assholes like that!" The father of a six-year-old, Richard, like most healthy parents, was revolted by the idea of incest.

"Yeah, it's hard to imagine people using their children like sexual objects."

"So how did Shirley become multiple?" Richard

inquired.

I told Richard about the satanic cult in New England. "You need to explain this satanic shit to me. I'm Jewish. We don't do the devil, you know." Richard's smile let me know that while he was likely to be tough on me and hold me to a high standard of performance, he was declaring himself a teammate and confidant. He was unaware of how much I needed that at the time, how much I needed his friendship. I was amazed. "I didn't know that! That's interesting. So, who do you guys blame when you screw up?"

"Our mothers. They're all neurotic. You've heard about Jewish mothers and guilt, right?"

"Sure. I hope I have the honor someday of meeting your mother and paying homage to the queen of guilt." I chuckled. "Well, back to the cults." I described the influential, organized groups that worshipped the devil to attain power, money, sex, drugs, success, whatever, and that once one was a member, quitting was nearly impossible and could be fatal. "I'm told incriminating pictures are taken of all of the participants to ensure a code of silence."

"And they really believe that a red guy with a goatee, horns, and a tail can deliver the goods?" Richard asked, incredulous.

"Sounds unbelievable, I know. They gather on certain holidays--Halloween's a biggie--fall and spring solstices, and full moons for their ceremonies." I stared out at the waves gently caressing the shoreline. The day promised to be another scorcher."

"So, what do they do?"

"Really sick stuff. Children are sexually abused from infancy by anyone or anything--including animals--to appease the devil. Anything that God relishes, Satan and his cohorts supposedly hate and viceversa."

"So, if God says sex should be monogamous, between committed adults, then Satan says sex anywhere, anytime, with whomever or whatever."

"Exactly!" I was certainly impressed with the mental acuity of my buddy. It felt good to be heard. "So, they attempt to please their 'master' with the hope of one day dominating the world. They maintain that in the afterlife they will inhabit hell, a place of celebration and partying, and eternal rule with Satan."

"So, sex, drugs, and rock-n-roll now, and eternal partying in the hereafter?"

"You got it."

"Where do I sign up?" Richard's wit, besides providing a refreshing perspective on the ugliness I was sharing, suggested that no matter what I told him, he was prepared to work with me. The humor was a defensive mechanism, used to cope with pain. Straightaway his mood sobered, and he stared through the sliding glass doors out at the Gulf of Mexico. He fixed his gaze on the sand and surf for what seemed like an eternity. His eyeglasses reflected three elderly women plodding along the shoreline. "Let's go outside. I need some air. We can walk and talk."

He kicked off his well-worn sneakers and headed toward the award-winning sugary sands of Crescent Beach. I locked the door behind us, then we wove through the baking vacationers on our way to the water's edge.

We headed north toward the public beach. Richard's eyes belonged to the variety of bikinis cradling an assortment of breasts, but I assumed his ears were mine, prompting me to continue.

I reopened the conversation. "Let me share my philosophy of treatment. Each alter is actually a pocket of emotions--especially extreme hurt and terror--thatcontains a memory or memories for the person. Escaping a trauma is like paying by credit card. Eventually the bill comes due."

"Yeah, with interest, I suppose." "You got it."

Richard and I dodged a wave that crashed farther up on the shoreline than we were prepared for, spraying our shorts with water.

"Now I need to remember the events and take the feelings as my own," I continued. "Unfortunately, I feel them as if I were five years old or however old when the trauma occurred. When I am ready to own what happened to me and work through the pain, I no longer require the alters and can integrate, one by one. I become whole, as I was born to be."

"So, how do you get to the memories? Hypnosis?" he asked. "Depends. According to my research, some patients have recurring fragments of memories and images. They need to let the memories surface. A therapist can facilitate with simple, nonleading questions like, 'Where are you? Who's there? What's happening?' and so on. Other people dream their flashbacks, while still others present with body memories."

I shared the story of Shirley's pseudopregnancy with Richard. "I use hypnosis in my practice when the patient gets stuck."

I was struck by an interesting thought: "When you come right down to it, dissociating really is only a form of self-hypnosis."

"Whose model do you follow? What school of thought?"

"I've been hitting the psych literature pretty hard lately, trying to understand Shirley and a couple of other clients who have presented recently with emerging memories and alter personalities. I'm reading a lot of guys who are biggies in the field -Braun, Ross, Kluft, Renee Fredericson, and others--but my own approach is based on the Gestalt theory of getting closure with unfinished business."

We both stopped briefly and grinned, watching a naked toddler pee into the onrushing foam of the Gulf.

"I use other therapies also," I continued, "like cognitive/behavioral theory to teach them how to change their thinking patterns and to quell anxiety. But I've learned this for sure: Without making peace with the past, there is no healing. No integration will ever takeplace."

"Fascinating. And you know what else?", he asked rhetorically. "My feet are blistered from walkingto freakin' Timbuktu. Can we turn around?"

During our walk back to the condo, Richard wouldstop suddenly every couple of hundred yards and fire a probing question at me. He was out of breath, so I set a slow pace and kept conversation at a minimum. Halfway back, he appeared ready to begin putting together the fragments of Shirley's mind like a ten-thousand-piece jigsaw puzzle. "So, my friend. Where are you stuck withShirley?"

"I think the treatment is working so far, because her memories continue to emerge one after another. What's interesting is that her recollections seem to present one at a time. When one is remembered and worked through emotionally, she seems to gain some peace about it. Soon after, another pops up. The problem is, I've run across an evil personality. I've seen her appear during three sessions now.

She finally told me her name is Colleen. She has issued me several warnings: 'Leave her alone. You don't know what you're doing.' She also says, 'I'm taking her back to the cult. Don't think you can stop me.'"

"Let's see, what else does she say? Oh, yeah, 'Do whatever you want, but you're not putting her in the hospital.'"

"What do you make of her?" We were finally back at the condo. I unlocked the door, and we headed inside to the kitchen for long drinks of water."

"That's where I need your help. I try not to let her threats rattle me, but I'm not handling her very well. I find myself arguing with her or restating my position."

"Getting into a power struggle probably isn't the best way to proceed," he told me unnecessarily, following me into the living room. It'll serve no purpose other than to incite and alienate her from you."

"But she keeps returning to talk to me, I pointed out, "so I guess I haven't lost her yet. She must want my help, or I doubt she'd continue to pop in for a few minutes of each session. Colleen has me baffled. She's why I called you."

Exhausted, Richard collapsed on the couch. "Hoo, boy, am I out of shape."
"You used to exercise a lot. What happened?"

"When I began to wage the war for my kids, everything got knocked out of kilter, including my daily routine. I'll get back to it when this custody mess is over."

"How 'bout some more water, my friend?" I hoped his breath would return to normal soon; I was beginning to feel alarmed.

"Nah, I've had enough. But if you have a tank of oxygen,

I'll take a hit of that."

"Listen, man, you better feel better soon or I'm dialing nine-one-one. I ain't giving you mouth to mouth. My pitiful love life hasn't made me that desperate yet."

He waved away my concern under the humor. I'm all right. Walking five miles has not only strained my heart, it has stimulated some thought. If you believe the alters are pockets of pain and memories, then why would Colleen be any different than the other personalities? Assuming your theory is correct, she's no more evil than any of them. Colleen has her own memories of horror, and she's getting ready to confront them. Any attempts she makes to intimidate you are because she's frightened to go near the memories that she took on for Shirley."

I resonated with Richard's suggestion. It made perfect sense. For me to help Colleen, I had to encourage her to tell me her story--how she came to be and what she did for Shirley. "As she shares her memories and especially the accompanying feelings, I'm sure she'll lose her power," I mused aloud.

"Not to mention her anger," he chimedin.

"And her efforts to intimidate me are self-protective, because she's terrified of dealing with the feelings. And yet she continues to appear in session because she truly wants help."

Richard nodded. "In essence she's at warwith herself."

"I'm embarrassed," I admitted. "The answer was right in front of my nose the whole time. Richard, you're a genius."

"I couldn't agree with you more. Now, if we can get away from Shirley for a while? How 'bout a pizza or something? I'm starving."

Richard and I chowed down on a large pepperoni pie

and then sat through a guy movie high in testo-Stallone. If there had been a plot, I couldn't concentrate on it. My mind was fixed on Colleen. At last, I felt empowered with a simple plan that could help Shirley finally make peace with that menacing alter. I considered this to be the turning point of her therapy. But as I found out later, my victory celebration was premature.

Chapter 5

Flashbacks

Helping Shirley process the horrors of her family's involvement in a satanic cult prompted me to think about my own family, its religious orientation, and how I managed to select a career in the helping profession.

Being a psychologist is a wonderful career with countless opportunities to make a positive impact on people's lives, but it never was my plan during childhood. Sure, I watched the Bob Newhart show just like the next guy, but my aspirations focused more on the ball field than the couch. I remember telling my eighth-grade guidance counselor that my intent was to play shortstop for theNew York Yankees. Maybe she'd heard that fantasy a time ortwo before; she was quite adept at gently inquiring if I had a Plan B the unlikely event that the Yankees weren't interested. I didn't then, but I do now.

Practicing psychology is Plan B. (Plan A remains intact just in case the Yankees ever comearound.)

I am the second of five children. My parents raised us in a New York City suburb of northern New Jersey. Although I didn't understand this growing up, my little slice of America was predominantly Italian-American. (Whoever wasn't Italian was Jewish.)

My parents converted to Christianity in the early sixties, and their beliefs prevented me from playing intwo Little League all-star games held on Sunday, the day of rest.

Both my parents were originally from New York City. My father, born during the Depression, in Astoria, Queens, grew up idolizing his father and respecting hishardworking mother, the unchallenged head of the Greek-American household. Work, not education was the priority for Dad.He became tough and very street smart in order to survive. At fourteen he drove a meat truck for his brother-in-law, and when Dad was behind the wheel, he concealed his age from the police by pulling a cap down low over his eyes.

My father's world caved in at age fifteen when his dad died suddenly of congestive heart failure. Never able to grieve his enormous loss, he angrily suppressed his pain and vowed never to love like that again. He never did. At seventeen, Dad dropped out of school in favor of the navy, beginning a career marked by hard work, low wages, and an omnipresent scowl. He was tough, angry, and hypercritical, and despite his loyalty to God and our family, we kids obeyed Dad more out of fear than from trust in his wisdom and authority.

His criticism bruised me more than the spankings and certainly lingered much longer. What hurt me the most, however, was the nagging realization that Dad never liked me. Oh, he loved me; I knew that I mattered to him. But sadly, the genuine fondness that a parent ideally bestows upon his offspring was missing. I spent my life trying to impress him and win his approval.

Mom was one of eight children born in Manhattan to Italian-American parents. She learned quickly from her mother that her life was to be one of self-sacrifice and complete devotion to faith and children. (If one of her children fails to attend church, for instance, Mom feels personally offended because she raised us to know better.)

Shortly after Greece met Italy, they married, assuring their children of at least two things: a fiery, ethnic passion and truly great food. While psychological research suggests that all behavior and personality traits are partially due to the genetic component, it appears that *at least* three additional factors contributed to my personality development: my parents' strict adherence to Christian principles, my dad's criticism of me, and my mother's perfectionism.

I developed into a people-pleasing perfectionist, sort of like Mom with sideburns, with a fundamental view of religion and a burden to make God and my parents proud. In grade school, I began memorizing Bible verses--a total of over nine hundred of them--to earn a free week of campeach summer. (To this day I fantasize about challenging the pope to a scripture recital contest.) In high school, I walked a tightrope between popularity and obscurity, wanting to be a "good Christian" without compromising social status. Walking on water would have been easier.

Adolescence was a barren desert of loneliness for me, as my Christian convictions convinced me of the need to stand apart from the partying masses. "'Come out from among them,' saith the Lord, 'and be ye separate and touch not the unclean thing,'" says Paul in II Corinthians 6:17. God, I concluded, drove a hard bargain.

As high school drew to an end, I made a safe if not wise decision to attend a Christian college. I blossomed in college under the perceived protection of sameness. If everyone was a Christian, then I could be myself. I developed many exceptionally solid relationships with peers, several of which have endured the test of time. Perhaps even more importantly, I learned a lifelong lesson during these years of transition from adolescence to adulthood: God did not require me to be anyone other than whom He created me to be. I could, in the words of St. Augustine, "Love God and do as you (I) please." There was no need to be someone I wasn't in an effort to be holy in God's sight.

Having accepted that my sports career would be restricted to that of a spectator, I opted for a major in psychology with the hope of one day becoming a professional counselor. I grabbed a master's degree in psychology at Texas A & I University, then headed to California for my doctorate. My parents, meanwhile, had semiretired to Florida, like all good New Yorkers are supposed to.

Southern California in the early 1980s was, to me, heaven on earth. Bodybuilding became a preoccupation of mine, and I pumped iron while eliminating carbohydrates in an effort to become Mr. Orange County. I didn't place in the competition, but few experiences compare with posing in swim trunks in front of dozens of *screaming* women--or at least that's how I choose to remember it.

School was equally rewarding. Abnormal psychology class would, I thought, prepare me for my budding career as a clinical psychologist. I learned about mental/emotional disorders ranging from depression to schizophrenia.

One day an inexplicable occurrence had more impact on my life and career than any excerpt from a text or gem from a professor. Class had just adjourned, affording a fifteen-minute break before abnormal psych laboratory commenced. I went outside for some air when suddenly a clear, distinct message resounded in my head as if broadcast from a loudspeaker: "*Go to Florida to bury your father.*"

The thought was not mine. I had no desire to leave the

Eden I had discovered in San Diego to relocate to a retirement community. And to bury my father? I must admit that the thought of tossing dirt upon him might have proved appealing after one of his critical tirades during my childhood. As far as I knew my father wasn't sick, nordid he require any special care or attention from his children. I had no desire to reside in close proximity to him, especially if it required leaving San Diego. I doubted that the message contained a command to commit patricide. So, what were those words supposed to mean?

The term "bury your father" was not unfamiliar to me. In the Book of Matthew, Jesus commanded a rich young ruler to sell everything, give his money to the poor, and follow Him. The ruler protested, claiming the need to stay at home and bury his father. Apparently, this indicated a desire to care for his father until the older man died.

An alternate meaning may have also applied to my situation: Perhaps what needed to be buried was not so much my father as my resentment of him--burial of the hatchet, so to speak.

In spite of my confusion, the power of that message left no room for doubt. I would be finishing my classes at United States International University as soon as possible and commencing an all-out search for an internship in the Sarasota area. Period.

It's possible to account for my subjective experience in any number of ways, depending upon one's orientation. I was content to believe that God had a plan for me that necessitated my relocating to Sarasota--or so I thought before giving up my faith.

God is, I'm certain, a very smart being. But if it truly

was His decision to send me to Florida, I thought, then He undoubtedly made a mistake. The internship I had been promised on the phone long distance dissolved the first day of my tenure in the Sunshine State.

There I was in Florida, with no car, no job, nomoney, and the only two people I knew in the entire state wereMom and Dad. Internships are usually arranged a year in advance, but miraculously, within two weeks, I was able to secure a three-month internship at an alcohol rehabilitation facility in Sarasota. The experience was invaluable, but the state-sponsored facility could no more offer me a stipend than a Michelob Lite. That could mean only one thing--move back in with Mom and Dad.

Moving back home with one's parents after havinglived independently for a number of years is about as workable as an adult climbing back into the womb. I learned firsthand about the concept of triangulation, where a threesome is composed of two people communicating something that only indirectly finds its way to the third. I learnedthat triads very often are reduced to two-against-one.

Unfortunately for Dad, my Mom and I often sided against him. He'd voice his disapproval of me and/or my lifestyle, I'd wise off in retort, and Mom would attempt to protect me or distract him enough to avoid a useless altercation. None of us was happy.

So, when the three-month internship had passed and no other takers appeared for a free forty-hour-a-week doctoral candidate, I figured it was time to get out of Florida. I was sorry I had ever come, and the supposed message from God was all but a dead issue. I never even gave it a thought.

But one last interview landed me a job at a psychiatric

hospital program in Venice, twenty-five minutes to the south of my parents' condo. The program elected to utilize my services for the remaining six months of my unpaid internship. I was forced to spend another half year living with my folks.

At times things got very ugly between Dad and me. His disapproval focused on my bodybuilding and attempts to create some semblance of a social life. Perhaps my immaturity and self-centeredness contributed to the problem, or maybe Mom was so thrilled to have a child back at home that she bestowed more love and affection upon me than on her husband. Dad spewed jealousy-based anger at Mom and me and contributed to our resentment. Thus, a vicious circle was perpetuated, and life in the two-bedroom condo on the golf course was strained by divisiveness and conflict.

God was another problem. Christianity felt more and more like a cross to bear with little remuneration. My understanding of God and spirituality contributed to a nagging feeling of guilt that dominated my life. Whatever I did, I wasn't good enough or holy in God's sight. More honestly, I never could resolve the whole sexual issue: abstain until marriage or "indulge," as my mother called it, sinning against God. I didn't like my options.

To this day, I don't remember what the last straw was or when, but just like the day at age seven when I petitioned Jesus to become my Savior, I now requestedthat He leave me alone--at least for a while.

I stopped praying. I stopped going to church. Ididn't say grace at meals anymore at Mom and Dad's. And best of all, I could finally consider being sexual without guilt. I briefly experimented with the concept of sex without commitment. I felt horrible guilt because I had beentaught that sex belonged exclusively in the marital domain, and even worse guilt because I knew I was using women for my own gratification. Other than that, I was having ablast.

By day, I listened to wounded women--the betrayed, the rejected, the abused. By night I was probably creating more business for my local colleagues with my attempts to. emulate Don Juan. I knew that the women I slept with were less than thrilled with the notion of "casual" sex, despite their assurances to the contrary.

In retrospect, this phase was probably a late bloom of my adolescent desires to sow wild oats. Fortunately, I didn't require too many oats before realizing that I was hurting people, and that was unacceptable to me.

Meanwhile, my relationship with Dad grew steadily worse. My resentment finally getting the best of me, I decided to part ways with my earthly father, just as I had with the Heavenly One. I wanted out--out of my commitment to God, out of my father's house, out of Florida.

With about six weeks to countdown before the completion of my internship, my parents purchased round-trip tickets to San Diego, purportedly to attend my doctoral graduation. I planned to stay in California somewhere--anywhere--to begin my career as a psychologist. In the meantime, however, I sent out dozens of resumes to agencies, hospitals, and mental-health clinics all over the country--even to places I'd never want to live--in an effort to get away from my parents and secure my first professional position.

There were no takers anywhere in the country, *noone,* and I wondered what happens to a man with a doctorate in psychology and no job offers. I was tempted to erect a stand, not unlike Lucy's from the Peanuts cartoon strip: Advice--5¢.

But then Dr. Gerald Bannasch, the medical director of the program in Venice where I interned,called me into his office.

"You're the new program director," he said beforeI even sat down. "You start in two weeks."

I froze before my butt landed in the chair. "I'mgoing to be in California in two weeks--to graduate."

He exhaled pipe smoke out of his beard-rimmed mouth, puffing out casual, yet life-changing words: You're not going. We need you to get started. You've got a program to run."

I treasured the opportunity to direct the program. As hard as I tried to escape God, Dad, and Florida, it wasnot to be. God made it clear that He wanted me in Florida by making me an offer I simply couldn't refuse--a paying job. The program continued to flourish until it became the Psychology Department of Venice Hospital, including an inpatient unit. Three years after accepting my position there, I left the hospital in favor of private practice.

At the time, I never even acknowledged God nor imagined that His hand was involved in directing my steps.

Then again, I had no idea what lay in store. If I had, I might not have stayed.

Chapter 6

Marital Missiles

In my experience, relationship conflicts and concerns are the primary reasons people seek help from a mental-health professional. These may range from bitter power struggles with an ex-spouse over child-rearing philosophies to the chronic irritants of coping with adult children who repeatedly return to the nest after failed attempts at negotiating independence. The most common impetus for making an appointment with a therapist is, not surprisingly, disharmony with a significant other.

Marital therapy, I've often believed, is a test in patience, perseverance, and long suffering--and it's tough on my clients, also. The therapist, however well-trained, may inadvertently be invited to wear the vertical stripes of a referee, the flowing robe of a circuit judge, or at times, the collar of the ordained. In spite of the hurts and misunderstandings, some of the most entertaining moments arise in the context of marital therapy.

Woman to husband in total seriousness: "Honey, why don't you tell your version of the incident first, and then I'll tell him the truth when you're done." But in many cases accusations, yelling, sarcasm, hysteria, even unbridled cruelty best describe the ugly reality of what goes on "behind closed doors."

Such was the case with Peter and Donna Carrington. A handsome couple in their early forties, the Carrington's captured the look of success. Peter, a successful stockbroker, was bright, sensitive, and articulate, with a good sense of humor and a warm smile. He dressed in the uniform of a financial professional, the traditional dark suit, white shirt, and requisite paisley tie.

Donna, a certified public accountant, was inclined to downplay her natural beauty. I made a mental note of that, as I am accustomed to seeing women in apparel that accentuates their feminine assets.

After three sessions of collecting history,symptoms, and the litany of problems that snarled the couple's marital relations, session four offered me the first solid clue to solving the Carrington mystery.

Donna opened the session with a question: "Why must I carry all the weight of our sexual relations, Peter?"

"You think you carry all the weight?" I asked her. "Yes. It's difficult always being the one to askif he'd like to be intimate."

"I initiate some, don't I?" he protested weakly.

"I can't remember the last time you made a pass atme." "Well, maybe I would if you could keep your handsoff me every once in a while," Peter said, making an awkward attempt at humor.

I knew that his diversion from Donna's line of questioning indicated his discomfort with the topic of intimacy. Just in case she missed it, he flashed a big smile.

She would have none of it. The softness that characterized her round, unblemished face disappeared. A laser exploded from her usually tranquil blue eyes—a look I would get to know very well--that all but impaledPeter.

"I can keep my hands off of you from now on if that's what you want," she threatened.

He held up his hands, fending off the attack. "No, no! I was only kidding."

Because of Donna's overactive hostility to Peter's defensive joking, I attempted to validate her pain. "You seem to be wounded by Peter's joke."

"Oh, a 'joke,' Dr. Cortman? Is that what you call a joke? I feel sorry for you if that seemed funny to you."

This was, of course, no time to react defensively to her sarcasm and contempt, although I had the distinct impression that Donna was inviting me—perhaps *expecting* me--to retaliate.

I opted to steer away from her pain and anger and gain a little more insight into the couple's pattern of interacting.

"Does this happen often between you?"

"And what, pray tell, is happening between us, dear Dr. Cortman? I'm sure you know. After all, you have the title *doctor.*"

Peter looked away, feigning interest in the framed diplomas on my wall. This was now the second time that he had conveniently "disappeared" during a critical period of the session. I assumed that this was Peter's modus operandi: When the going gets tough, he could be countedon to make himself emotionally inaccessible to Donna.

I decided to reinvite Peter to the session. "When your wife is as upset as she is now, how do you typically respond?" (As if I didn't know.)

He never got a chance to respond.

"He's a man, Dr. Cortman," Donna seethed. "And you know how men are. If a woman gets angry, she's a bitch and not to be taken seriously. Peter doesn't take meseriously, and I'm sure you don't, either."

I began thinking of the wisdom of my friend Bob, an anesthesiologist, who only treats patients who are asleep. I had heard enough of the contempt, the sarcasm, and now the "nobody-loves-me" self-pity. And yet I knew thatthese were merely an ugly façade for the fragility Donna was incapable of revealing.

Instinctively, I asked Peter if he would mind if I spent some time alone with his wife. I again assumed, correctly, that he would be pleased to have a reprievefrom the so-called therapy. He immediately acquiesced, heading off to the safer environs of the waiting room.

I moved my chair close to Donna's, risking the possibility of an increase in the threat to her. Yet Imade it clear to her with my relaxed and informal body language that I bore no threat. I asked her a simple question. "What hurts so much, Donna?"

Tears welled up in her eyes as her countenance declared that the hostility had all but melted away.

"I'm sorry, Dr. Cortman. It's not you. I'm sorry. I'm sorry."

"It's okay," I assured her. "Is there anything that I need to know to help you?"

I don't know why Donna appeared confused or upset; I wasn't sure which. Somewhere in all this, I surmised that perhaps she would do better in individual therapy, at least for a while. To get anywhere, I would need a better rapport with her. I would need her to trust me in order to understand what was lurking below all that sarcasm and venom.

"Would you be okay about spending the next session here without Peter? I think it might be easier to get to the bottom of things if we took a temporary hiatus from marital therapy."

I was wrong about one thing. The three of us would never again return to marital therapy. Donna's pain ran deeper than any of us imagined and was only marginally connected to the marriage. A journey into the pits of hell was about to begin.

Chapter 7

Courage

If there is one characteristic that sets apart the highly successful client from the marginally successful one, that would be courage. Courage manifests itself in the capacity to face one's past, however monstrous it mayhave been. Courage is about owning one's present as well and avoiding the very common pitfall of remaining stuck in the past. Juggling the two--past and present--is among the greatest challenges that beset the team of client and therapist.

Journaling proves to be extremely helpful in dealing with the past because via the written word, experiences gain expression, often for the first time. While I encourage most of my clients to keep a journal, the practice is an invaluable resource to virtually every person attempting to make peace with a painful childhood.

An English minor in college, Donna Carrington was already adept at written communication. Poetry, short stories, and letter writing were a part of her repertoire. But journaling about her past afforded her a peek into a childhood long since buried, a past that was now breaking through the frozen surface of repression as we began our individual work together.

Again, and again Donna's words were chilled by a fury that seemed excessive when compared to the benign topics she addressed in her journal. Should Peter fail to notice her new haircut or forget to notify her when staying late at the office,

Donna's blood would boil. The burning rage, however, was more often directed at herself than at her husband.

While despising oneself is common among people with low self-worth and/or suffering from depression, the tendency is also characteristic of childhood-abuse victims. I made a mental note but said nothing, so as to ensure that if any such information should arise, it would not be the product of my suggestion.

One Friday afternoon, Donna's eyes brimmed with obvious pain as she peered up from her journal entry. "I don't think I want to live anymore, Dr. Cortman. It'sjust not worth it." Her self-contempt enveloped her words, turning her fierce anger inward, as she had so many times before.

"How often do you think about suicide, Donna?" I inquired gently in an effort to get a handle on justwhat we were up against.

"I've thought about it for as long as I can remember. Nothing ever changes. There's no hope for me."

She sounded as if she were trying to convince me so I would condone her decision to drop out of life. I made a concerted effort to communicate my concern for this very disturbed woman. "You've thought about suicide throughout your life, but have you ever attemptedit?"

"Yes, once, many years ago." Her eyes rolled upward and to the left; those who espouse a therapeutic school of thought knownas neuro-linguistic programming believethat position conveys that the individual is recalling something from the past.

"Tell me about that."

"It was a number of years ago. I was in my late twenties at the time, I think." She paused as if this brief response would suffice.

"Tell me more, please."

"I-I was very hurt by the realization that I could never have children." She began to grow teary and covered her eyes with her right hand, as if to hide her shame.

"Go ahead, grab a tissue and tell me about it." "There's not much to tell. I had a hysterectomy."

Her voice changed, depicting some type of defense at work. Her sadness was quickly replaced by defiance, not unlike her attitude during the initial meeting with Peter. Judging from Donna's protective response, I gathered we were once again treading on dangerous ground. Still, I needed to know if she was a danger to herself at this time, so I forged ahead.

"How did you attempt to take your life?"

"You need to remind me of that, don't you, Dr. Cortman?" She was almost taunting me. Her contempt was no longer turned inward. I considered shifting the questions to assess if she might be violent toward me.

Donna glared at me. "I took some pills and ended up in the hospital, but they let me out within a week." She sounded less hostile, but still protective, brushing her blond locks away from her face.

"What kind of pills?"

"Look, Dr. Cortman, I am not about to commit suicide now. Isn't that what you want to know?" She had read between the lines.

"Well, yes, that is what I *need* to know. How about if I make a verbal contract with you that if you're thinking about it seriously, you call me? I'll give you my home phone number for an emergency. I would rather you call me in the middle of the night than do anything to hurt yourself, okay?" Although my phone number was listed at that time, I didn't make a habit of inviting clients to call me at home.

As if touched by my concern, Donna's mood melted back into the warm, soft, and scared woman who had entered the office that day. "Thank you. I won't take my life, I promise, and I will call you if I get desperate. I promise!"

Now I understood Peter a little better. His wimpy behavior may have been his strategy for dealing with his unpredictable wife. Would another approach have mademore sense? I wondered. I also wondered about the severity of Donna's mood swings, a condition known as *lability*.

"Does your psychiatrist know you're thinking of taking your life?" In the initial interview, Donna had revealed that she had been depressed on and off for many years but had never done any significant work in therapy. Since moving to Florida, she had secured a psychiatrist and was taking Prozac.

"Well, he knows, but, well, I don't really talk to him." She sounded embarrassed, if not apologetic.

"Do I have your permission to contact him if I deem it necessary?"

"I have no problem with that." Her voice was as soft as a fluffy pillow, coinciding with a pleasant countenance.

As we had passed the fifty-minute mark--the customary length of a psychotherapy session--and with the weekend coming up, I felt relieved that we had made a verbal contract regarding suicide.

Somehow, I understood several things about Donna as she stood to leave: First, she would keep her word if she were a danger to herself; second, her pathology ran *much* deeper than one could detect from a casual meeting; and third, she possessed the courage to do the work she needed to do.

I had planned a low-key weekend--kicking back and wallowing in self-pity because I was unattached. In spite of the ugly realities, I witnessed daily in couples counseling, I yearned for a mate. I had finished with my Don Juan phase, and the timing seemed right: Most of my friends were already married, engaged, or headed that way with a special person. I, too, was hungry for a woman who wanted a relationship to work and would be willing to invest the energy and emotion necessary to making that happen.

I had dated scores of women during my extended bachelorhood, but for one reason or another, no one ever seemed destined to accompany me down that church aisle of permanence. My most recent disappointment had been a graduate student and part-time waitress, charming and attractive but elusive. The Saturday before, we attended an early afternoon wedding. I learned that my date had taken the evening off from work, but her Saturday night plans did not include me. My overly sensitive ego was squashed, and out of self-protection, I vowed never to go out with her again. Although she called me once during the week, I held true to my promise, and our relationship ended.

Now, I called my buddy Marc and invited him to join me for dinner. Unfortunately, he was booked for a first date with a woman who had recently relocated to Sarasota from Ohio.

"Why don't you join us, man?" he asked. "Julianne has a friend visiting her from Youngstown. You can round out the group."

"Lilah," I said. "I don't want to meet some fat, ugly chick who's going home to Ohio tomorrow." These sexist projections were uncharacteristic of me. I was, however, recovering from one woman's perceived rejection and willing to punish all the rest of them for hersins.

Marc begged to no avail. "Too bad, man. Julianne's boss rented us a limo for the night."

I changed my mind. I could feel sorry for myself some other time. I wanted to be chauffeured around Sarasota. I hung up the phone and went to take ashower.

Ninety minutes later, when I settled into the spacious back seat of the limousine and rested my eyes on the out- of-town guest, my romantic side contemplated such phrases as "love at first sight," "meant to be," and "girl of my dreams." My prediction had been correct in only one thing: She was going home the next day. She was hardly fat and ugly. Laura was petite and trim, with soft brown eyes, blond hair, and a face as beautiful as Michelle Pfeiffer's. She was also sweet and soft spoken, and most importantly, she laughed at all my jokes. I liked that in a woman.

As we got to know each other over dinner, myclinical self-analyzed the situation. The men she had dated abused chemicals, ran from the law, slept with her friends, and needed her to be their shelter from life's unrelenting storms.

Laura told me she was emerging from a toxic seven-year relationship marked by drugs, infidelity, financial woes, and the kind of exasperation that culminated in an attempt to make her boyfriend a hood ornament on her Chevy Z24. She was lonely and down on herself.

Laura was different from the image I held about my life's partner. Though she liked cooking, sewing, decorating, and other domestic arts and crafts, she was not educated beyond high school. She worked hard as a cosmetologist in a beauty salon in a working-class neighborhood.

And yet I wanted to get to know her better and was frustrated that she would be leaving the next day. I thought about the high-functioning, career-minded women I had dated who moved out of state for a promotion. *Well, at least Laura won't do that,* I thought, miserable. *We already live twelve hundred miles apart.*

*　　*　　*

Donna's word, I learned the following Wednesday, was good. She waited on hold for more than five minutes while I finished my 10 A.M. session.

"Dr. Cortman," she said in a sweet, helpless child's voice. "I'm not making it."

"What do you mean, Donna?"

"I just don't think I can do this, you know?" "What is it you don't think you can do?"

"I can't deal with these dreams every night. It's ... they're haunting me. I can't take it!"

I could feel her desperation pouring through the receiver. "Are you a danger to yourself?" I wondered if that was where she might be taking this conversation.

"Don't you see? No one ever wanted me around." She began to sob, drowning in a self-destructive flood of rejection and worthlessness. "I just want to die."

The crying gained intensity, as Donna all but collapsed into uncontrollable anguish.

If I were to be at all helpful, I had to maintain a dialogue. "Okay, Don--" I attempted to get a word in.

"Dr. Cortman, do you really think you can help me?"

she interrupted almost as if she was placing her entire hope for the future in my hands. This is often a very seductive trap for the therapist, especially the neophyte, since many of us have a need to be needed that is temporarily gratified by a dependent client. I chose not to take the bait; I declined the role of savior--this time anyway.

"Yes, Donna, I know *we* can get you through this *together,* and for now I think it might be a good idea to consider checking into a hospital. It will give us the opportunity to work more intensively on your issues while keeping you safe from your suicidal thoughts. I know a facility that has an excellent women's program. I'll see you at least twice a week, and we can work on getting to the bottom of what's going on with you."

Silence.

"Donna? You still there?" I hated to think my wonderful speech was all for naught.

"I'm scared, Dr. Cortman."

I might as well have been talking to a child, given the sound of her quavering voice.

"I know. Will you promise to check yourself in this afternoon? I'll contact your psychiatrist."

"Okay, I'll have to call my supervisor at work." She sounded considerably calmer now, and the tears had subsided.

I hung up with a sense of relief. As I dialed Donna's psychiatrist, again I asked myself how a woman as attractive, intelligent, and successful as she could maintain such a penchant for self-destruction. What were the repetitive dreams about? My instincts told me that the first in a series of clues would be revealed in our initial hospital session.

Chapter 8

Donna's Dream

I don't normally do 7 A.M. appointments, but an early morning meeting was the only way I could keep my promise to see Donna twice that week in the hospital. I met briefly with the charge nurse, Nancy, a too-perky person who was evidently unaware of what an ungodly hour it was. Nancy informed me that Donna was complaining of "horrible dreams" that she was hesitant to discuss. She said she'd wait for her "session with Dr. Cortman." I learned that her vitals were stable (nurses always say that) and that she was not deemed a danger to self. She reportedly was cooperative.

"Donna, do us both a favor and breathe. Slow down. Let me see if I can decipher what you're saying, okay?" I echoed her words--all of them--then added, "You won't tell anyone about the dream because you don't want it to be true. And now you'd like me to offer you a perfectly plausible psychological explanation of your dream to suggest that it is only a dream, and you need not worry about it. Am I close?"

There are several reasons to provide this extended feedback to Donna or any client at a time like this. Initially I wanted her to calm down. Secondly, if I could demonstrate that I fully comprehended *what* sounded to her like incoherent ramblings, she would feel less isolated and, more importantly, could believe, *"I'm not crazy."* I attempt to provide this feedback in a nonchalant "of course you're feeling this way" style, which says, "I've seen your problem before, and it doesn't intimidate me. Since…I know it's treatable, maybe, just maybe, you can find one grain of hope somewhere, and that is all we need to begin our healing." Surprised, Donna exhaled in what seemed like relief. She clutched her Styrofoam coffee cup with both hands, took one final gulp, and went for it.

"In my dream, I'm about four, maybe five years old, and … I-I have a better idea. May I read it right from the journal?"

"Sure, however you want to do it." I had once heard that the degree of resistance that a client employs in tackling any given issue directly parallels the amount of fear and pain lodged in that issue. In other words, Donna was playing dodge ball from this dream because she so feared the implications of its message. She took another deep breath, looked at me for reassurance, then began reading.

"Donna, it's getting late. Come on, it's time to clean up for bed."

"Coming, Dad." I scurried off to the bathroom, excited by the promise of a dose of attention from my father. It wasn't typical for him to get involved in the bathing ritual. I don't remember where Mom was on this night, but I can't place her in the house. He towers above me in the dream. I can feel how small I am in comparison to him. He looks at me and remarks what a big girl I am and how it's time for me to take showers instead of baths now. Baths are for babies.

"You're not a baby anymore, are you, Donna?"

"No, Daddy, I'm not a baby."

"You're Daddy's big girl. So, it's time for you to take a shower, and I'm gonna teach you how to do it, okay?"

"Okay." I was so excited, I could hardly stand it. My father had so little time for me normally, and now he was talking to me and making me feel so special and grown up. I remember feeling so wonderful that he was proud of me.

"Okay, I'll turn on the water--not too hot now and not too cold. Take off your clothes and get in. Here's a washrag. Now, watch me soap up the rag. You need to scrub your face first while you stand under the water and let the water rinse the soap off your face."

I was enjoying the experience so much until Dad climbed into the tub with me. I was taken aback at first. He startled me by touching me from behind. Still, I trusted that he knew what he was doing. "Here, Donna, let me do it." He started with my hair, rubbed vigorously on my face, and then moved his hands down my neck and onto my chest. Having Dad pay this much attention to me felt so good, I didn't know what to make of his touch. As he continued down my torso to my waist and beyond, I felt a sense of panic as he approached my genitals. I didn't know what to expect.

He began to rub me on the outside, then stopped to lather his hands and then continued on my genital area. It occurred to me at that point that Dad did not use a washrag like he had instructed me to. I remember thinking that it may have been due to the fact thathe was an adult. Regardless, I forgot all about it when he directed me to turn around. When I did, I was frozen solid by what I saw. Dad's penis was right in my face. It was so big. I didn't know what to do! I just stared at it until I was completely numb. I could hear Daddy talking as if in a tunnel, but I felt nothing anymore.

Dad grabbed my hand and placed it on his penis. He held my hand and moved it back and forth, guiding me.

"Move rapidly, but not too fast," he said. "What a good girl. Yes, that's it. Yes, that's it. Now I want you to do something else for Dad. You like it when Dad is happy with you Donna?"

I just nodded, still reeling from the strange aura that overtook me and the numbness that followed. I didn't even enjoy the fact that Dad was being so nice to me.

"I want you to open your mouth, Donna. Here, don't say anything. Just put this in ... there you go. Good girl!"

Daddy, don't! Daddy, don't! You're choking me! I can't breathe. You're choking me." I never said any of those words out loud, but I heard them screaming in my head. My dad had his own agenda, and he placed his strong right hand behind my neck and held my head in place while he thrust his penis in and out, in and out, again and again. I couldn't breathe, but it didn't seem to matter to him. I felt nothing. Nothing. No terror. No hurt. No rage. It was as if I was far, far away, or as though it was happening to someone else.

I don't know how long it lasted, how long the warm water poured down my back while my dad slammed his penis into the back of my throat. At some point he stopped and his body shook. A warm, salty fluid burst into my mouth. Again, it was as though I was aware of the sensations but could not feel them.

I had no idea why my father went to the bathroom in my mouth. I didn't understand at the time what was really happening, nor was I aware of the significance of what was happening to me. Right after he ejaculated on my tongue, he told me to rinse out my mouth in the shower. He toweled himself off and instructed me todo the same, tossing a pink and white towel at me. He now seemed distant from me, and he wouldn't even look at me anymore. All the special attention that I enjoyed so much was now gone. I didn't understand that.

During that scene of drying myself off while my father wrapped his towel around his waist, I began feeling again. I was so hurt, so confused, and I felt dirty, although I had just showered. Even with all the scrubbing that my dad did, I emerged from the tub feeling as if I needed a bath.

I felt excited when he walked over to me again, picked me up, and sat me on the closed toilet seat.He looked me in the eyes and said, "Now, Donna, what happened in the tub is our secret." His eyes grewcold and stern. "You will never tell anyone about this--not even your mom, not your brother. No one. Never. Do you understand? Do you?"

I shuddered at the piercing look that burned through me. I nodded helplessly in response.

The last part of the dream I remember was my father walking out the door of the bathroom and pausing just a moment to say, "Remember, no one, or you'll never see your mother or me again."

I didn't dream the entire dream each night. It was more of a progression throughout the week. I hope this is now the end of the dream."

Again, Donna exhaled as she emerged from her journal, closed the journal, and said, "Dr. Cortman, could this have really happened to me?"

"I don't know if it happened to you or not. How do *you* feel about that possibility? Do you have a sense about whether or not this dream contained a real memory?"

"I-I get a sick sensation in the pit of my stomach. It was so real." The tears flowed again. "Could it have happened without my remembering till now?"

"Yes, it's a well-documented phenomenon. The mind can contain the memory of a traumatic event for decades, like meat in a freezer, only to be defrosted with feelings that one experienced at the age when it happened. I've worked with dozens of people who have repressed traumatic memories. The key seems to be allowing the memory to surface, working through the feelings, and integrating the trauma into one's life by accepting it."

While Donna took a tissue from her purse and blewher nose, I continued my explanation. "I believe that good therapy provides a safe place for a client to vent and is also an avenue to teach her about herself and, where relevant, about psychological research and theory."

"As far as the dream," I went on, "there are many hypotheses on dreams, including Freud's classic theory that dreams are the 'royal road to the unconscious mind.' Other schools of thought consider dreams in different ways.Would you like me to continue?"

Donna was intelligent and very desirous ofinformation that might help her to put this recurrent dream to rest. "Yes, please." She had stopped crying. She opened her purse and removed yet another tissue, wrapped it around her index finger, and dabbed the corners of each eye.

"The Gestalt theory on dreams posits that each person, character, or part of the dream represents some aspect of the self and contains some special message."

"Other people believe that universal symbols in dreams mean the same thing, no matter who dreams it. A bridge, for example, would indicate a period of transition in a person's life. Or dreams may be a wastebasket foruseless information and data gathered during any given day. We can take bits and pieces of perceptions and weave them into very bizarre, unintelligible stories that may not have any interpretive worth."

"What do you think?" she asked.

"Personally, I think the dreams that are worth examining are the recurrent ones. They definitely hold meaning. In your dream, there is some meaning to the image of your father sexually abusing you. It may have happened exactly as you remembered it. Or parts of it may be true. Or perhaps there's some reason for you to create this image for yourself to contend with."

"Why would I do that?"

"I have no idea. But we'll find out, I promise. You know the truth of what happened to you, and you can deal with it, whatever it is."

On the way to my office, I collected my thoughts. I had my hunches, but I did not want to influence Donna by sharing them. It was very important for her to determine the truth herself. As I pulled my silver 300ZX out of the parking lot I grabbed my Dictaphone so as not to lose the gist of the session. One aspect of Donna's dream remained lodged in my mind like food stuck between molars: If this had beenonly a dream, how had Donna so accurately described *dissociation,* a psychological term for disruption in the usually integrated functions of consciousness, memory, identity, or perception of the environment? She had gone into numb-out, despite being cognizant of what she should have been feeling. She spoke of the incident as if it were happening to someone else. She mentioned another voice screaming in her head.

I didn't know what to make of it yet, but one thing was clear: Donna had a most interesting dream life. And she was just getting started.

Chapter 9

The Hanky Man

While I was treating Shirley and Donna, I spent a good deal of time traveling between Sarasota and Warren, Ohio, to see Laura. Unable to forget her after that one glorious evening together, I decided to get to know her better and, I hoped, clarify my feelings. Laura did the lion's share of the commuting, as the white sands of Siesta Beach were more alluring to her than the subfreezing winters of Ohio were to me.

I had met Laura's family and her big-haired cosmetology friends and done my best to endear myself to everyone important to her. One particular weekend visit to Ohio spawned a relationship that would prove to be one of the most interesting I've ever known.

A distinguished-looking man in a gray pinstriped suit and sunglasses climbed over me to get to his window seat, and a fragile elderly woman with blue hair was to my left. The cramped seats in coach made small talk almost unavoidable without seeming rude, but the fellow,somewhere in his early sixties, stared out the window without a word until the tall, slender flight attendant came with her drink cart. The gentleman ordered a club soda with lime, then turned back to his window. After the flight attendant took my request for a V-8, I added, "And please make sure my filet mignon isn't too well done."

The woman flashed a toothy grin, playing along asshe

handed me the plastic cup with ice. "Will scalloped potatoes be okay, sir?"

"Yes, but no green beans, please, and how about some cheesecake for my friends here?" I said, accepting the tiny packet of pretzels.

The elderly woman to my left smiled at the interaction, while the pinstriped suit to my right continued to stare out at the luggage trucks without mustering so much as a facial expression. I became intrigued if not challenged and wondered if I could get this guy to talk. "Business or pleasure in Cleveland?" I inquired, knowing he couldn't dodge a direct question.

"Business." That was it. No eye contact. No movement of the head. *Okay, Chris,* I thought, *this guy is in his own world and prefers to be left there.*

I reluctantly whipped out my paperback, *Secret Survivors* by E. Sue Blume. With the unusual number of incest survivors composing my practice, I was absorbing whatever I could in the way of books, lectures, and journal articles to shore up my skills and sensitivity to my clientele. Several pages melted away quickly.

"How 'bout you? Business or pleasure?"

He speaks! With all due respect to Ms. Blume, I was all too happy to talk. As a therapist, I have a need to converse with people, even when off the clock.

"It was totally pleasure. I was seeing my girlfriend."

"Mm-hm." More silence.

I decided to try again. "What do you do for a living?"

"Retired." He wouldn't give an inch.

"Oh, yeah? From what*?*"

"I worked for the government. still do, to some extent."

He looked at me for the first time, though still behind his shades. His hairline, slightly receded and parted on the left side of his head, revealed thick gray hair indebted to a generous portion of mousse.

"In what capacity?" I slipped into my intakeinterview mode.

"Intelligence." Great. Another one-word answer. "You mean like the CIA?" He wasn't going to get off that easily.

He frowned, shed his RayBans with his right hand,and revealed his blue-gray eyes. He squinted as if the light was far too powerful for his sensitive eyes. "Yeah, like the CIA, but not the CIA. You've never heard of our organization. No one has."

He had piqued my interest. "Wow! Were you involved in international espionage?" I probably sounded like a thirteen-year-old.

He snorted a laugh. "Yeah. A lot of international crime, contraband, that sort of stuff." He quickly changed the focus back to me. "You some kind of socialworker?"

"I'm a psychologist, actually. But how did you come up with a guess like that?"

"Your book. I figured you had to be working in the mental-health field to be reading about incest."

"Fair enough." I thought more about it. Ihadn't noticed him even glancing at my book. "How--?"

"In my field . . . what's your name?"

"Chris Cortman." I happily extended my hand. He didn't shake it vigorously, but he did offer a name.

"Charles Evans. In my field, Chris, you learn to observe everything. You've never been married. You rely heavily on a good sense of humor to hide your social anxieties. You lift weights to compensate for your short stature, and you walk on the outside of your feet. How'd I do?"

I must have had my mouth open in amazement. "My mother doesn't even know me that well. Oh, there I go, using humor to hide my social anxieties." Neither of us laughed. "I'm impressed, Charles."

I really was. I was glad that I had worked so hard to draw him out of his shell. During the two-hour flight, I managed to coax a good story or two out of Charles, who carried a deep disgust for government corruption. He referred frequently to the underworld in his anecdotes but described the government as "the biggest mob."

With all the insight that the man espoused about underworld activity, I couldn't resist asking one more question: "What do you know about satanic cults, Charles?"

We were scheduled to land in less than a halfhour, and the plane's descent was wreaking havoc upon my hypersensitive left ear. I swallowed, feigned a yawn, and snapped at my gum in an effort to equalize the air pressure.

Of course, Charles didn't miss a trick. "If you hold your nose and blow, sometimes that will release the pressure. Why do you wanna know about satanic cults? Considering joining one?"

I chuckled. "Nah, I couldn't handle all thelate-night meetings."

"Yeah, I know some about them. Why do you wantto know?" He sounded reluctant to go there.

I explained, using a highly condensed version ofthe wave of horror stories that made *Friday the 13th* movies look like Disney flicks.

"First of all, your patients are not making itup. It's out

there. Secondly, these are some dangerous,freaky people. We once ran across a case in the Midwest where a mob group ordered a hit on one of their own--a priest, of all people! Well, to avoid having to whack their own man, they hired these satanic guys to do it for them. But instead of shooting the guy execution style, they tie this guy down, disembowel him, eat his heart, and paint their fucking pentagrams on the wall-- with his blood! The mob guys vowed never again to hire those assholes." He snorted. "They were too sick, even for the mob."

Charles was on a roll now. His face turned a shade of salmon that caused me to wonder if Charles knew the priest personally.

"And these are not gas-station attendants. Congressmen, judges, surgeons, district attorneys--even members of the clergy are involved." He paused, pulled a fresh handkerchief from his sport coat pocket, and dabbed at the beads of sweat below his hairline. The topic evidently evoked powerful feelings in him.

"Is there a national organization or just a number of independent cult groups?" I could hear my words echo inside my head due to the imbalance of air pressure. I wondered if perhaps I was talking too loudly.

"I don't know. Maybe I'll find that out."

Now he mopped his brow and forehead. Did he sweat whenever he spoke? I wondered. Was his suit too hot, or had my questions excited some nerve?

"How many of these groups are in existence, do you think?" Knowing that I might never again have the opportunity to speak with someone with inside information, I had to push this for all it was worth. His powerful words were very validating for me. Previously I had had only Shirley's testimony; now her recollections were confirmed in the spontaneous answers of a government official.

"Like I said, I don't really know much about their organization. I only came upon them by happenstance. I admit, just talking about them arouses my curiosity. But I don't know any more than what I've already told you." One final wipe of the brow and the Hanky Man put away the square of white linen.

I received his messages, verbal and nonverbal, to drop the inquiry. No matter. By now the 747 was landing gracefully upon the runway at Sarasota-Bradenton airport and rolling toward one of the few hangars illuminated after 9 P.M.

Upon landing, Charles darted out of his seat and through the space created in the aisle when I offered to help the little lady with her luggage. He offered a "Nice talking to you, Chris," and charged down the aisle beforeI could respond with any more than a "Yeah, you, too,"to the disappearing back of his silver head. There was no point trying to catch up with him. Charles had chosen to vanish into the muggy night likea vision I had created for my own enlightenment and then destroyed for my own protection.

But no, Charles was real. And there was no reason to believe that I'd ever see him again.

Chapter 10

Roller Coaster through a Haunted House

To a certain extent, I dreaded my old friends' visit to Florida as much as I looked forward to it. Gregg Fisher and his wife, Shawn, were devout Christians, and I knewthe topic of religion would surface at some point. It was inevitable. I was the "backsliding" Christian, and they were God's little messengers, sent to remind me of how far I had strayed.

Gregg, the popular president of our senior class in college, had already been enroute to answer his'calling' as a man of the cloth when he fell for Shawn, a cute and bubbly blonde with a zest for God and life. Newlywed, they suddenly took sick with mysterious symptoms that no one could diagnose. Eventually both were forced to drop out of graduate school and return to their family.

They had appeared on daytime talk shows, participated in research studies at the National Institutes of Health {NIH), and gone to all kinds of doctors, from endocrinologists to homeopathic physicians to psychiatrists. After ten years of submitting to ineffective medical protocols, they were finally diagnosed with Epstein-Barr virus--now called Chronic Fatigue Syndrome.

I admired these old friends because of their positive attitude. They had no job, no recreation, no energy, no income--and yet they had more faith and more *happiness* than I had ever known. They made me sick.

Watching Shawn and Gregg made me think about my

ongoing relationship with Laura. The Fishers were so much alike; Laura and I were polar opposites. I enjoyed parties and large groups of people. She preferred animals to people and loved a quiet evening alone. She was self-conscious and withdrawn in social situations. (Given her beauty, people often mistook her reserved behavior for aloofness, conceit, or arrogance. If they only knew how she trembled inside!)

I was breast-fed on the Bible; Laura had rarely seen the inside of a church. I lived and died forsports; Laura *came* to hate sporting events after living with a "small-time bookie" who refused her access to the telephoneor television during routine athletic contests. I was characteristically cool; Laura was fiery andexplosive.

On and on I explored our differences, to the pointof scaring myself. As I surreptitiously studied the Fishers' interaction, I came to realize that Laura was everything I wasn't. She was the anti-Chris!

Then I took off on a tangent. *Does that mean that opposites really do attract?* I asked myself. "Of course, they do," Imuttered, "but that doesn't mean that opposite interests--or sameness, for that matter--offer a solid foundation for marriage." I began to conclude that our differences were challenges to overcome, not reasons to marry or to separate.

All in all, the Fishers and I had a terrific visit, and as they prepared to leave, I felt hugely relieved that the question of religion never arose. Shortly after I had said my final good-bye to Gregg, however, Shawn sidledover to me.

"Chris," she asked, "what happened between you and *God?"*

Here we go, I thought. *I knew God would find a way to stick His nose into my business.* I answered truthfullyyet vaguely, just wanting the topic to go away. "I guess nothing happened, and that was the problem. I got tired of feeling guilty all the time and dealing with the perception that my prayers were only hitting the ceiling. I got tired of either feeling like a hypocrite or worrying that I was disappointing God. It just got old, you know? And really," I added, "I'm still the same guy I was, I just don't go to church anymore."

Shawn wore the look of a desperate woman, which made me feel all the more like the depraved sinner. "Is there anything we can do or that I could do besides praying for you--we pray for you all the time, Chris--to help you with this?"

Resentment and defensiveness formed my response: "Shawn, it's gonna take a miracle for me to believe in God the way I used to. I'm sorry, that's just how I feel right now."

Six weeks later, a demon-possessed woman sat in my office, and several of my new patients claimed to have firsthand experiences with demonic entities and even Satan himself.

I wasn't ready to label any of this "a miracle," but I'd be lying if I denied the life-altering implicationsof sitting across from a woman possessed.

Donna had been in therapy for seven months and long since discharged from the Palms hospital. She made enormous strides in our sessions by means of a series of nightmares that tormented her. On more than one occasion, she dropped off her journal with Sandy, my office manager, and requested urgently, "Please have Dr. Cortman read this before our next appointment."

Curious and obedient, I took the book of dreams home to the beach one Friday evening in mid-July. Delta Airlines promised to deliver Laura to me by 9:22 P.M. I was a man with a plan: Go for a run, read a few pages and learn about Donna's psyche, grab a shower, then head to theairport.

My run proved uneventful. I decided on the shorter route of three and a half miles, rather than the full six- mile length of the beach. I grabbed a tall glass of mineral water along with Donna's journal, plopped my sweat-soaked body down on a beach chair, and began to catch up on the inner turmoil of Donna's troubled life.

*   *   *

Monday, July 17--For the eighth straight night, I dreamt about my father. Each dream contained images of suffocation and the smell of dirt, and each night I awoke screaming, terrified by the look of intense rage on my father's face. For the first time I was able to piece together an entire scenario. God help me if it's true. I am no more than five or six in the dreamsand wearing the same maroon-colored jumper, a white blouse with ruffled sleeves, and my favorite black shoes with oversized silver buckles.

I was happy to be spending a day alone with my father. How I loved him, Dr. Cortman. He was tall and handsome. Short, jet-black hair, green eyes, and a firm chin. Rarely a smile, always a cigarette. New sky-blue shirt and chinos. Somewhere in my romantic, childish mind, I imagined that he had dressed up for me. I reveled in my role as "Daddy's Little Girl."

I picked a handful of pansies from our next-door neighbor's garden, near the backyard fence. I wasn't supposed to go there, but I wanted Daddy to have a special surprise. I don't know if any little girl ever loved her daddy more than I loved mine.

I climbed into the old white Ford, proud to be big enough to get in all by myself. I clutched the flowers in my right hand and slid across theleather seat as close to my father as possible.

"Where'd you get those?" he barked, referring to the flowers.

"They're for you, Daddy." I was beaming, myeyes aglow with love, admiration, and excitement.

Suddenly, *whack!* He backhanded me across the face. "I told you to stay away from the fence! What the hell is wrong with you? Are you stupid? Damn you, Donna! Gimme those flowers."

"I'm sorry, Daddy. I wanted you to have flowers." "Don't ever, ever pick them again. Do you understand me, young lady?" "Yes, Daddy."

"Next time, you won't get off so easily."

My left eye was throbbing and spinning stars floated about my head. Tears streamed down both ofmy cheeks, but I knew better than to make a sound. I didn't want to ruin the rest of our day together.

Besides, he did take the pansies.

My father drove in silence. We eventuallystopped at a gray house with black and gray awnings. The lawn was poorly maintained. An open garage door revealed a beat-up Chevy. Not surprisingly, the garage was a mess with rakes, oilcans, and broken bicycles strewn about.

If this was the final destination, I would be very disappointed. "Why are you stopping? Where are we?"

"Stop asking so many questions, will you? You sure have a big mouth for such a little girl, you know? Just wait here."

"Okay." I tried my best to conceal my hurt and disappointment. Daddy grabbed the pansies and yanked back the handle of the driver's car door, slamming it behind him.

I watch as he knocked on the front door, already partially ajar, while holding the flowers behind his back. A woman, probably in her late twenties, flung open the door and exclaimed, "Oh, hi, honey!

Daddy brought out his surprise flowers and said, "I got these for you."

My heart sank. I wondered if he knew I could hear every word of their conversation. He was lying. "*You're lying, Daddy! You're lying!*" The woman was tall, with strawberry blonde hair. She hugged and kissed Daddy right there in the doorway. "Oh, Dale, you shouldn't have. They're beautiful!"

Daddy reached back and closed the front door behind them. I waited in the car. And waited. (I don't know how long dreams last, Dr. Cortman, but I had the unmistakable feeling of having waited in that car a long, long time.) My eye throbbed. I studied the odometer and breathed in the merciless odor of Daddy's open ashtray; chock full of cigarettes butts. Funny thing, I could even see the crushed ends of his Camels in great detail.

Finally, Daddy emerged from the front door with this woman walking behind him. He was in a rush to get away from her. She held the flowers in her right hand. As they approached the car, she noticed me rising from my slumped position on the front seat.

"Oh, your little girl! Isn't she adorable? What's your name, darling?"

The nearer the lady came to the car, the more I could

see imperfections in her heavily made-upface. Now her hair was a mess.

Daddy was all business. "Oh, that's Donna."He seemed embarrassed.

"Hi, Donna. Would you like one of my flowers your daddy gave me?"

I impulsively protested, "Daddy didn't get you those flowers. I picked them for him. They're Daddy's flowers, not yours!"

Daddy's face turned the crimson color that I learned to be wary of. He turned and said, "I'm sorry for my daughter's rude behavior, June. Listen, I gotta run. I'll see ya."

In retrospect, I gather that this was a wham-bam-thank-you-ma'am afternoon.

"Bye, honey! Bye, Donna!" June's frantic waves went unacknowledged by Daddy and me. I was mad at her for having the flowers I picked for Daddy. I was mad at him for giving them to her. Mostly though, I was scared. He was very angry.

Daddy sped off down the block and after a few turns, took me down a deserted side street. He came to a sudden halt and commanded me to get out of the car. I followed him out of the driver's side door and around to the back of the Ford. He inserted his key in the lock of the trunk and popped up the great big lid.

"You don't deserve to ride in the front seat with me, you rotten brat. I'll teach you to talk back and embarrass me."

He reached down for me and in one fell swoop tossed me into the trunk. I landed directly on the jack, my lower back slamming on the cold, hardmetal. Pain shot through me. "You will never, ever, fuckin' disrespect your father again." His rage continued as he slammed the trunk door down and left my ears ringing and myback pulsating.

He screeched the tires in peeling off down the back roads of an undeveloped suburban area. I was tossed about in the great trunk like a tiny ship in an angry sea. Battered, bruised, and terrified, I finally clung to the old spare tire as if locating a buoy upon which to gain some stability. More tears escaped my eyes.

At last, the trunk opened. "Get up," heordered.

His jaw jutted out; his neck muscles protruded. He yanked me out of the trunk and then reached intothe very back behind the tire iron and came out with a shovel. I had no idea what this was for.

He had parked in a wooded area. Behind Daddy's head, tall evergreens partially blocked the sun's rays. He led me to a path in the middle of a desolate wooded area. He reached a patch of ground that suited him for some reason and began digging while I watched. He tossed shovel after shovel of dirt into a pile on his left near a great oak tree. He muttered under his breath, "You're gonna learn, girl. You'll fuckin' learn."

I shook from the chill in the air and more so from the unbridled rage in his eyes. When he dug deep enough, he paused as if to admire his work. He picked me up and threw me in the freshly dug hole. I lay there stunned. Paralyzed by fear and wounded by my Daddy's rejection, I didn't know what to think or feel when Daddy shoveled the dirt on top of me. One shovelful after another he dumped, filling the hole, while repeating the mantra: "You're gonna learn, girl. You will learn."

Soon the dirt covered me so heavily that I couldn't move. My eyes and mouth were shut tightly now after making the mistake of leaving them open at first.

The smell of dirt has mysteriously plagued me at times throughout my entire life. I now know that it began on that Saturday afternoon.

I was so scared that I would die, I wet myself. Having been punished for wetting my panties before, I wondered if it would just be easier if I diddie.

After several minutes, Daddy began shoveling the dirt off me until at last I could breathe, see, move. I was actually happy to see him.

"Get up. Go shake off. I don't want any dirt in my car. You understand? No dirt at all. And get it all outta your hair. Aw, shit, you're wet! What the fuck didya do now? You pissed yourself like a little baby. Donna, you're hopeless."

He stopped and thought a minute. "Well, you're gonna have to pay for that, too. C'mere, you little whore."

He pulled out his still-wet penis (I now know from that blonde) and put it in my mouth. He held my temples firmly with both hands and thrust back and forth, gagging me with every forward movement.

"Oh, yeah, baby, that's good," I could hear as he pounded and pounded into the back of my throat. I was confused and hurt that Daddy was doing this to me again. My back was killing me, my pants were soaked, and my throat was sore from the repeated pounding. I wished he would've left me in the dirt to die.

Fortunately, he stopped soon afterward, his body shaking as his penis pulsated in my mouth, sputtering and excreting a nasty but familiar substance onto the back of my tongue. "Oh, God, yes, he said in a victorious tone. He even rubbed my head for a moment until he withdrew and said,

"Don't you dare spit out Daddy's little gift to you. You swallow that, girl. Understand? And not a word to anyone about this, or I'll whip your ass so bad you'll wish to be dead."

What he didn't know was that I was already wishing for that. He found an old rag for me to sit on so I wouldn't dampen his upholstery. He reminded me if questioned to say that I had been playing in the dirt at the park ... had fallen a few times and hit my eye on a swing. "Above all," he emphasized, "you tell your mother we had fun today. A lot of fun. Understand?"

"Yes, Daddy."

*　*　*

Oh, Dr. Cortman, another miserable night. It's 3:47 according to my clock radio. It's not that I can't fall asleep. It's just that sleep invites dreaming, and dreaming these days is a roller-coaster ride through a haunted house. Can it be that the most dangerous place on earth is the dark, unexplored layers of my unconscious mind?

Either I really am crazy or the dreams about my father are true. The scariest thought of all is, I would be relieved to know that the former iscorrect! But I don't think I'm crazy. I don't act like acrazy person. Worst of all, these nightmares *feel right!* From the very first nightmare of my father in the shower, I knew they were true. How am I supposed to live with the idea that *my own father fucked me?* Dammit, Dr. Cortman! Dammit! The pain is too great to bear!

Please, please, please tell me it's all in my mind. Tell me he would never, ever do this to me. He loved me. Tell me he loved me. Please! Why wasn't I lovable? What was wrong with me? What did I do wrong?

Now it's 5:36 A.M. I've been in the bathroom crying. Every fiber of me screams with rage andburns with despair. I took out the razor blades again.I wanted to slice my wrists. Let the blood flow. Peace. Peace at last. But I couldn't follow through. Why not? Because something within--a force, a strength, something--made me drop the blades before I could do any real damage.

I can only hope and pray for one thing: Please, God, send the daylight soon. Let this night be over.

I set the journal aside and wondered how much more she could take. Would I lose her? "oh, God, help her," I prayed. "Touch her wounded soul. Have mercy, sweet Jesus."

That was the first time I had turned to God in many years. My plea came as a complete surprise to me.

I thought of that "part of her" that she described that somehow keeps her alive. I needed to believe that her hope, her faith, her very survivorship, were qualities that *I*, too, had to connect with, build upon, believe in. If I were to help Donna and Shirley, I would need more help and guidance than my research and my friend Richard could give me.

Chapter 11

Donna's Distress Call

"Donna Carrington's on line one," Sandy informed me on the office intercom. "She's been on hold and is very agitated."

"Thanks," I replied, preparing myself for what could be another in a series of crises for Donna. *Whatever it is,* I thought, *I don't need this* today--not after back-to-back sessions with underachieving, unmotivated adolescents who didn't care if they saw me or not. "If I had wanted to pull teeth, I'd have gone into dentistry," I muttered, bathing in self-pity. One more deep breath, a mind-clearing exhale, and I punched the blinking button on the white telephone.

"Hi, Donna, what's up?" I said in a positive way, attempting to convince both of us that everything was going to be all right.

"Oh, Dr. Cortman, I'm a mess. I'm not sure where I am. I don't know how I got here. I'm lost. I'm scared. I—"

"Please deposit one dollar and thirty-five cents for the next three minutes," interrupted a recorded message.

"I don't have any more money." Donna began to sob. "Okay, okay. Calm down. What is the number on the phone? I'll call you back."

After a short hesitation, she read me the numbers. "Is that the eight-one-three area code?" I hoped she hadn't vanished in one of those fugue states I'd read about in graduate school, where people sometimes turn up in other parts of the country with no recollection as to how they got there.

"Yes, eight, one, three. Please don't hang up, Dr. Cortman."

"I have to, but only long enough to call you right back. So, hang up, and I'll call you immediately, okay?" I did not want to sound condescending, rendering such simple instructions, but her condition impressed me as being regressed, childlike.

"Okay. Please don't forget to call me." "I won't forget."

As I dialed Donna's pay phone number, I realizedthat the exchange she had given me numbers for was generally assigned to Port Charlotte, thirty to forty minutes to the south of Venice. What was happening here? Seemingly before it rang, the phone was answered. "Hello? Donna?"

"Yes, who's this?" She didn't sound the same asduring the previous call.

Who is this? My insides screamed. Who the bloody hell do you think it is? Of course, I restrained myself. "It's Dr. Cortman. Are you all right?"

"Of course. I'm fine, Dr. Cortman. Nice of you to call and ask."

I felt like Lou Costello in the famous "Who's on first?" skit. Before my frustration escalated, I recalled the phone conversation with Shirley when I first learned about her multiplicity. "Do you know where you are?'

"No, I don't really." She sounded soft, controlled, and curiously, without a hint of panic in her voice. "Doyou?"

"Possibly Port Charlotte. Can you describe your surroundings?"

"I'm near a busy road, two lanes going each way, lined with numerous restaurants, especially fast-food places. I am right next to a 7-Eleven."

"Okay." I glanced at the clock. It read four fifteen, and my four o'clock client was inclined to be ten minutes early for her appointments; she had waited long enough. "You are on Route Forty-one, Donna, and all you need to do is go north for a half hour or so and you'll reach Venice. Then I'm sure you'll recognize the area and make it home safely. Are you okay to drive?"

"What kind of a question is that, Cortman? You know I don't drink."

This voice was a change from the previous two. I wasn't sure why it sounded familiar, but I remembered that caustic side of Donna from another time. Satisfied that she could drive home safely, I repeated the instructions before requesting, "Call me tonight from home, no matter what."

"Thank you, Dr. Cortman." Nice, polite Donna again. As a fail-safe system, I asked Sandy to call the Port Charlotte police and ask them to keep an eye out for my dear, lost Donna.

*　　*　　*

During my next break between clients, I contemplated Donna's amnesiac journey to Port Charlotte. Where had she intended to go? How had she lost the time? Why had I felt as if I were talking to three different people--a terrified child; a calm, courteous adult; and a defensive, angry individual? What had triggered such an episode?

The best answers I could find resulted from my comparing Donna with Shirley, my only other client who lost time and switched her presentations as dramatically as Donna had today. But there were some glaring differences: Shirley routinely referred to herself in the first-person plural ("Sorry we're late!) and with names she had created for her alters--"personalities," as she preferred they be called. Donna demonstrated nothing like that ... at least not yet.

Donna's Friday appointment was purposely scheduled for four o'clock, normally the last session of the week; we could comfortably run over the usual time allotment, if need be.

She arrived dressed to the hilt after a day at the accounting firm: a tan suit, tangerine blouse, matching shoes and bag. Her greeting was warm and friendly, which with Donna, was never something to take for granted. Abig smile brightened her face, reassuring me that all was in order.

"You seem well, Donna," I remarked, demonstrating more optimism than conviction. "Is that *so?*"

"Yes, I feel very well, thank you. It's fun to come here." Her smile was flirtatious.

"Therapy is fun?" I echoed, resisting the opportunity to wisecrack in response.

"Oh, yes. I enjoy coming here. Do you know what we're doing this weekend?" Her excitement was uncharacteristic, although after the distressed phone call of two days before, I was no longer certain as to what really was characteristic of Donna.

"No, what will you be doing this weekend?" She giggled. "I'm not supposed to tell you. Uh-oh, I gotta go."

"Go?" Bewildered, I stared at her blankly. But before I could get any clarification, I watched Donna's eyelids flutter several times and then open widely, barring an intense expression devoid of the amusement she had presented upon entering the session.

"Dr. Cortman?"

"Uh, yes." I wondered who she was expecting.

"I should apologize for Sally. She's such a flirt."

"Sally?"

"Yes, she was just here. Didn't you talk to her?" "And who, may I ask, am I speaking to now?" I didn't expect to be talking to other facets of Donna. While she had left numerous hints of her multiplicity, I didn't know I'd ever hear her refer to herself in the thirdperson.

"It's Dianna. We've spoken before." "Really, when?"

"On the phone a couple of days ago. You gave me directions. You were most kind. I thank you for helping us, Dr. Cortman. Many of us were very frightened. Could you tell?"

I sidestepped the question, asking one of my own. "Who was so frightened, Dianna?"

"Well, mostly the children. They don't do well when they don't know where we are. Being lost always scares them." When she looked intently at me, her blue eyes wearing nary a hint of Sally's amusement and playfulness, I wondered if I had just met Donna's inner self-helper.

"How many children are there, Dianna?" I wanted to know what she knew about whom she was sharing Donna's mind with. More importantly, I wanted to know what I was up against.

"I don't know the exact number of children, Dr. Cortman, but I do know this: The children carry the bulk of the pain. They are the ones who hold the memories for all of us. You have earned their trust thus far, but much more work awaits you." She stopped abruptly, her eyes darting about nervously.

"What's wrong, Dianna?"

"Uh, well, there is someone who is not pleased with the fact that I'm talking to you." Abruptly her expression became anxious, paranoid. She cocked her head, seemingly listening to something I could not hear.

"Who is that someone, Dianna?" I was eager to undercover the keys to her private inner turmoil, but that was not destined to happen that day.

Her eyelids fluttered for about five seconds, heralding another obvious change in demeanor. So, Donna changes alter personalities whenever she flutters her eyelids, I thought. Had she done so in previous sessions without my noticing? Or only now did she feel safe enough to start showcasing her alters?

"Who is here now?" I continued, as the fact-gathering newspaper reporter.

"What kind of a question is that?" she demanded. "I've been coming to you nine months, and you ask who's here?"

She was not confused, I decided. Donna hurled sarcasm at me in order to shift the focus off of her personalities. Apparently, I had gotten too close for comfort.

"I was just talking to Dianna," I said matter-of-factly, "somehow you don't seem to be the same person, so I had to ask."

"Ha! I'm no Dianna! She's so prissy! Miss Goody Two Shoes herself. That'll be the day when I sound like her."
"Exactly my point," I replied. "Which is why I keep asking who you are. Or would you prefer to remain anonymous and mysterious?"

"I'm not trying to be mysterious," she said in a huff, and crossed her legs in an exaggerated Hollywood gesture. "Don't flatter yourself, Cortman." Her pitch heightened; her tone amplified with each new thought. "I don't even give your kind a second thought. I couldn't give a rat's ass if you find me mysterious or anonymous or anything else for that matter. Just remember, you don't know shit about me."

"Wait just a second. Excuse me for interrupting your tirade, but what exactly do you mean when you say, 'my kind'? Are you talking about half-Greek, half-Italian psychologists from Jersey or what?" My intention was to lighten the mood and avert the focus from whatever she found so threatening. I hoped to lessen the intensity level so she might be able talk without the defiance, sarcasm, or worse yet, yelling.

"No, I don't mean shrinks. God knows we have seen enough of those in our time."

"We?" This was the first time I'd heard Donna use the first-person plural to describe herself. I leaned forward as therapists sometimes do when demonstrating acute interest or caring.

"Yeah, we, us. Okay, so now you know, Sherlock. Donna is not one person. There are many of us. Have been for a long, long time. So whaddaya gonna do, Cortman, lock us up again? Think we're crazy now, do ya?"

"No, relax. No one's getting locked up. I appreciate your honesty. And if it's okay with you, I'd like to ask a few more questions. If you'd prefer not to answer them, that's fine, too."

She shrugged apathetically and muttered, "Knock yourself out, Doc."

"Thanks. First, instead of calling you 'You,' 'Miss X,' or 'Mystery Lady,' how about if you give me a name, even if it's not your real name. That way, I'll know whenever I'm speaking to you." (As if there'd be any mistaking this "beloved" part of Donna.)

"My name's Mary. I assume you have no problem with my calling you Christopher." Apparently, Mary needed to remain on equal footing with me.

"None whatsoever," I conceded, pleased to be getting somewhere. "Thanks for trusting me with your name. Do you mind if we go back to that previous statement of 'your kind'? I'd really like to understand that if possible."

"It's men. That's 'your kind.'" She nailed me with angry eyes and raised her voice. "As long as she's been alive, men have been hurting her. Using her. Screwing her. Or, as in the case of the asshole she married, ignoring her. Men are not to be trusted. I can't believe there's a good one out there, no matter how they appear on the surface."

Once again, I intended to chime in and lower the intensity. But I was smote by a sudden awareness that Gestalt therapists call an "Aha experience". I *had* met Mary, in the very beginning of our marital-therapy sessions with Peter! Hers was the angry, defiant voice that prompted me to excuse Peter from the session to talk to her alone.
In fact, I'd spoken to her several times.

"Didn't we speak on the phone from Port Charlotte the other day, Mary?"

"Yeah, but it wasn't my idea to call you. I knew I could get us home. And I did," she proclaimed proudly.

Who were the other two alters? I wondered. Perhaps Dianna and ... a child, I'd guess. "You don't like to ask for help, especially from a man. My guess is it makes you vulnerable to abuse."

"Aren't we perceptive, Christopher?" she taunted nastily. You *are* a good listener."

"But I'm also a man, so trusting me won't be easy." I leaned back in my swivel seat and kicked off my loafers, tucking my right leg under the left. If leaning forward conveyed interest earlier, I now leaned back to communicate safety and harmlessness. I had my work cut out for me if I were to become Mary's first trustworthy man. I chuckled silently as I compared myself to Captain Kirk and the starship *Enterprise,* boldly going where no man had gone before.

"Who else did I speak to? Dianna?"

"Why don't you ask her? It's not my job to inform on the others."

"Okay, let me ask you something else instead. When did you come to be? I mean, I'm assuming that Donna was born as one person. When did she, uh, create you to help her?" I attempted to be as respectful as possible while still communicating safety.

She just shook her head quietly. Then, hunching forward, she buried her eyes in her hands momentarily. As she looked up, pain overcame her face. "She... she's not ready, Dr. Cortman. Please. She's not ready yet. Please be patient with us."

"That's fine. There's no rush. We can move at whatever pace you can handle. Hey, I'm new at this, too. I'm learning all the time. Thanks for sharing what you have, Mary."

But somewhere in the moments of hiding her face in her trembling hands, Mary had slipped back into the sanctuary of Donna's psyche. Someone gazed up at me with tender eyes and a soft expression. Her furrowed brow underscored her words. "Oh, my head is killing me, Dr. Cortman. What happened?"

I assumed correctly that Donna had returned to the

session. "What's the last thing you remember?" I asked, hopeful of gaining clues to figuring out when she becomes amnesiac.

"Truthfully?"

"That would be the preference."

Donna laughed at my response to her rhetorical question, then winced from the headache pain. "I don't even remember coming here today. What happened?"

A quick glance at the miniature desk clock revealed only a few minutes left in the session. I needed to summarize the events while being sensitive to how she might feel about the information. "I met some other parts of you *today--alter personalities,* they're called. I gather you have a teenager, plus a kind and optimistic person and a protective woman. Learning about you affords me the opportunity to help you."

"But what happened? Did I ...I'm confused." She pressed her fingertips to her temples. "You're saying that I have other people inside my head?"

"Not other people. Other parts of you. It's all you. And you will learn about every part of you when you're ready. Continue to journal, but with one addition: If any part of you writes, I'll ask her to sign her name after the entry. Got it?" Donna nodded.

"One more thing. If you want to ask about what happened today, go within for the answers. I believe you'll know what you're ready to know. And don't forget--you can always call if you need to."

*   *   *

My ride home that day was dominated by Donna's new voices, prompting a slew of questions: How many alters were there? Did they all have discernable names? jobs? Memories of their own? Why had they been headed to Port Charlotte? And just what frightened Dianna away when she was revealing too much?

I settled on Mary as being Dianna's intimidator. But as I subsequently found out, I was dead wrong.

Chapter 12

Multiple Lessons

From the early days of treatment with Shirley, I acknowledged that she was emerging as significant a person to me as I had become to her. She was the accidental professor; although she presented as helpless and insignificant, no one has ever come as close to schooling me on the traumatized mind as she.

Her decision to trust me resulted in an unusual display of openness and intimacy. Few people I've ever worked with have allowed me the consistent access to their inner world as Shirley did. "If I don't let you in," she once explained, "I simply won't make it."

First, she and I both learned to understand the purposeful and beneficial nature of dissociating. Withdrawing from a traumatic situation is always preferable to suffering through it. I have treated numerous patients who, as children, were exposed to compromising sexual episodes. More than a few of these boys and girls managed to escape the horror of the abuse by temporarily separating themselves from their body and emotions. This clever response granted them the advantage of watching the experience from the outside, often from the ceiling. This is dissociating, but it is not multiplicity.

With *repeated* exposure to trauma, as Shirley taught me, the frequent need to escape prompts the creation of other "people" to serve as substitutes for the youngster. Sometimes an event is perceived as so destructive to the self, the original child is believed to have died. Shirley was the first person ever to reveal to me that "little Shirley" had died. She required others not only to take her place but to function appropriately in any given situation.

I marveled at how creative she needed to be just to survive. I listened in amazement to a poem she wrote describing the transformation of a paternal rape into a day at the park:

As he kisses my face I am alerted

At once to make my way for the park. He caresses my thighs, gently at first, And I know the pain can't be too far.

I am no longer there when he penetrates me. Running free, I ascend a great oak tree.

He pushes, he pounds, and he drives within me, Making sounds that I do not hear.

For I ride on a swing, climbing.

Higher & higher with a breeze that blows through My long hair.

Perspiration streams from his brow, Falling down on my face like the Gentle rain bringing coolness

Shirley also taught me about the versatility of the alter personality. Whatever role had to be assumed or function undertaken, an alter could be created to fulfill the task. A five-year-old child does not possess thewisdom and experience of a senior citizen, but Shirley forged an identity to provide her with such. "Stella," Shirley'slone alter who could qualify for social security, was imagined to be perched in a rocking chair, with any one of the hurting children upon her lap.

Alters could be either gender; Shirley had a "rage" alter bearing the name Joseph. When she needed an extra burst of fiery anger with a penchant for destruction, Joe might appear out of the shadows. I imagined him as across between the Tasmanian Devil and the White Tornado.

Some of Shirley's alters were designed to be her protectors. Deniers like Pauline were keepers of the secrets. She appeared on several occasions to spar with me or advise me that everything I had just heard from Shirley or her alters was untrue. Others, like the aforementioned Teller, were designed to provide information and iron out the wrinkles in her presentation. Julie took care of business, while the alter named Daddy terrorized the children inside exactly like the man for whom he was named. Some alters, like Colleen, sought a safe return to the cult. "Mary" on the other hand, aimed to sever all ties with evil and follow God. Numerous children cried in the night as the memories surfaced. A depressed alter, Sandy, harbored immeasurable despair and hopelessness; eventually she committed suicide in Shirley's mind.

Shirley also introduced me to the concept of co-consciousness. Certain alters knew about the presence of other ones and could hear and observe whatever might be happening. Shirley, however, was not co-conscious with all of her alters, a situation that often led to pathetic (albeit humorous) episodes of lost time and belongings.

More than once, she was lost on her way home from my office. Too often she wasted precious hours looking for belongings that other alters had either misplaced or deliberately hidden. One afternoon Shirley called in tears, pleading to know where her car keys were so she could get to work on time.

I needed to teach her some very basic cognitive and behavioral skills, such as keeping a record of business and financial transactions and even to leaving notes to herself on the kitchen table, with requests such as: "Anyone know what happened to the book we were reading on Feeling Good?"

Many other types of here-and-now-focused treatment culminated in instructions on how to relax, how to make certain only adult alters drove the car, and how to cope with an unstable ex-husband.

Examples abounded of her inability to have one hand know what the other hand was doing. One unforgettable day, the office felt too unsafe an environment for a therapy session, so Shirley and I strolled to the picnic tables outside the Sarasota courthouse.

"I can't handle this money thing anymore," she told me. "Maybe we aren't making the progress I thought we were."

"What's going on, my lady?" said I, keeping the cheerful tone in my voice.

"Well, I don't seem to have around the money I ought to, considering the number of hours I'm working at Bronco's. I don't know where it's disappearing, but I ain't spending it on anything that I know of. I'm so fucking pissed!" She banged her fist on the rough tabletop, and tears of frustration filled her eyes.

Shirley had always been fiscally responsible with me, even after negotiating a reduced fee. She was never one to squander anything. She lived on the most basic provisions and rode a small motorcycle to save on gas.

I knew by now that someone could shed light on this situation; I just didn't know who. "Why don't you pick a spot on the table and stare at it," I suggested, "and breathe deeply and concentrate on my words. Relax."

As always, Shirley responded quickly to the hypnotic instructions, despite the passersby on their way into the courthouse. Within moments her eyes opened. Her facial expression communicated, "I'm here. Now what?"

I went right for the information. "Do you know what's going on with Shirley's missing money?"

"Yeah," she answered. "About once a week or so, she gets a phone call from Doris, asking to speak to me."

"Uh-huh. And who are you?" "Elaine."

"And what do you do?"

"I send Doris at least one hundred dollars everytime she

calls."

I wondered who knew how to elicit this type of mindless obedience from Shirley. "Does anyone else know about this, Elaine?"

"I don't think so."

"Well, thanks for coming. I appreciate your sharing. It's okay to return me to Shirley now ... unless there's more you want to tell me."

She shook her head, closed her eyes, anddisappeared.

If Shirley had been "pissed" before Elaine's appearance, she was doubly irate after it. "I hate her so bad for doing this to me. She knows I barely earn enoughto support my kid. How couldshe?"

"Who is Doris anyway?" I finally inquired. I didn't expect the response that I got.

"Doris is my mother." She looked at me incredulously, as if I should have known her mother's first name.

"Your mother calls you and triggers you to send her your money?" I was in disbelief.

"Never again," Shirley said bitterly. "Never again will she get a fuckin' dime from me."

Speaking of money, Shirley taught me another thing about myself--treating her was more important to me than getting paid for doing it. After more than a year of treatment, Shirley asked to cancel a month of sessions due to financial reasons. I refused, letting her know that we had come too far to stop. In fact, never again did I ask for another penny from her. All I ever wanted was to see her dream become a reality: "I would just like to know at the end of any given day what I had done that day, without losing any time."

Shirley and I were both novices in regard to the

integration of alters. I explained integration to Shirley by furnishing her with the following analogy: "Imagine that you're a snowman. Let each alter represent a snowball. When an alter integrates, it is as if that snowball is smashed into the snowman to become an inseparable part of it. The snowball and snowman are now one entity, stronger than before the fusion. Nothing is lost in their union. The snowman retains all the properties of the snowball."

The last point, the concept of Shirley's capacity to retain the skills and characteristics of each integrating alter, could not be overstated. For example, Lorraine, the first alter to attempt integration, was terrified that her services as designated driver would be lost forever. I learned in session about her responsibilities when one of the child alters reportedly wrested control of the motorcycle and took all of Shirley for a painful spill.

My best efforts were necessary to convince Shirley/Lorraine that she would be capable of successfully negotiating the ride home without Lorraine at the helm, especially because her version of integrating was to say good-bye to each alter and imagine him/her walking out of her life forever. Again, Shirley chose to trust me andsaid farewell to Lorraine.

We were both moved by the emotional story that Lorraine shared before departing: "Shirley's father used to chase me around on his motorcycle during afternoon gatherings with the group. He wasn't about to run me over, but I didn't know that at the time. He was doing it to show off his ability to scare his daughter to the other men. He would come so close to us and then turn the bike away at the last second while the other men roared with laughter. I took these experiences for Shirley. Later, I took a more important role--I rode the motorcycle and did all the driving for us no matter what condition we were in. When some of the others were drinking heavily and doing drugs, I made sure there were no accidents and no DUIs." She spoke through tears.

I guess I saved Shirley's life. But Idon't think she needs me to be a separate person. Please make sure she's okay without me. And don't let the kids drive, all right? Good-bye, Chris."

And just like that, Lorraine was gone. And Shirley was still capable of driving her motorcycle like a pro.

As we continued to work together, Shirley and I devised strategies essential to keeping her on track. For example, we needed to create a safe place for her to retreat to when she felt too overwhelmed by both past and present stressors. I suggested she use the same park she had written about in her poem as a refuge from emotional storms.

"This is your safe place, Shirley," I said. "No one can visit you there without your permission. No one can hurt you at the park. It's always secure and sunny. When you feel ready, you can leave the park and face whatever you need to."

I wasn't surprised that she retreated there often. We created other boundaries, especially regarding personal welfare and protection. During one difficult session, Shirley reported that a man in the cult had taught her to deal with overwhelming emotional pain by using a razor blade to slice neat gridlike patterns in her arm. The cuts, he had said, would allow some blood to spill and thus provide immediate pain relief.

While I worked to validate Shirley's feelings, I said something that made a lasting impression upon her: "It's not okay to hurt yourself, Shirley. You don't deserve to be abused by anyone ever again--especially not yourself! I understand why you feel what you feel, but you need a more constructive manner to release your pain. You can draw, write, cry, dance, exercise, scream--exactly what you do doesn't matter--but it's *not* all right to hurt Shirley anymore."

She claimed to have been unaware that hurting herself was "not okay." After that conversation, she abused herself only one more time.

Suicide was an even more serious concern. Multiples wrestle with "wanting to dine as regularly as overeaters grapple with craving carbohydrates. The most natural reaction to pain is an attempt to remove it. Take a pill, get a shot, drink alcohol, fall asleep. Whatever it takes. Those who suffer from chronic debilitating pain--physical or emotional--are many times more likely to consider suicide than the pain-free population. It makes perfect sense: If I no longer exist, I will no longer suffer. But I instructed Shirley that suicide, like the self-mutilation, was not an option. In its stead, I offered her as many alternatives as I could think of, from support groups to my home phone number.

I have since treated numerous self-mutilators who report similar rationale: Bloodshed relieves the emotional pain by bringing the hurt to the surface. Not surprisingly, every self-mutilating patient I've ever seen reports a history of sexual abuse as a child.

Incredibly, Shirley always had room in her recovery for a sense of humor. She tolerated my attempts to lighten the mood by poking a little fun at the concept of multiplicity. Once, she arrived for a session after eating lunch out by herself. "Did you ask for separate checks?" I inquired.

Or the standard joke people ask me when they learn of my specialization in treating multiples: "Do you charge each personality separately?"

But more importantly, Shirley injected her own dry, sometimes crass wit into her otherwise no-nonsense approach to therapy. The Valentine card she sent me as a surprise said it all: "Life is tough, times are hard. Here's your fucking Valentine card." I was touched by the sentiment.

She also sent a note she had uncovered in a card store. It read: "I'm lost--I've gone to look for myself. If I should return before I get back, please ask me to wait."

Shirley's capacity to laugh at her condition was like the premise of the *M*A*S*H* television sitcom--if we don't find things to laugh about, we will surely have to cry. And laugh she did, but never to the exclusion of tears.

Which leads to perhaps the most critical of the eternal lessons Shirley taught me. No injury, insult, loss, trauma, or horror existed that could not be healed through grieving. More specifically, an outpouring of excruciating pain via buckets of tears repeatedly lifted Shirley's spirits from the depths of despair and hopelessness to a level of faith and hope. I marveled at her resiliency. If Shirley, by courageously facing the unconscionable horrors inflicted upon her and grieving them, could find peace, then who among us was doomed to a life of hopelessness and depression?

But we were still only at the beginning of along, dark Journey.

Chapter 13

The Bald Man by the Tree

Once an individual commences the process of remembering childhood trauma, he or she might as well be opening Pandora's box. One ugly memory after another rushes to the surface without prompting or digging frantically into the past. I was fascinated to witness the presentation of "new" memories taking on a range of formats, including dreams, visual flashbacks, body sensations, or even disturbing repetitive thoughts, to name just a few.

Donna seemed to be doing the bulk of her remembering in her nightmare-filled sleep, but on this particular autumn day, she tried an altogether new method. Barely past the first few minutes of small talk, she began to complain about the conditions in my Venice office.

"I'm cold, Dr. Cortman. Is it cold in here?" Shuddering and shivering as if in obvious pain, she rubbed her hands together to create heat. Her teeth chattered, her eyes grew far away as her focus apparently constricted to a spot on the predominately gray and mauve pattern of the wallpaper behind me. Her frozen presentation was so convincing, I almost expected to see clouds of vapor emanating from her nostrils. But, of course, a climate-controlled thermostat regulated the temperature in this office complex at seventy-five degrees Fahrenheit.

Subjectively, Donna was freezing; objectively, a few degrees cooler might have been better for optimal productivity. I offered her my jacket to wear, concerned that she might be fighting off a germ.

"No, thank you." She continued to rub her hands together furiously. "It's so cramped in here, Dr. Cortman, isn't it?"

"What do you mean 'cramped'?"

"There's no--there's no room in here. I can't get out!"

"You aren't trapped," I reassured her, completely missing the boat. "You can get out at any time."

"No, no. I can't get out." Her stare burned a hole in the wall behind me.

Suddenly the light went on in my head. My office was not too cold, nor too tight, nor too difficult to escape. *Donna isn't here!* I realized, then asked, "Where are you, that you can't escape?"

"I don't know. It's dark and very cold. I'm scared. I want to go home." Donna's eyes, still steadfast in her self-induced trance, grew moist. Her eyebrows drew together.

"You say it's dark. Do you see any light?" I was playing Lieutenant Colombo, as suggested by an internationally renowned psychologist in a workshop I had attended recently.

She said nothing for thirty seconds, then, "Yes. I see light above me. It's smelly in here and loud. Everything echoes." She shuddered again, seemingly suffering from a combination of cold and fright.

"What kind of smell," I inquired, not sure anymore if I were was talking to Donna or to a child alter. I decided the "who" was far less important than the "what."

"It's, ah, it's sorta musty. Yeah, musty smell and water."
"Water?"

"There's water below me. Oh, I can hear some dripping

in the water. I'm looking, looking up, trying to see Daddy. Daddy, Daddy, let me up! No. No. I mustn't cry! I don't cry anymore! Daddy says big girls don't cry. Hewon't stand for it. Pull me up, Daddy, pull me up!"

Though still not clear as to where she was, nor what she was experiencing, Donna seemed to be remembering her exact thoughts at the time.

"Wait. Shhhh," she continued. "They're talking and laughing. They're laughing! Why? I want to get out of this well!" Donna struggled about in her seat, her arms andlegs flailing desperately in a possible attempt to ascend from the depths of a well.

To some extent, I guessed, this made sense. Cold, dark, musty, echoes, water and light from above--these were all consistent with her reported location. Her father laughing from above. Well, that wasn't inconsistent with what I had been hearing for months about this allegedly sick bastard. But something else was even more troubling: Who were the "they" laughing with her father? Could other people possibly have been involved in this scene? I hoped it was a misunderstanding--you know, something that is terrifying to a child but not deliberately abusive on the part of adults. My attempt at self-consolation was in vain; I wasn't buying my own explanations. Still, I sat quietly and let Donna continue.

"I feel like I'm suspended by something," she continued, her tone and word choice reflective of an adult state. "I can feel something here," she described, pointing to her waist and then circling it with her right hand. "Perhaps a rope?" she contemplated. "Yes, they tied a rope around my waist and lowered me into this well."

For the first time since the onset of her trance she broke

her stare from the wallpaper and turned my way, possibly to ground herself in reality. "Do you think I'm making this up?"

A pathetic look encased her countenance; she appeared helpless and vulnerable, making me acutely aware of the awesome power I possessed as trusted therapist.

"Why don't we just process what is here first," I suggested, "and then we can analyze the material later as to its veracity and its meaning. If it's at all possible to continue, please do."

Donna removed her glance from the kind expression I sought to render and turned her head slowly to her left, almost instinctively, relocating to the same area of wallpaper to climb back into the well. I had seen this before with other trauma survivors. Once a "memory"was activated, a person could go in and out of the memory numerous times, as if coming up for air while diving repeatedly in a shallow swimming pool.

Seconds later, Donna resumed her shivering. "'Are you ready to come up now and obey your father?' Ooh, I hate the sound of his loud voice echoing in my head." Donna pressed her hands over her ears, and tears hung on her lower eyelashes. "I don't want to be brought out of the well to him." Her fear joined forces with grief, prompting me to hand the Kleenex box to the now sobbing woman, face buried in the palms of her hands.

"It's all right. Go ahead and let it out," Ireassured her. "You're safe now."

"No! I mustn't cry. I must be strong. I need to obey my daddy."

The tears ceased. She returned to the wallpaper and the well and continued her description. But this time, her voice was devoid of emotion, robotic. I knew another "switch" had taken place, but to inquire about an identity would only sidetrack Donna from the main focus of processing her memory.

"He's pulling *her* out," began the narrator. "He has the wicked smile of the Cheshire cat. She hates him. She's so afraid of what he'll do next. Three other men are with her father. She hates them, too. They are in with him."

"What does 'in' mean?"

She may have ignored the question. "They're up to no good. 'It's my turn,' says the bald one, and he grabs her by the hand. She goes far, far away where he'll never find her. Amy takes over. She's the one who pleases the men. The others don't like her... The man takes Amy behind a big tree. The bald man zips down his fly and pulls out his—"

The narrator paused, her eyes flicking a glance at me before the eyelids fluttered in the telltale alert that another personality was on its way.

"What are you, some kinda pervert, Christopher? I'll bet you get your jollies off these sex stories. You're no different from any other man. You've got one thing in mind, don't you?"

"Mary, is that you?" I asked, hoping I was correct. "Oh, it's Mary all right, and not the mother of Jesus, in case you're confused."

"Thanks for clarifying. So, what brings you here today?"

"Why do you make her tell you these things? We went all these years without talking about them, and we survived. None of the other therapists she's gone to ever knew any of this. Who do you think you are, Dr. Freud?"

Her scowl, I gathered, was designed to intimidate me. "Somebody in there must be very frightened, Mary, or you wouldn't have appeared when you did. I think your attack on me is a rather deft maneuver, designed to remove the focus from the memory."

Her bluff called, Mary vanished through the same door whence she had arrived--the eyelids fluttered, and another alter appeared.

"Dr. Cortman, I'm sorry we make this so hard for you. Please understand we are all so terrified of facing our past. It's very bad, you know--so much worse than anything we've told you so far."

"You sound like Dianna."

"Yes." A quick smile of appreciation lit up her face.

I felt gratified. "Hi, Dianna. I could sure use some direction here. Should we return to the well and deal with what happens next, or has Donna had enough for the day?"

"Let me consult the wise one. I'll be back."

I had not yet encountered a "wise one." Dianna went inside for approximately five minutes, eyes closed, head tilted downward slightly. I could still see her eyes dart back and forth, like a person in REM (the rapid-eye- movement state of sleep) or, more accurately, like certain hypnotized subjects. At last Dianna reappeared with a determined set of her chin.

"Stephanie was good to meet with me, Dr. Cortman. I feel like she has a plan."

"Is Stephanie 'the wise one'?"

"Yes, she's old and quite tired. None of us know how long she has left to live. But she's gentle and so wise. She listens to our sessions, and she believes you can help us. She wants us to keep coming to you."

And so there it is, I thought. *I've got two thumbs up: one from the teenager and the other from the wise old woman.* But Mary, the man-hater, would probably prefer to castrate me than to look at me.

"Tell me about this plan."

I no longer felt fazed by sitting with a woman who claimed that her name was Dianna (although her legal name was Donna), who got advice from an old person in her head named Stephanie, after insulting me as another called Mary. Of course, all this after confusing my office for the inside of a well. Thankfully, most of my clients do not do this to me in a typical session.

"Stephanie figures it best to journal the remainder of the memory and have you read it. We are emotionally spent today. And if it's all right with you, we'd like to leave, even if our time is not up."

"Sure. I would never keep you here against your will. You are not trapped anymore." I lectured, intent on encouraging continued openness through perceived safety. "But I'd like to ask something of you."

"What would that be?"

"Before Donna returns to the room, please pass the information from today's session on to her so that she doesn't come back so confused. Could we try that?"

A silent nod preceded Donna's reappearance a minute later. Her face and shoulders sagged with weariness. *It's been a long day,* said the forlorn look she carried back with her from the dissociative trip.

"Oh, my head is pounding," she complained. (I now understood this to be standard symptom for switching alter personalities.) "I talked to Dianna. I know what I need to do. No offense, Dr. Cortman, but can I just go?"

"None taken. You did very well today. Please have a great weekend when you're not journaling, and maybe we can have even more fun next week."

She smiled wanly at my lame attempt to end her difficult day with some humor. "I can hardly wait," she replied.

Demetrio's is no one's idea of a four-star restaurant, but when it comes to fine, hearty Italian food in generous portions, you can't beat it. Not quite a regular in the brightly lit eatery, I am inclined to spend a lonely evening or weekend lunch with a book, some clinical paperwork, and a plate of spaghetti and meat sauce. Greek salad (no pepperoncini), buttered French bread (hold the garlic), and a Diet Pepsi complete the feast. (Everyone knows that a one-calorie drink can negate the effects of a five-pound plate of pasta.)

The joint was slow for a Thursday night--a nice, quiet atmosphere for immersing myself in Donna's new green and white journal--her second since beginning therapy--containing the promised completion of the memory of the well. Aware of the power of Donna's memories and their capacity to ruin almost anyone's appetite, I decided to start on the salad before devouring the first pages of her entry. I tore into a slice of bread, exhaled through both nostrils, and decided that I was ready for just about anything she might remember.

*   *   *

Don't ask who this is writing, Dr. Cortman. It's not important. If you want to know what happened to that little girl, then keep reading.

I was five at the time, I'm fairly sure. I say that because I was picked up from kindergarten by my dad instead of my mom or my maternal grandmother. I was so excited to have him there and all to myself.

I climbed into the front seat and slid across as close to Dad as I could (we didn't use seatbelts back then) and began to show him some of the finger paintings I created in school. Not surprisingly, Daddy's comment was, "Yeah, that's nice, Donna," in a less-than-convincing tone. In fact, he never even took his eyes off the road to see any of my work. He seemed tense, preoccupied. I didn't understand this at the time", but I felt the rejection as if pierced by a sharp blade in my abdomen. I sighed angrily and putmy paintings down on the seat to my right and waited. We would be home soon. Or so Ithought.

Daddy was not heading anywhere near home. He turned down some unfamiliar roads and headed into a desolate wooded area. Glancing nervously at his watch, he muttered a monosyllabic curse at whatever was wrong. Soon, he pulled up near a dirt path and followed it for the better part of what felt like five minutes. Eventually, we came upon a parked police cruiser, with three men leaning against it, smoking cigarettes and laughing as if they hadn't a care. Right on cue, Daddy pulled out a cigarette from his own omnipresent package of Camels and fired it up, as if to convey sameness with the others. He sprung open the driver's side door and directed me with a menacing glance to stay put. I complied anxiously, never taking an eye off of him.

"Where ya been, man? We've been waiting more than ten minutes for ya," said the tallest, a brown-haired man with a pointed nose and dark, beady eyes that shifted nervously. If he were a caricature, he would've been sketched as a rat.

"Yeah, sorry, Mike, the little bitch was running late from school. What am I gonna do, complain to the teacher that my little whore has a date with three of my buddies?"

All of the men laughed at this, snorting smoke through their nostrils. Two things became clear to me: Daddy was off the hook for being late, and I was an integral part of the men's plans for the afternoon. I began to shake as I heard my daddy's voice barkingout an order. "Donna, c'mon out here. Hurry up."

Although a little girl stumbled out of thestill- open door on the driver's side of the Chevy, it was not Donna. She escaped into the darkness upon hearing her father's command. Some other nameless children replaced her for the time being, as designated sacrificial lambs being led to slaughter. *We* walked toward the men obediently, maintaining a steady focus on the top of their dirty shoes. We didn't know exactly what they had in mind, but weknew it wasn't good. The child alters were numb,pint-sized robots, ready for programming by a wicked master.

"Let's go already... first cause I gotta go back to the beat. What do ya want for this, Dalerten bucks?"

"Gimme a break, Mike. A guy's gotta make a living. Look at her. She's adorable and experienced, too. I want twenty bucks apiece or forget it."

I look back at the irony, my father attempting to sell me for sexual favors by emphasizing how "adorable" I was--the only time I ever heard a compliment from him, and because he wanted to double his asking price for my services.

"That's a lotta cash, Dale," said another of the men, one with nasty stains on his boots and his too- short khaki workpants. "Can I give you a credit at the shop?',

"Yeah, sure, I may already owe you something for that pot roast last week. By the way, that was a great piece of meat." Turning to the others, he said, "But I want cash now from you guys."

Within seconds, Ratman whipped a bill from his wallet, and the transaction was complete. Shamelessly, he unzipped his fly and presented me with an already erect penis. My daddy was right about one thing--I was experienced and knew exactly what was expected of me. Emotionally, I might as well have been on the planet Pluto. They couldn't hurt me--at least not then. I went to work like the professional I had become. I knew how to work the equipment. The better I maneuvered my mouth, lips, and hands, the sooner it was all over. I took care of Ratman the Cop and then the butcher guy with the stained shoes.

But after the financial exchange with the third gentleman, a quiet bald man in a drab brown business suit, something happened: Daddy came and touched me gently on the head, as if to convey his pride in me or pleasure that I was making him a better chunk of change than he'd make in a day's work. That was all it took--the affection-starved Donna returned to the scene, gathering in the brief moment of physical approval from the man she loved so much. She was completely oblivious to the events of the past fifteen minutes and wondered briefly what the awful taste was in her mouth.

Turning her head toward his touch, Donna offered a great big smile to her beloved daddy. Embarrassed by her loving response in front of his comrades, he decided to regain his machismo by yanking her by the hair and turning her head back toward the man in the suit. Donna was stunned by the unexpected outburst of violence by her father, but before she had ample opportunity to descend back into the darkness and emerge as one of the alters designed for sex, she was greeted by the bald man's exposed penis. He stroked himself furiously, probably in an effort to sustain an erection so as not to seem inferior to the others, who had already demonstrated their masculinity.

But Donna was unaccustomed to dealing with sexual situations. She emitted a yelp and frantically ran from the pathetic, stocky man as fast as her tiny legs could carry her. As she found out quickly, that was a mistake.

Once again, her father was humiliated in front of his peers. That spelled rage for him and doom for Donna. He easily ran her down from behind and snatched her off the ground with both hands, slamming her into his muscular chest. Donna was gone now, the protective children gathering about to shield her from his likely retribution.

He slid his powerful forearm against her throat, all but collapsing her windpipe. She gasped for air while simultaneously creating a part of her who could survive with little or no oxygen. He carried her as a proud hunter would carry his game, slung over his mighty right shoulder, her head facing down.

"You won't disrespect your father, bitch. You will fuckin' obey me. I'll see to that. You're gonna learn a lesson today, girl. I am your father, you little shit. You do not run away from me, you fuckin' whore. Do you understand me?"

He did not want an answer. He was not done posturing for the boys. His anger seemed to grow with every curse until he realized that a mere scolding would not suffice. I guess he needed to punish and torture me to regain his status with his peer group.

We began to prepare for anything. "Gentlemen, this kind of behavior cannot be tolerated. The little whore has got to learn." He emphasized the last three words as if he were a concerned parent fretting over his dear child's inability to master her A-B-C's. "There's that abandoned farm a minute down the road. You know, Eddie Humphrey's old place? You know the well over there. I once seen it used to straighten out some of the other kids who got too smart for their britches. Let's take a quick ride down there, whaddaya say?"

"Listen, Dale, I don't give a shit that your daughter needs a lesson. I paid you twenty fuckin' clams, and I expect to be compensated."

"Compensated"? "What the hell does that mean? Speak fuckin' English, asshole. No one here cares that you went to college! And fuck you, I'm gonna raise my daughter the way I want to, and you can kiss my ass if you don't like it! Got a problem with that, Dave?"

Dave would not contradict my father. If he attempted to, he'd have to back up his words, andhis underdeveloped physique was no match for my muscular father, especially not when my daddy was becoming psychotically angry. Dave backed down.

"I support ya, Dale," shouted Ratman, "but I'm gonna have to get back to work soon. I don't fuckin' want to get fired 'cause Donna needs a lesson, you know?"

"Why don't you just tell your boss you were helping out a child who got lost or something, Mike? I mean, who the hell will know?" Those pearls of deception from the butcher appeared more than adequate to appease the simple-minded Ratman, who preferred to attend our lesson rather than return to a boring afternoon on the beat in our quiet old town.

"Okay, let's go down there in the cruiser, but we gotta hurry, no shit. C'mon, already!"

My father was right. Within a minute we parked alongside an old stone well with a wooden beam across the top. A frayed yellowed rope wrapped around the beam and hung down into the mouth of the well.

The men climbed out of the vehicle purportedly designed to serve and protect the people. We all walked quickly to the well, the men squatting and gazing into the opening to determine the appropriateness of this site for educational purposes.

"I don't know if we can count on this rope to hold her without breaking, Dale," offered Ratman, "and this fucker goes down a long way. I don't think we should risk it."

"Damn right, we're gonna risk it," he was corrected. I'll tie it around her waist. It'll hold, and if not, hell, we'll report her missing. No one's ever gonna know we were here. They'll never find her."

I slammed my hand down on the table, reacting with fury to the words I was reading. Tomato sauce flew through the air, splattering my white shirt and pants with red dots. Embarrassment rode piggyback upon rage. But I needed to close down these emotions quickly--just like Donna--and pretend that this was just an accident caused by almost spilling my Pepsi. I realized that Donna's hell was getting to me, even with my clinical walls and protective moat surrounding my emotional fortress. This is not supposed to happen. Was I losing my emotional invulnerability?

As disgusted as I felt about Donna's horrible abuse, I was almost as upset that I had let it get to me. I prided myself on being able to remain detached, unaffected, despite caring for my clients as much as I possibly could.

I put on a happy face and paid cash to avoid the extra minutes required by using my Visa card. I wanted out of there. I hurt. *How could a father. Aw, what's the point of going over it again? Could this really have happened? Hm... can I be sure? Suppose she was making this up--subconsciously, of course-- to explain a life of unhappiness and failure.* I wondered if this was a possibility, however remote. After all, I had no proof that any of this was real.

I put my car into gear and roared out of the parking lot and on to the Tamiami Trail. As I headed north, then west toward Siesta Key, my mind raced. Could a person really remember with that degree of detail? Could whole conversations be completely recorded?

But I'd had numerous survivors of sexual abuse in the past several years who had taught me that very thing-- traumatic memory could be recorded and often in great detail.

And how can a therapist help anyone if he doesn't believe the things painfully shared with him? No, it wasn't my job to play judge, jury, or even private detective. I was to be facilitator of the healing process. In order to do that, I mused, I needed to provide a safe, supportive atmosphere where my clients could determine forthemselves what reality was for *them.*

As I pulled my car into the driveway at the beach house, I was confronted by one more thought: *Why couldn't I feel, express, and release my own emotions as I expected my clients* to do *routinely?* That made more sense to me than continuing to believe that I needed to remain unyieldingly stoic in the face of these horrendous accounts of child abuse. That seemed more logical and made me feel okay about being human. I could forge ahead with Donna. And Shirley. And all of the others. And I could sleep that Thursday night, too.

Chapter 14

The People Are So Happy

The Big Brothers/Big Sisters program ranks as one of the finest volunteer organizations in Sarasota County. I have been blessed with the greatest "little brother" (he's now six feet, one inch tall) of all time, or so he reminds me. with the undeniable success of my pairing with brother, Fred, I am readily inclined to recommend the program to childless adults, specifically those who are lonely and/or down on their confidence.

Donna's hesitance to participate in the program was born out of her lifelong perception of inadequacy ("What could I possibly offer a little girl, Dr. Cortman?"). Eventually, however, she was capable of suspending her doubts due to her unfulfilled dream of having children and my unrelenting encouragement. Additionally, Donna and Peter were on the verge of separating, despite several months of marital therapy with a local clinical social worker. Imade this referral for them after concluding that Donna and I should concentrate on her individual therapy.

She was matched with eleven-year-old Melissa, a young lady with a deceased father and a hardworking mother of three who had little time to invest in her children's development.

Donna and Melissa blended together like peanutbutter and jelly and virtually every weekend enjoyed shopping, movies, and other girl stuff. The match was made before I had any knowledge of Donna's dissociation or multiple personalities. Normally this would not have spelled a problem for the newly acquainted "sisters," but Donna's behavior was rapidly deteriorating. The ugly memories of her father's sadistic abuse were gaining in power and momentum.

One weekend Donna switched personalities atSarasota Square Mall and left Melissa behind in a store. "You ruined everything!" she wailed on the telephone, telling me of the disaster.

Fortunately, I was at home, cleaning my condo for a visit from Laura. I could easily picture Donna's face overcome by sorrow, shame, and tears.

"Try to calm down. Take a deep breath and tell me exactly what happened." "I left her in a little shop and went to the food court. She looked all over for me and finally found me sitting alone at a table, smoking a cigarette." One more exaggerated sob came from Donna. "And I don't even smoke!"

"Is Melissa okay?"

"I suppose. I came up with some quick lies and excuses, and I think she believed me. But I don't know if I can be trusted with her anymore. Dr. Cortman, what am I supposed to do? My whole world is caving in on me!"

"All right, Donna, listen," I interjected. Time to think on my feet--literally, since I always stand when talking on the phone. Clearly Donna's memories and newly emerging alters were wreaking havoc. "You need to take back control of your life. These alter personalities are all a part of you. They're under *your* control. You don't feel that way because you have only recently discovered them. You need to set limits for each one of them as much as possible."

"How?" In truth, I wasn't sure. "Maybe by creating a

mandate. Maybe in writing. How about a contract that the alters sign, that limits their access to certain activities in your life. You don't have child alters filling out your tax forms at work, do you?" I didn't wait for an answer.

"Whoever left Melissa at the mall deserves to be heard. I'm sure she has a story to tell. But I suggest you make a rule: Only you, Donna, can be out when with Melissa."

I continued my impromptu rambling. "Every alter gets a chance to express *when appropriate:* at home, while journaling, dreaming, or in session with me. But *never,* ever, with Melissa."

My clarity and confidence grew with every instruction. "As for right now, you can get right back on the horse. You and Melissa can plan something fun for next weekend. That way, you demonstrate that leaving her behind was a fluke and will never happen again. Or you can let Melissa and her mother know that you're not feeling well and need a little time to recuperate. Truthfully, I like the first idea better. You and Melissa are good for each other if you can control who spends time with her." I glanced at my watch and winced. Laura's plane would be landing in twelve minutes.

"I-I think I need to keep seeing her. If I stop, I might not return to the relationship. Thank you, Dr. Cortman, for being there for me."

"Donna, wait. One more thing. You may want to ask the wise one—what's her name?"

"Stephanie."

"Yeah, ask Stephanie for her input on maintaining control of the alters and what to do about Melissa. And then we'll talk again in our session Friday, okay? See you then."

Friday's session with Donna promised to modify my

perceptions of her treatment and my life to this day. I remember it as one of the most haunting therapy hours I've ever facilitated.

She presented in a smart navy business suit with matching bag and shoes. Blond hair draped over to one side, and eyeglasses replaced her contact lenses. But Donna's gentle smile was nowhere to be found. No small talk today. No mention of the unyielding autumn heat. She was all business and settled into the midnight-blue leather recliner, a different seat from the chair she had chosen when remembering the story of the well.

"I will have no peace until I read this to you and deal with the memory. I've been dreaming this in fragments for several weeks." She paused pensively for a moment, then continued. "I am still embarrassed by my behavior last weekend--or whoever it was that left Melissa."

"Whom do you think it was?" I had been my curious since the phone call, although I had a hunch.

"Probably Mary."

I was not surprised. "What do you think that was about?"

"I'm not sure. I suppose it's connected to what I'm about to read to you. I feel as if a rebellion'sbrewing inside me." She dropped her gaze to the mauve carpet and whispered. "I'm scared."

"I know you are. I appreciate your honesty andadmire your courage. Did you consult with Stephanie about controlling the alters?"

She remained silent for a moment. "Dr. Cortman, can I just read this to you?"

"Sure, Donna. Go ahead."

"People shiver and shake moisture off their umbrellas and raincoats as they hurry inside the butcher shop. They are casually dressed men and women escaping the cold and the dark--all Caucasian in our white-bread town. I greet them at the door like a seasoned hostess, even though I'm only six at the time. I smile confidently and take their coats, then awkwardly attempt to hang them on a small coat rack placed near the entrance to Randy's Meats.

Randy, one of the few butchers in our town, stands behind the counter in his blood-soaked white smock. Underneath, he wears a plain white T-shirt, aged khaki pants, and work boots. He flashes an infectious smile each time a couple more people move past him on their way to his store's basement. It's as if he's flattered that they have braved the elements just to come to his celebration.

My adult mind knows that the shop should be closed; it's clearly after hours. Randy's position behind the counter appears to be a guise of sorts, to convince any passersby that he's still cleaning up after a busy day.

I am not alone in greeting the guests. Another little girl my age for some reason, I know her name is Stacey--- enthusiastically welcomes the newcomers.

Before long, Randy heads toward the front door, a spring in his step. He locks the door and shuts off the front lights. Virtually all the guests have gathered downstairs.

He glances my way for a moment. "Go downstairs, Donna." Then he tells Stacey, "You come with me."

Like a robot, I march down the stairs into the cool, candlelit dimness, prepared for virtually anything. The adults wear long black robes, and some have outlined their eyes with kohl. In the center of the room stands a wooden table covered by a white cloth, perhaps a sheet.

I find my father and mother in the crowd, and I silently grasp my mother's hand tightly. Mother is plain and usually fades into the background. Daddy is the flamboyant one, a leader. The sight of his heavily made-up face terrifies me.

Silent minutes drag on. The candlelight mesmerizes me, so instead I study the chips in the floor tile. Eventually Randy descends the basement stairs, holding on tightly to Stacey, who wobbles on unsteady legs. She has been clothed in a gorgeous white dress that resembles a wedding gown, and Randy has exchanged his bloodstained apron for a blackrobe. Randy lays his rag doll upon the table. My adult mind tries to make sense of her limpness. She undoubtedly had been drugged. I imagine that Stacey is relieved to be lying down.

Randy motions for a couple of men to assist him in tying Stacey's legs, spread-eagle, with a rope to the old table. She moans in a deep guttural sound. I am mostly anesthetized via my self-protective numbing, but somewhere within I, too, suffer with little Stacey, helpless and alone in a roomful of adults.

Randy prepares an adjoining card table, covered with a red-velvet tablecloth, with several objects necessary in performing his ritual. He places a large pewter goblet on the left side; in the middle table he sets a thick, black-covered book. The great book's leather cover is embossed with an upside-down cross. On the right side of the small table, rests a dagger, its long blade glistening in the flickering candlelight.

Randy looks around the gathering until his eyes connect with my father's. Daddy nods, evidently authorizing commencement of the ceremony. Randy beckons the group to approach the table. Seventeen adults and I gather at Stacey's feet, then fan out to surround the table. Everyone grabs and holds hands to form a circle.

I cling to my mother's hand on my right and a tall, familiar man to my left. In a flash, it occurs to me that it is Ratman, the cop. My numbness is momentarily pierced by the image of his large penis gagging me, but I quickly dissociate further and transmute the Ratman into a robed stranger.

Randy samples the liquid from the goblet, then winces. At my father's signal, Randy forces Stacey to drink. Barely conscious, she never opens an eye before clumsily swallowing the drink. Some runs down the sides of her mouth--a dark, thick substance.

A moment later one of the heavily made-up men finds his way past the circle of enjoining hands and near the pseudo-altar. He carries a howling black cat to Randy, who slits its throat with the dagger. A few spastic kicks from its limbs, and then all movement ceases. A chant swells in the room, as the cat's blood pours over Stacey's face. She seems oblivious to the bloodbath. (My adult self has an explanation for this, Dr. Cortman. Not only was she drugged; I now believe that she was also inclined to dissociating.)

My father commands that the cat be removed, and Randy runs to fetch an empty metal pail. He and his assistant worked diligently at holding the cat's lifeless body in a variety of positions to ensure that each and every drop of remaining blood is caught.

The group chants again, but this time in verse:

A child is offered.

See the blood on her head. Accept our praise and

Randy, chanting with the rest of the group, smears the blood on Stacey's face to create a five-point star, encircled. The symbol was familiar to me then, as it feels familiar now. I don't know why.

Randy retrieves the dagger. Sparkling stones, most likely diamonds, line the handle. He runs the blade gently up and down Stacey's dress, then he holds the garment up from her body, slices the silk from her neck to her privates, and pulls the material away. She is not wearing any underwear.

Ratman drops my left hand in favor of his own pride and joy. Within seconds, however, he places my left hand upon his penis. I turn to my mother for help, but she is oblivious to what is happening or totally unconcerned. I already know that my father provides no protection, so I turn to thereliable sanctuary in my own inner world.

(I find it very hard to describe what transpired at this point. From the very beginning a variety of rapidly switching children help me get through this; but when Ratman placed my hand upon his penis, I did a free fall through time and space. I vanished to a remote speck in a faraway galaxy where no one could find me or, worse yet, hurt me. At the same time, I knew exactly what the cop expected and how to satisfy him.)

Triggered by the exposure of Stacey's genitals, others also engage in sexual stimulation, either masturbating or fondling a partner, and not necessarily the person they arrived with. The sexual play reaches a feverish pitch as Randy climbs onto the table. To the delight of all the adults in the room, he forcibly mounts the child and penetrates her.

Ratman is aroused to the point of grabbing me to perform oral sex upon him. Within seconds I am left with a mouthful of Ratman's semen. I feel nothing at all, as I called again upon Amy, the alter responsible for sexual performance. Dutifully, we swallow the ejaculate.

Likewise, Randy does not require much time before dismounting Stacey. Within seconds, my father climbs upon the table and replaces Randy. Stacey whimpers softly under the weight of a man a full four times her size. Upon completion, my father lets out a loud yelp that prompts a greater flurry of excitement in the room. My hand is grabbed again, this time by the bald businessman who forced me to commit fellatio upon him at the well. Mercifully, my dad's booming voice ends the orgy. He commands the attention of all the robed participants, who once again encircle the altar. Daddy clutches the great black book in his hands and opens it to a place with a bookmark. The thought of Daddy as high priest seems preposterous, but from what I can now piece together, that's exactly what he appears to be.

As the group holds hands, my father speaks these words: "I would like to thank you all for taking time from your busy schedules to join us in a celebration of worship to the master. Our great lord and conqueror, Satan, has granted us the privilege of serving him in ceremony. Today we gather for the dual purposes of honoring our master and promoting one of our members, Randy, to second in command of our sect."

He turns to Randy and asks, "What bring you to offer the master in obedient sacrifice tonight?"

"I bring my beloved daughter, Stacey, firstborn of her

mother, Marilyn, and me. I present her for the glory of our great master and ruler of the earth forever and ever. All hail Satan!"

"All hail Satan!" the group responds. "All hail Satan! All hail Satan!"

As the group chants louder and louder, Randy bends over Stacey and kisses her softly on the lips. He whispers to his daughter, and she opens hereyes. This seems to please her father.

As my father hands Randy the dagger, Stacey lays eyes upon the imposing blade and responds with alook of horror. Then her eyes roll back into her head,and whether she passes out in fright or reenters a self-induced trance, I'll never know. Her eyes never open again, although Randy speaks in her ear. Finally, he prepares himself for the sacrifice, placing his left hand on her forehead and tilting it gently to expose her frail little neck. Perspiration gathers uponhis brow as he decisively slits his daughter's throat from right to left.

The crowd roars. The circle is broken by celebratory hugs and kisses. But the job is not done. Randy thrusts the blade violently into her chest and guides it toward her abdomen. He literally splits his child in half with the diamond-covered dagger. Blood flows to the surface, leaving Stacey to drown in a crimson pool.

The men reach barehanded into the bloody torso and expose her rib cage and organs. I did not look away; I don't know why. I also know that I knew exactly what to expect when the child was rent in half. I think I had seen this before.

But this time my father calls me by name to approach the bleeding child on the altar. He then instructs me, "Pull out her heart--you know what to do."

Even with all the switching I did to this point; I am ill prepared to handle the assignment. So, one more time, I go deep inside to find a part of me that can handle such a gruesome command. (We all know her; none of us ever dare to speak her name.)

Once the switching is complete, we reach carefully into the bloody torso and yank at the delicate, still-beating organ. It is powder blue and about the size of a plum. Without prompting, our new alter bites into the warm meat and tears off a piece with her teeth. She seductively licks her lips and hands the remainder ofthe heart to the leader himself.

He, too, bites off a piece of heart and passes it on to Randy, who follows suit. All the adults and I dine on a small bite of Stacey's heart.

The men work hard to drain and preserve as much of Stacey's blood as they possibly can in some large metal bowls used by day in the butcher shop. The work mostly done, Randy reaches underneath Stacey's limp body and scoops her up from the table. He raises her high inthe air, looks to the ceiling, and then triumphantly proclaims to the group: "This is my daughter!"

Glancing around the room, Dr. Cortman, we notice one more thing: the people are so happy!"

Donna peered up from her journal, eyes bloodshot. A chill shook me, and for a long time I could not get warm. For as long as I draw breath, I will never forget Donna's voice and her shocking words, "the people are sohappy."

Chapter 15

The Pretender

I slid into the booth and shook hands with Charles Evans, the elegant fellow I'd met on the plane corning home from visiting Laura several weeks before. The lunch crowd at Shoney's was bustling and loud.

"So, you had a good weekend?" Charles's attempt at small talk was awkward and strained.

I responded vaguely while wondering why the "semiretired government agent" had chosen to contact me by telephone. What in the world did he want from me?

"Hi, gentlemen!" the waitress greeted us. "Know whatcha want?"

Charles ordered a cup of coffee, but I take lunch seriously. As the only hour between 8 A.M. and 7 P.M. when I don't see clients, lunch is to be revered, and food is the way to celebrate it. I ordered the meatloaf platter, no gravy.

Charles downed the last gulps of coffee without a sound. I imagined that existing without making noisehad been part of his training, in case he was assigned to a stakeout of the Colombian drug cartel.

"So, you're a Jersey guy, eh? Yeah," he responded, probably to the puzzlement on my face. "I did a background check on you. Come from a large, middle-class family, religious people. Good people, nobody's in trouble. Older brother has had a few pizza restaurants. Another brother works for UPS, right?"

"Federal Express." I felt very ill at ease. George Orwell's notion of "Big Brother," the all-knowing, all- powerful government, played out before my eyes.

Charles fell silent as a new waitress brought me a diet Coke big enough to suck from all afternoon and refilled his coffee.

"What's this all about?", I asked. "Am I in some kind of trouble?"

He held up his hands. "You, no. You check out squeaky clean. But you know what surprised me? You had a gay roommate in the eighties. But that is neither here nor there. Truthfully, you are of interest more to the satanic groups than to the government."

I realized at that moment that virtually everything Charles said had been designed to evoke a reaction from me. With that awareness, I decided to pull the plug on emotionally responding to him. I wanted to reduce his power to upset me.

"Oh?" I said nonchalantly while my stomach roiled. "And what do Satan's people want with me?"

"You're treating some of their people."

"I told you that on the plane!" I felt violated, for my clients' confidentiality is of the utmost importance to me. "Are you telling me that people who are remembering abuse from cults twenty to thirty years ago are still being monitored by these groups?"

This information was deeply troubling, since I had assumed that my clients' ties to the cults had been severed for several decades. To think that some anonymous person spied on them--and on me--left a hollow sensation in my gut.

Atypically, I barely acknowledged the waitress as she set down my luncheon plate. "Are you suggesting that these survivors are of some value to the cults?"

While Charles had succeeded in jolting me, he was powerless against the forces of my appetite. He watched as I tucked into the meatloaf and instant mashed potatoes, then exhaled and reached for his trusty hanky. "Listen, I was checking to see if you could be trusted. The satanic people-- God, I hate saying that name--the *cult* members have a different agenda for you."

He swabbed his face as he talked, and his piercing eyes had the same intensity as on the airplane. "Do you remember the question you asked me on the plane, about whether a large, cohesive organization existed or ifthe cults were independent groups?"

"Yeah," I said, talking with a mouthful of food. "Well, my research suggests a national, if not international, structure. I told you before, big people are involved. Because I'm fairly certain I can trust you, I did find out the names of a couple of celebrities involved in this thing."

"Yeah, who?" I inquired, pushing my dish to the side after once again reinstating membership in the Clean Plate Club.

Charles excitedly ran off the names of an actor (not much of a surprise), a politician (who could probably stand in for the devil when the "evil one" was out of town), and an entertainer who, I must admit, disappointed me. Where Charles obtained the names and information I would never know, and how accurate the information was remains a mystery.

"I don't get it, Charles."

"What now?" He didn't seem to like my questions.

"The cult members follow up on survivors they have

had in their clutches as children, right?”

"Right."

"And by keeping track of them, they know who is in treatment and talking about it, right?”

"Oh, yeah. They have easy access to all of your files to find out who is talking and who isn't."

"How?”

"Are you kidding, Chris? You're dealing with professionals here. If they want your files, they'll get them. Same with government. We can get information if we need it. Don't be so naive as to believe that as long as your records are locked up in a filing cabinet no one else will read them. You need to know that."

A wave of nausea swept through me. The idea of people reading my private patient files was virtually overwhelming. Still, I acted as if nothing was amiss.

"You're saying that the cult group knows what I'm up to 'cause I know too much about them. But why is the government checking on me?”

"It isn't. I have, and only after meeting you on the plane. I started to think about the questions you asked me and looked into them. I'll tell you--just keep all this between us--I was stonewalled everywhere I turned. No one wants to talk about cults or even admit they exist. The government closes its eyes to the whole thing, probably because of the power held by some of the members. Anyway, I found out some things on my own that were truly disturbing, so I figured I'd get back to you. First, I needed to check you out and see if you were kosher. Then once I found out that you weren't gay anymore--"

“I was never gay!” I shot back too loudly. Diners from several neighboring tables turned and looked at me. I felt embarrassed, as if I were in the middle of a sitcom, waiting for the audience to break into hysteria.

"I know," he said with a "gotcha"-type laugh. "Chill out. I was just yanking your chain. But I did want to give you that information."

"So that's what today's meeting was all about?" I intuited Charles had more to say.

"Well, there is another thing." The hanky was working overtime by now, clueing me in to the magnitude of the next issue from Charles. "A cult meeting is planned soon, in a very impressive mansion in Sarasota County. Because drugs are involved, it's my deal, although my orders are to intervene only on that matter--drugs--no matter what else might be going on."

I nodded at the insinuation of child abuse and possibly human sacrifice. Although I was intensely interested, I remained oriented to the clock, aware that it read 12:57--three minutes before my next client.

"I'm heading this up and will have a couple of agents with me. One's a government official, and I'm cutting a deal with him, to observe from a room that overlooks where the ceremony takes place. The people won't be able to see us, but we'll see them. Anyway, I figured I'd ask if you wanted to go."

"What?"

"Yeah, I'll see to it that it's safe. The mansion's owner knows we're coming--not *you,* but I can get you a fake I.D. for the night--and you can see for yourself what goes on. Maybe it'll even help you understand your patients better."

"Charles, I appreciate that your intentions are pure, but" I shook my head as my abdominal war waged on. "I'm out of my league here. I'd have no business in being at that mansion, and honestly, I don't think I want to be in the presence of such evil. Of course, I'm very curious, but, nah, I know this isn't right for me. Thanks for the offer, though. You really stuck your neck out for me, Charles."

"Okay, I understand," he said graciously. "I'm sure you're right. You don't belong there." He glanced at his watch. "Hey, it's almost one o'clock! A good time for us to break up this little meeting so the good Dr. Cortman can get back at the usual time, about five minutes late."

He grabbed the check and reminded me that myfederal tax dollars would help to offset the cost of my meatloaf.

During my three-minute ride back to the office, I was aware of being watched, of being a menace to the underworld, and of a nagging doubt that Charles Evans might not be who he claimed. What if he were a part of a cult? What a clever strategy that would have been! He "coincidentally" sits next to me on the plane, baits me for information while I think I'm questioning him, and then I'm invited to a cult meeting. Would they kill me? force my participation in their activities?

Don't go there, I told myself. Those thoughts were too upsetting. I was overreacting, just being paranoid. Or so I hoped.

I was an emotional wreck, trying to process every feeling known to man. But I had to set my fears aside and focus completely on my one o'clock session.

As I peeled my hands from the steering wheel and turned off the ignition, I noticed how sweaty my palms were. Why not, considering the number of bombs Charles had just dropped on my once-peaceful life? Evil people were watching me reading my files and taking interest in my work!

And then a bone-chilling revelation as I opened the

door to my office: They are right here in Sarasota County!

Chapter 16

Early Awakenings

"Hello?" I growled in my sleep-induced coma. "Chris, is that you?"

I recognized my friend Richard's voice. "Hold on,I'll check. Yeah, it's me." I squinted at my bedside clock--six o'clock, Saturday morning.

"Are you all right?" I asked, concerned.

"I'm fine, thanks. I just got a phone in my car,and they gave me my first thirty minutes free. I figured I'd give you a call."

"I'm trying to feel flattered," said I, rubbing my eyes. "How's the divorce going?"

"Horrible and getting worse. Her attorney has accused me of everything from infidelity and child abuse to the creating the fuckin' national debt."

"Which ones are you guilty of?"

"Only the national debt." His voice turned serious. "She's really punishing me for wanting out. I'm not sure how the hell to handle this anymore."

"What's your attorney saying?"

"He wants me to play it cool, not to stir anything up. Let the judge see what kind of pathological bitch she is. So far, it's not working. I haven't seen Annie and Max in over a month. Thank God Joshua is old enough to make up his own mind, and he's with me."

"Sounds tough, Richard. I'm sorry she's preventing you

from seeing your kids."

"Yeah, thanks. So, what's new with you?"

"You really want to know, or you just asking to be polite?"

"If I was worried about being polite, would I be calling so early? I'm interested."

I decided to tell him about Charles Evans. "Well, I'm on a plane coming back from Ohio--"

"You're still seeing that blonde Buckeye? I don't know how you do it."

"What do you mean?" I asked.

"Relationships are hard enough when you live in the same house, let alone trying to trust someone fourteen hundred miles away. Or maybe that's the saving grace-- you're not in each other's face all the time. Who the hell knows?" Richard's false bravado had wilted with the topic of relationships and trust. I gave him a moment, enough for him to say apologetically, "So you're on a plane home from Ohio."

I could picture Richard shaking his head in disbelief as I related my story of Charles, ending with declining the invitation to the mansion.

"But then, just last week he calls me again," I continued, "and he says, 'Good thing you didn't go tothe meeting. You would've recognized three or four mental-health professionals at the meeting.'"

"No way! Who?"

"He did tell me the names, but I can't divulge them.I don't know this guy well enough to be sure his information is accurate."

"I would've gone to the meeting," Richard said."It's hard to believe this shit is real."

I sat up and planted my feet on the carpeting. I knew I wouldn't fall back to sleep after this conversation. "Charles told me the group sacrificed a baby and a four- year-old during the meeting."

"As in killed?" Richard sounded as if he wanted me to come up with a different definition of *sacrifice* torelieve him of the horror.

"And Charles's description of the events matches my patients' childhood memories." I shared the specifics of removing a child's heart, for Richard's understanding.

"Oh, shit, Cortman," my friend said in disgust. "Don't tell me what I know you're gonna tell me. You're not about to tell me that they eat the fucking hearts, areyou?"

"Passed it around until it was gone. And drank the blood."

From the research I'd been doing on the meaning of cult rituals, consuming the heart and drinking the blood supposedly transferred power to the participants. The rite was a bastardized version of Judeo-Christian dogma. "Without bloodshed, there's no remission of sins," I said, quoting a Bible verse from my memorization days.

"Christians believe the blood of Christ cleanses them from every transgression," I continued, remembering a hymn, "'There is Power in the Blood, Power in the Precious Blood of the Lamb.' The lamb is the symbol for Christ, who Christians believe willingly offered himself as asacrifice for their sins. But how did you know they ate the hearts, Richard?" I asked. Richard is Jewish.

"I know a little about sacrificing because civilizations have been putting people on altars for sacrifice for thousands of years--you know, tossing virgins into volcanoes, giving babies to the gods to assure fruitful harvests, shit like that."

"Yeah," I added, "I even saw a program on the Discovery Channel about the Mayans or Incas--I can't remember now--that sacrificed thousands upon thousands of children and adults to their gods and saved the skullsfor some reason."

"In the Jewish religion, Abraham was willing to sacrifice Isaac, his son, to demonstrate loyalty and devotion to God."

"And according to Christian theology, God sacrificed his son, Jesus, out of love for his people."

"But nobody eats the heart," Richard pointed out. "True, but in Christian churches, communion is offered to imply devotion to Christ. You eat bread to symbolizethe body, and wine or grape juice to represent the blood of Jesus."

"So, what are you planning to do about Charles?"

I could tell Richard was concerned about me. "Keep my ears open and my mouth shut. Between Charles and my patients' accounts, my naivete about life in America has been shattered. Of course, I'm inclined to believe what they've told me because that's what I've been trained to do, but these stories are just "unbelievable."

"You're never tempted to check up on your patients' accounts--you know, names, newspaper stories, or maybe police reports of missing children?"

"Of course, I'm tempted, but I'm not going to act on it. I don't see that as my role. I'm a psychologist, not a private detective."

"Maybe ignorance is bliss," Richard remarked. "But if you ever stumble on any evidence to corroborate their memories, well, keep me posted." His voice took on a different tone, as if he were setting me up for something.

"Maybe something good can come out of all this."

"And what might that be?" said I, taking his bait. "Well, you have underworld connections--cults, special agents, undercover spies. With the people you know, can't you have my wife bumped off or something?"

"You're watching way too much TV, man. Besides, we're supposed to be in the helping profession. I'm pretty sure murder is against APA ethics."

Richard struggled to keep from laughing. "Butyou're Italian, Chris. Don't you have an uncle Luigi with a bad attitude and an itchy trigger finger?"

"Sorry, pal. The best I can do is an uncle Louis who does a neat trick to make it seem like his thumb disappears. Is that helpful?"

"I just wish I didn't have to deal with her control tactics anymore."

I missed his cue to take things more seriously."Don't you have any connections? A congressman or politician in your pocket? As loaded as youare--"

He snorted. "Yeah, that's a good one. My money has been eroded by legal fees--hers and mine. In his infinite wisdom the judge decided that I should be responsible for all of the attorney bills. I've blown seventeen grand already, and we're not even close to a settlement. Andwhat do I have to show for my investment? I don't get to see my kids. I'm telling ya, I'm beginning to understand these guys who go nuts and shoot their ex-wife. I've fuckin'had it!"

"Whoa, slow down, Rambo!" I told him. "You're not going to lose it, are you? You're starting to scare *me.*"

"Nab, I'm all talk. Jews aren't street fighters. We don't have a Mafia. That's why I have to call my *paisan* for action."

"If you do find a hit man, don't call him this early. He might not be so understanding." I got up, went into the bathroom, and relieved myself. "Seriously, what do you think you need to get through this?"

"I dunno. I wish I had a good vice to turn to, but I don't have any money to support a habit."

"So, what are you saying? You need a loan to support a dope habit, which will calm you, so you don't shoot your wife and spend the rest of your life in prison? Is that what you woke me up to tell me?"

Richard resisted laughter long enough to return serve. "Yes, thank you, Dr. Cortman. Finally, a man who understands me. How can I ever thank you?"

With the mood-changing laughter, I no longer worried about my buddy losing it… today.

"Enough about the divorce. Catch me up on your multiple-personality patient."

"Sure," I said, "But now I'm up and you're gonna go with me on my morning rituals." I crammed ayellow toothbrush into my mouth and began my update. Shirley had been suffering more bizarre symptoms, remembering horrible things, then feeling better after processing thememory.

"Last week she said, 'I can't get organized to cook, work, even do my laundry.' She told me she could barely make it to her appointment and hadn't done dishes in overa week."

"How'd you cure that one?"

"I asked to speak to someone inside who knew what was going on with her. This required only a light trance, and someone emerged who explained that she was so angry with what she was remembering, she couldn't be trusted not to kill her father. Shirley owns a gun for protection, andone part of her wanted to blow her father's brains out, while the other wanted to continue healing and let itgo."

"Sounds like me and my desire to whack my wife." "Right. Anyway, some part of her decided if she couldn't function, then she couldn't kill anyone. Shirley needed to be made aware of all this consciously. She expressed her rage appropriately, and that was that.She was back to functioning normally--at least normally for Shirley."

"That's amazing, really," he marveled. "And it makesa lot of sense. The normal psyche may process extreme conflict in a similar way--by distraction and the creation of other smaller conflicts."

"Let me give you another example. She complained about losing personal records, being unable to find her way home from work late at night, experiencing a lot ofconfusion. By now I know what to do. I put her in a light trance and ask to speak to whatever part of her knew something about this."

"Out comes an alter calling herself Magic. She was created to feign 'being out of it' in cult meetings after being administered a small dose of a sedative. Believing she was too sedated, the group leaders wouldn't give her more drugs. Thus, Magic could maintain control and awareness of what was going on throughout the entire meeting."

Richard had a knack for getting right to the point. "What does this have to do with screwing up her personal records?"

"I'm getting to that. Lighten up and try some decaf. All Magic knew how to do was trick people, and with no one to trick, she did it to herself."

"What did you do with that?" Richard asked. "I asked Magic if she could use her talent for trickery for Shirley's betterment. She thought for a minute and said, 'Well, I could trick her into thinking thatshe has more patience with her daughter.'"

Richard laughed appreciatively. "That's great!"

"Isn't it?" I agreed. "Magic was done at that point. The self-sabotage took care of itself." "What's up with that evil one?"

"Colleen? Even that's resolving. Instead of competing against her, I asked her to tell me about her past. We're not done there yet, but the whole mood has changed. You really helped me with that. I appreciate it."

"Well, it's good to have you there for me, too.Even if you don't have any Mafia uncles to help me. Everything else okay?"

"Pretty good, thanks," I replied. "Still trying to decide what to do about Laura."

I explained that I had introduced Laura to my family and hoped for an enthusiastic welcome but met with displeasure. My ultraconservative Christian parents were not happy that I was so involved with a young lady whowas unchurched and nonreligious and had, as my father put it, "been around the block a time or two."

"There was no overt disapproval," I told Richard."My folks are genuinely nice people and are good to Laura.But the enthusiasm and excitement that exude fromparents thrilled to see their son meet his bride? That's obviously missing. Laura detects their disappointment, and it wounds her deeply."

"Your parents aren't dating her. You are."

"Still, relationships are hard enough, as my clients have taught me, without having to wrestle with unhappy in- laws."

"How about the rest of your family?"

"My siblings all genuinely like Laura and have said *so*. She's genuine and down-to-earth. Nothing pretentious about her. Even my hard-to-please sister--who didn't like any of my previous girlfriends—likes Laura."

"Well, you know what I think. Women are more dangerous than pit bulls and farcostlier."

"That sounds most objective and rational, Richard, without a hint of bitterness."

"Yeah, well, I'm done with women."

"So, you called to ask me for a date?" I thought I had him.

"You're cute, Chris, but not my type. Besides, *my* father would never approve--you're not Jewish."

I snorted a laugh. "My loss, I suppose, but I'll get over it," I shot back. "Listen, I think I consumed all thirty of your free minutes, which is good because you're too broke to wake me up again. Besides, I need a shower-- the thought of being your man has made me feel very unclean. Thanks for calling. Keep your chin up and know that I care about you."

Chapter 17

The Black Mass

Like everything else in life, psychological caseloads seem to come in cycles. At any given time, I may be treating more than my share of one type of client or diagnosis-- grieving widows, anorexics, men wishing to reconcile with their estranged mate. Clearly that had been true for me with patients suffering from Dissociative Identity Disorder, as my caseload now included seven such people.

And while they consumed more time, patience, and energy than the remainder of my practice combined, my "multiples" were special to me. Somehow, *they* revitalized *me* and continually restored my faith in the healing process.

Several months had passed since Donna recalled the murder of the butcher's daughter. Not surprisingly, she protected herself by means of the "denial alters,"whose sole purpose was to dispute the veracity of the harsh accounts she bravely shared with me.

Fascinated, I observed the war raging in Donna's fragmented mind: Alters that promoted remembering battled alters that secreted the information from the conscious mind; alters that trusted me with the most defenseless aspects of their being versus hostile alters that sought to remove me permanently from her life; alters that pursued a newfound spirituality versus alters that held fast to a subterranean world of darkness and evil. (While I didn't realize it at the time, this described Shirley's battle as well.) Eventually I recognized that this civil war of the psyche was the key to understanding much of the conflict in all of the clients I was now treating with abusive histories.

Donna's nocturnal turmoil continued to dominate her life in early 1992. The horror in the butcher's basement was only the beginning in a series of nightmares that featured stories of unconscionable evil. One such memory included the participation of a Roman Catholic priest in what she described as a "Black Mass."

On this particular Friday in early May, she came into my office and, without a word, handed me her journal and motioned me to read. She settled in the recliner across from my desk and watched me open the book.

"I am probably nine years old. We're inside the sanctuary of Our Lady of Lourdes, the church my family attends each week for mass. But this is not Sunday morning; it's the dead of night, and a generous supply of black candles distributed throughout the room provides the illumination. The smell of burning incense permeates the room. Perched above the altar is a derisive Christ. Jesus is portrayed as a villainous creature; his bestial face twists in a mean laugh, mocking those who would trust in him.

Father Delvecchio leads approximately twenty black-robed people in the mass. The sermon is very formal, and the priest is wearing a dark red garment. On his head, His Holiness wears a scarlet cap from which two horns of red cloth emerge.

A naked woman lies upon the altar, with Wendy, a child of four, resting on her abdomen. By her side is a golden chalice. Father Delvecchio offers the elements, then prepares to sacrifice the girl. I knew Wendy well and attempted in vain to befriend and encourage her during some of the most trying of punishments. Wendy displayed her weakness in obvious demonstrations of cowardice.

The priest slits her throat to the delight of the congregation. He drains her blood into the chalice and mixes it with flour to create a "black host" for consecration.

The mass commences as the congregation sings the responses to Delvecchio's lead. The priest kneels before the altar and hails Satan as a most reasonable and just god. He describes his lord as the "master of slander" and "dispenser of the benefits of crime" then "administrator of luxurious sins and greatvices; cordial of the vanquished; suzerain of resentment; accountant of humiliations; treasurer of old hatreds; hope of virility; king of the disinherited; the son who is to overthrow the inexorable father."

He calls upon Satan to grant glory, riches, and power to his worshippers. He curses the "execrable" Jesus and labels him as the imposter and breaker of promises.

"Jesus was to redeem mankind and has not," says Father Delvecchio. "He was to appear in glory but did not. Jesus was to intercede between God and man but did not. As priest, I force the do-nothing king and coward God to descend into the host" "--a wafer just like in a Catholic mass--" "to be punished by the violation of His body."

The priest urinates upon the communion wafer as the congregation cheers, then he masturbates and eventually ejaculates onto the host. He hurls it onto the floor and angrily shouts the familiar, "Vanish into the void of the empty heaven, for thou wert never, nor shall thou ever be."

The crowd rushes to the altar and like animals attack Wendy's corpse, clawing and tearing and chewing and swallowing. An orgy follows, with Father Delvecchio performing oral sex on several of the men. Two women accost me--one of them heavy set--for my participation in a threesome. We switch alter personalities, especially upon the demand to perform cunnilingus upon the larger woman. Amy takes over and services the lady.

*　　*　　*

Donna's journal entry contained more material, but I was distracted by a low growl that caused me to look up. Donna disappeared into the darkness within. Another low growl rumbled in her diaphragm, and her eyelids fluttering rapidly communicated a change in personality. Unlike the others, this alter never looked up, never made eyecontact with me.

Eventually the eyelids ceased blinking. I could see her eyes roll back in her head, as if Donna had entered a deep trance. What emerged before me was a dramatic thirty-second presentation of an alter I had never met. Its voice, deeper and lower than typical for Donna, sent chills down my spine.

"We are the society of Luciferians. On this day we assemble before the mighty and ineffable Prince of Darkness and in the presence of all the dread demons of the pit. In this assembled company, I acknowledge and confess my past error, renouncing all past allegiances. I proclaim that Satan-Lucifer rules the earth, and I ratify and renew my promise to recognize and honor him in all things without reservation, desiring in return his manifold assistance in the successful completion of my endeavors and the fulfillment of my desires.

"As my father before me and my grandfather before

him, I, Lucinda, proclaim service to him, the overcomer. For we are the chosen. Ave, Satanas!!!"

I would be lying if I said I wasn't rattled by Lucinda's appearance. The name was an obvious derivative of Lucifer. Evil crept steadily through my soul like the early morning fog in San Diego and settled palpably in the office.

Then the bizarre presentation ended as it had begun, with the rapid flurry of the eyelids.

As I sat frozen and astonished, Donna dropped her face into her hands and moaned the cry of an individual delirious with fever. The moans grew softer until they diminished into whimpers. The metamorphosis culminated in Donna's reemergence. She looked up slowly until she found my eyes. Her blond hair, matted with sweat, fell off to one side just above her right eyebrow. The deep creases in her forehead suggested worry or confusion that bordered on panic.

"D-Doctor Cortman, I-I… Oh, God, my head. It's just throbbing. I'm sorry… Did I do anything wrong? I'm sorry if I--"

I interrupted her with the reassurance she had come to count on.

"You're going to be fine. Your head hurts because you've been switching. That's happened before. If youlike, I'll get you some water, or if you'd prefer, you can use the bathroom to collect yourself. Whatever you need."

"I think I need to get out of the office now. May Igo home early?"

Although she had ample time left in the session to accomplish more, she was not up to it. And I never wanted to give her, or any abuse survivor, the feeling of being trapped.

"Feel free to go. I understand you're frazzled right now.

I'd really like it if you'd call me later, just tolet me know you're okay. You did well today. I want you to know that."

She rose from the leather recliner to herunsteady feet. "Do you think I'm gonna make it? I'm so scared!"

I surmised from her childlike demeanor that she was very fragile right now. I assessed her capacity to travel home safely and sent her on her way with a verbalcontract to call as soon as she walked through her door.

I stayed at the office for another fifteen minutes to finish up some paperwork for managed care. Leaving mywork at the office had always been important to me, but now, with the advent of Shirley, Donna, and theother challenging cases, maintaining boundaries between my personal and professional life seemed more necessary than ever before.

I also needed to calm down. I thought about the preceding session with Donna, trying to understand why I was still so upset. Then it hit me--the Satanism! Donna's graphic and detailed description lent overwhelming credence to the notion that this was real, organized, and in opposition to everything that I had learned and embraced in my youth. I felt violated by the mockery of Jesus and outraged by the accusations levied against him. I was furious to hear that people--including an ordained priest-- had the gall to teach that Jesus had failed in his quest to intercede between God and man, that he was, according to this cult, a breaker of promises.

I found myself wanting to defend my Christianity-- wanting to embrace once again that which I had left behind. I felt a tugging within that I couldn't begin to describe.

It sent me straight to the phone to call my old friend Gregg Fisher. Had only six months passed, I reflected, since I told his wife, Shawn, that only a miracle" could bring me back to God? As I punched in his phone number, I knew I wasn't ready to label any of this miraculous, but I'd be lying if I denied the life-altering implicationsof sitting across from a woman who sounded possessed.

When he answered, I quickly apprised him of myentire situation. I wasn't sure about what I was looking for; I just hoped he'd understand.

"Fish," I said, addressing Gregg by his college nickname, "I don't know what to make of this demon thing. Did you and Shawn summon up this diabolical attack justto scare me back into thefold?"

He laughed his infectious cackle. "Of course not.But whatever it takes to get you back…" He laughed again, assuring me that he was only kidding. Then his tone became serious. "I don't think that any of this is an accident-- not your message from God to go to Florida; not your walking away from Him; not the whole satanic thing. I believe that God has His hand in all of this and thatit's all for a reason that will ultimately be in our best interest and for His glory."

I had heard Gregg say this before, and many times.He and Shawn believed their Chronic Fatigue Syndrome was no accident or coincidence. Compared to the way they gracefully handled their suffering; Job was a whiner.

"I understand the concept," I responded. "But howdo you keep on believing in Him after over ten years ofhell on earth? I can't talk to you and Shawn without feeling guilty and self-absorbed. I don't know what it's like to suffer or have problems compared to you two, and here we are talking about *my* life!"

"That's 'cause there's not a whole lot happening in Ours," he joked. "Our whole church group prays for you,

Chris. When we got home from our vacation in Florida, we told them about you and your satanic struggles. Some people are called to be on the front line of the battle, while others support the war efforts from behind."

"So, what are you telling me? I am dealing with Satanism, multiple personality disorder, and the underworld because God has a plan for me? You think He put a bug in my ear in California to come to Florida and fight His battle on the front lines? Am I supposed to buy all of that?"

"Sounds like a possibility," Gregg replied. "But I don't claim to know or even understand the mind of God. I just know that when He calls you to go, you go. And if He called you to Florida and then all this stuff happened to you, then you needn't worry--He's in the midst of everything, with His protective hand upon you. There's no safer place to be than in the middle of God's will."

He would have made a convincing preacher. "Safe, huh? Easy for you to say!" I paused, about to reveal something I had kept to myself for the past few nights. "I've been sleeping with the light on in my bedroom and my right arm wrapped around a Bible. What's worse, I switched my alarm clock radio to a Christian station. And I don't even like Christian Rock!"

Again, the familiar and reassuring chuckle. "Corpus," he said, using my college nickname, "everything will be fine. I truly believe that. God will not abandon you through this, just like you won't abandon yourpatients. It's okay to get right with Him. He's not mad at you, you know."

"What, did He call you before, to say He's forgiven me?" My pride and stubbornness prevented me from rushing toward the very thing that I--and my patients--neededmost.

"God is forgiving," Gregg continued. "He's still awaiting

your return to Him with open arms. It's consistent with everything the Bible says. You know His Word as well as I do."

Silence overcame me. I had run out of wisecrack responses to his persuasive words. I knew Gregg was right about at least one thing: God had not moved. I had. And even after eight years of ignoring Him, He was undoubtedly willing to forgive and forget my angry rejection of my faith, like a parent would embrace a teen-aged runaway. That was consistent with my understanding of God--loving unconditionally, ready to forgive if I would only ask.

But asking, that's the hard part, I thought. *Especially as a male.* It wasn't easy to admit that I was wrong. That I needed forgiveness. That I was weak, needy, scared, and in over my head. How emasculating! But, I reasoned, God was not interested in humiliating me, merely humbling me enough to make Him necessary in my life once again. Did He really have a specific plan in mind for me? I didn't know.

I gratefully said good-bye to Fish, then turned off the lights. As I locked the office door, I continued to wonder if God had a specific plan for every one of us. Could God be so involved as to have an individual plan for the six billion inhabitants of planet Earth? Could He be that big?

On my ride home, I recalled the verse about God knowing the number of hairs on every head (Matt. 10:29-31). I pondered that, because it seemed unfair that He would have a plan for only certain select individuals. I didn't feel comfortable thinking that He had a specific role for me and a few others. I would be labeling myself as special, and that seemed too egotistical.

Big ideas floated through my mind and heart all evening. I finally admitted that I didn't have any idea what

God had in mind for me or the rest of humankind. As I drifted off to sleep, I decided I was comfortable with that. I didn't have to know His mind. He wasn't my patient; I was His child. And sometime in the night, I chose to trust Him again.

Chapter 18

Special Delivery

Saturday morning, I couldn't get Donna off my mind. I was concerned but not acutely frightened about her short-term safety. I did not believe she was a suicide risk. no more thanusual.

Something else bothered me--Lucinda. This alter caused me to suspect that some part within Donna was still devoted to Satan and his followers. *Lucinda may have been the alter personality that I was warned of,* I realized. Maybe she was like Shirley's alter, Colleen, who had learned to love the ways of the cult.

Was I on the right track with treatment? Was she really getting better? Tough questions. Like many mental health professionals, I believe that people in treatment often feel worse before they feel better. This is especially true when clients bravely attempt to face unresolved trauma. Obviously, the uglier the trauma, the more difficult it is to overcome. And Donna wascontending with some awful accounts of abuse. But did bringing up her memories really help her? Might she be better off forgetting and buryingthese so-called memories under a mound of psychological repression?

My answer was no. *She* was resurrecting this story line; I never asked for it, expected it, required it, or suggested it. I had asked her simply to take me to thepain that disrupted her life and sabotaged her relationshipwith Peter.

I reminded myself of the brief respites between the

nightmares, when Donna demonstrated signs of hope, assertiveness, and even contentment. She was improving. Furthermore, the memories were finished after she related them and appropriately grieved. This process proved consistent in Shirley's treatment as well as all theother abuse and/or trauma survivors.

I concluded then what I still believe to be true: Emotional healing seems to be the byproduct of remembering, feeling, expressing, releasing, and then learning to think differently--usually in that order.
The ringing phone interrupted my thoughts. "Dr. Cortman?"

"Donna?"

"Yes."

"Are you okay?"

"Yes, but we don't think we'll be coming back to see you anymore. And I should have told you earlier, this is Dianna that you're speaking to. Sorry."

Dianna, I recalled, was the spiritual aspect of self who was always a pleasure to converse with.

"No need to apologize, Dianna. But what do you mean you won't be returning for treatment?"

"We think we're doing a lot better now. You have helped us so much, and we're most grateful. We feel certain that we've received all we can hope for from therapy. We will handle it by ourselves from here."

"Dianna, something happened yesterday in session that was very upsetting to all of you, I'm sure. I don't know how it was processed or what impact Lucinda had on all of your but I'm certain there's more to the story than you're telling me. With all due respect, I don't buy that you are dropping out of treatment because you've improved as much as you're capable of, or that it's coincidental that you're quitting the day after Lucinda surfaces for the first time in therapy."

After a long pause, Dianna responded, Here goes, Dr. Cortman. Lucinda feels threatened by you. You have gotten way too close, and she's threatening to do horrible things to us if we continue with you. We just can't riskit.

Lucinda doesn't make idle threats. She makes good on her word as if it's a covenant. We're all very frightened of her."

"What is she threatening?" I asked.

"I'm not sure I should say. Ah, I-I guess I can tell you. She's threatening to sacrifice our cats in a bloody ceremony of evil. She says she might do it anyway--even if we do stay away from you--to reaffirm her commitment to her master."

Well, there goes my weekend, I thought. But that was not a helpful way to react, so I attempted something a little more therapeutic. There was no way I was about to give up on treating Donna. No way! I tried to assess Lucinda's capacity to carry out the threat. "If shewanted to hurt your cats and you tried to stop her, what do you think would happen?"

"Oh, I could never stop her from doing anything, Dr. C. She is much too powerful."

"Well, I didn't mean *you,* Dianna. I meant anyone attempting to resist her." I continued, hoped for a different response this time.

"It wouldn't matter. Lucinda is the most powerful of all the ones inside. No one can successfully oppose her."

Stuck in a no-win situation, I figured I'd have someone awaken the old lady inside, the wise Stephanie. Maybe she'd know what to do. I asked Dianna to do my dirty work.

After a moment, she returned with some unusual, if not confounding words of wisdom from Stephanie: "What you know, you know. Stick with the truth."

Great, I thought. *I need some practical advice, and instead I get a Chinese proverb.* I shook my head in frustration, then I considered the advice. What *is* the truth? The truth is, every alter has a story to tell and some pain to express. *Every* alter. Even Lucinda. *Bring her on,* I thought. *I'm ready.*

"Okay, Dianna, tell everyone that your resignation from therapy has been denied and tell Lucinda I'd like to talk to her directly next time. Let her know thatshe's welcome in my office anytime."

"We want our appointment to be in Sarasota, not Venice."

An unusual request. I paused, thinking. "Allright. I'll have time Tuesday afternoon at four. Tell Lucinda I look forward to meeting her."

"I will. But ... I don't know what she'll say or do."
"That's all right. Just tell her I'll see her then."

A thirteen-year-old with attention deficit disorder began my workweek. He interrupted me mid-sentence with: "Did you know you have two different color shoes on?"

I never took my eyes off him. "Please tell meyou're joking, Jeremy."

He wasn't.

I could not have predicted how my boneheaded mistake would deepen my rapport with the boy, possibly because he could see that I had greater problems than he did. Whereit really scored a major victory, however, was with a woman who had recently survived a stroke but suffered an appreciable loss of certain cognitive functions. After one look at my feet, she wasn't certain which one of ushad sustained the brain damage. Suddenly there was hope--for her, at least.

Just before lunch on Monday, flying insects swarmed my office, disrupting the therapy sessions. I called the landlord, who called the exterminator, who informed us that the bugs lived in our plants. He suggested--get this--that I wash every leaf of every plant with soap. I followed his instructions, which had no impact on the insects but made me the proud owner of the cleanest plants in Venice.

Just after lunch I treated a woman who was so severely depressed, she claimed that even her good cholesterol was bad.

At two o'clock I turned my attention to my next client. Phil, a fifteen-year-old dropout, feared his own violent fantasies. He confessed to having two pets--a snake named Slam and a hamster named Thud. I figured I had my work cut out for me with Phil.

My appointment with Shirley was uneventful until a half hour after she had left. She called me from a phone booth near a local gas station. I must have allowed her to leave my office in an alter personality not accustomed to driving. She was without a clue as to how to get home, despite having made the trip from my office dozens and dozens of times.

I could think of only one thing to help her: hypnotize her over the phone in order to bring another alter--onewho drove--to the position of host. A tad unorthodox by APA standards, but with the advent of phone sex and phone psychics, I figured why not? The idea worked like a charm, and Shirley was home within a half hour.

But Donna was by no means so compliant--not this week. She walked in clad in some impressive threads, which would have been suitable for a fancy restaurant, the ballet, or a night on the town. Turns out she had dressed to impress me.

"Dr. Cortman," she said in a sultry voice upon entering

the office from the waiting room. "You look especially attractive today."

"Thanks, Donna," said I, not buying a word of it (although I knew my shoes matched that day) but wondering what was up with her. Now I knew why she had chosen to have her appointment in Sarasota; I never had a secretary there. My office manager, Sandy, worked all five days in Venice.

"How about if you and I get to know each other a little bit better today?" she suggested while commencing to unbutton her blouse.

"Whoa, stop! This is not going to happen," I responded quickly and as emphatically as I ever get in session. "I'd like to get to know you in a different way. Why don't you tell me your name?"

She was startled, as if she had not anticipated such a clinical reaction to her striptease. Nonetheless, she complied with the command to cease her disrobing. "My name is Janie," she replied.

"Hey, Janie. Thanks for telling me your name. Why don't you tell me about yourself."

She hesitated as puzzlement settled across her face. I guessed Janie was not used to talking much. In all likelihood, she was a woman of action. Too bad she had run into a man of words. "What do you want to know?" Any hint of seduction had vanished with my questions, replaced by discomfort.

"Tell me how you came to be. You know, the time Donna first called upon you to help her."

"I remember that. She was in college and trying to register for a specific English course. The course was closed, so she called upon me to help get her into the class." She smiled proudly at the recall of her first conquest. "We got an *A.* "

"So, Donna created you to help her accomplish things that she's incapable of herself. And you get the job done by having sexual relations with someone. Did I get that right?"

"Yes, you could say that."

"Okay, and how often does she call upon you to, uh,to help her, shall we say, take care of business?"

"Not very often. Twice since college and neversince marrying Peter."

That was a relief to me. And no doubt Peter,working diligently in his office, breathed a sigh of relief for reasons unbeknownst to him.

"So, why would Donna send you here today to visit me? She's hoping for an *A* in therapy?"

"Donna didn't send me here," she stated, as if I should have figured that out by myself.

"Who did?"

"I can't tell you. That's not my job."

In a flash, I knew who and why Janie was summoned to seduce me. "Lucinda sent you to have sex with me, so I can be reported and lose my license to practice. Then Lucinda wouldn't have to contend with my efforts to help Donna heal."

But before I could finish my conclusions, Janie fluttered her eyes and was gone, never to be heardfrom again. I had dodged a serious bullet. For now.

Donna spent the remainder of that session with me, and no more new--dangerous--material was shared by other alters during this session. Once again, Donna was spent, although she didn't know why.

I elected to tell her about Janie for several reasons: first, Donna needed to know that sexual advances, even if expressed by an alter, were completely unacceptable; second, she needed to know as much as possible about Lucinda's tactics because that knowledge would decrease Lucinda's power. Finally, I wanted her to understand my commitment to her healing--I would not withdraw my efforts, not even for sex.

But she would test that resolve in the next few days in ways that made me seriously question my commitment to our therapy.

"Dr. C., I'd like you to see something in my journal. I don't know who wrote it, but I swear to you that I didn't."

"Okay, I believe you. Let me see the journal."

She reluctantly handed me over the green and white book, open to the page with the entry in question. Satanic symbols, all in black marker, dominated the page. Below the pentagrams and inverted crosses was an encoded message. I had seen coded messages before in Shirley's journals, so I assumed that children reared in cults were taught to write satanic communications backwards. Donna's code proved just as easy to decipher:

I am Lucinda, princess of darkness. I am the one who dominates Donna's life. I control her decisions, her choices, her destiny. You, Christopher, must stay away from her, for you serve a different master. I serve the true master, the conqueror, the lord of all evil. We will reign with him, and you will be destroyed.
Now hear my words of warning--leave us alone immediately or there will be death at your doorstep. So saith Lucinda.

If my description of Janie's attempted seduction weren't

enough of a humiliation to Donna, certainly Lucinda's threat was. As the therapist, I focused on Donna's emotional reactions and paid little heed to Lucinda's encoded warning. When I sent Donna home that day, I hoped she would not regress into a depressive funk. Worse yet, I feared a return to suicidal thinking.

As for myself, I figured Donna/Lucinda wascompletely harmless. I dismissed the death-at-my-doorstep message altogether. I just couldn't find it in me to be afraid of this frail middle-aged woman.

Friday evening found me in a good mood. The crazy week had finally ended, and Laura's visit was only three hours away--enough time for a run, a shower, and a quick straightening up of my home. On the tile floor in the foyer just inside my front door was a shiny black gift bag, and attached to the handle was a black helium balloon. Black tissue paper poked up from the top of the bag. I had seen this gag before, most recently when a friend had turned thirty.

But this was June, and I had no special dates to celebrate. I wondered who had access to my condo. With a mental shrug, I carried my mail in one hand, the bag in the other, up the stairs and into the living room. My curiosity got the best of me before I began opening the mail. I reached into the bag and yanked out the tissue paper. *Something heavy inside,* I thought, and unwrapped my little surprise.

The beady eyes of a decapitated rat stared at me. Repulsed, I dropped the package, and the corpse rolled from the tissue paper and spattered blood on my gray carpet. If it was meant to be a joke, it wasn'tfunny.

My heart raced and thumped uncomfortably in my chest. Fear became anger and, within an instant, rage. I wantedto hit someone. Who the hell had been in my house? I wondered; my fists balled. Who would--?

I solved the riddle at once--Lucinda. How did she get in? What else had the evil lunatic done in my home? Visions of her sacrificing the rodent on some homemade altar flashed before my eyes. I conjured up other images--of summoning evil spirits, of worshipping Satan. I wanted to call her up--I knew her home phone number by heart bynow-- and tear into her.

No! I reminded myself. *You need to get a grip. You're her therapist.* The incident indicated the need for clear boundaries. Maligning her was unacceptable. Appropriate expression of feelings--that was the way to proceed, I concluded.

Just then the phone rang. I was really in no mood to deal with anyone, but I pounced on it, half hoping Lucinda was on the line.

"Chris?"

"Yeah, hi, Dad. How are you?" I was especially not in the mood to talk to my father, who was inclined to be critical of me.

"Good, thanks. How 'bout you?"

"Truthfully" I'm a little ticked off right now." While discarding the rat in the garbage, I gave Dad the rundown of my evening at home so far.

"How'd she get in?"

"I don't know." I told him the "death at your doorway threat," which prompted memory of Dianna's earlier statement that Lucinda carries out her threats.

"Well, I'm not sure how to tell you this, but that's the reason why I called."

"Huh?"

"Yeah. Your mother and I had a card hand-delivered to the house when we weren't home today, and we opened it up and found a Catholic communion card, with all the words changed to indicate worship of Satan. In fact, let me read some things. Oh, yeah, Natas--that's *Satan* spelled backwards. And those five-pointed stars encircled--what do you call them?"

"Pentagrams."

"Right. It's decorated with pentagrams and other silliness giving praise to Satan. Oh, and this coin about the size of a silver dollar, with a winged creature and some name on it. Hey, Vi"--he called to my mother--"what does that coin say?"

I heard her voice in the background. "Motley Crue."

"That's a heavy-metal rock band," I explained. Somewhere in the midst of our conversation, my rage had been transformed into compassion and pity for my folk.

"So, was that it?"

"Yeah. I figured it had something to do with you, with all the weird stuff you've been into lately."

"It's my stuff, all right, Dad. I'm sorry you and Mom had to get mixed up in it. Are you guys all right?"

"Your mom was a little shaken at first. She's not so worried about us. It's you she worries about. We both want you to know that it's fine to walk away from these patients if things get too ugly. There's no shame in removing yourself from evil. Know that your mother and I pray for you every day. And we have faith that if you are in God's will, then you're exactly where you need to be, no matter how scary it gets for you."

"Thanks, Dad. I appreciate that vote of confidence. It means a lot.

"I'm sure you caught the irony of the rodent."

I paused. "Whaddaya mean?"

"Wasn't it you who almost got kicked out of college for putting a dead mouse in the salad bar in the school cafeteria, or did one of your brothers pull that stunt?"

I had to laugh. I hadn't thought about that for a long time. "No, I'm the one."

"Well, now you're on the receiving end. What goes around, comes around." He chortled, knowing he had landed a good one.

I laughed again, releasing the remainder of the tension from my body and soul. "You know what, Dad? I'm glad you reminded me of that. I guess I have no right being upset about this, when I authored the prank in the first place. But I never decapitated my mouse. I didn't even kill it. Someone gave it to me already dead. I just stuck it on the salad bar. How's that for rationalizing?"

"That's great. I'm glad that you learned so much in school." He was yanking my chain, and I was getting a real kick out of him.

He continued. "Listen, I'm gonna get going, but if you need anything, even to talk, I'm here. I'm proud of you, son. Good night!"

My voice and my lip quivered as I said good-bye. My father's words touched me so deeply, I almost started to cry. I was amazed at how powerfully they registered. Even with all the psychological training and experience, I was reduced to a little boy when my daddy told me he was proud of me.

*   *   *

I checked all the current psychological journals in vain--none offered suggestions regarding how to confront clients who deliver decapitated animals to your housewhen in an alter personality. I was going to have to wing it. I picked up the phone.

"Hi, Donna, how are you? It's Dr. Cortman." "Dr. C., what a surprise. How are you?"

"Well, not so great. I'm a little upset by the package you left me this afternoon."

"What are you talking about?"

"You have no idea about what I'm referring to?" "None at all."

"Does a decapitated rat wrapped in black tissue paper ring a bell?" I expected contrition. I got denial.

"You must be confusing me with someone else. I don't even know where you live, and I certainly wasn't in your house this afternoon. I really don't know what you are accusing me of, but I do know that I don't appreciate it. I'm going to hang up now."

Click!

Great, I thought. *I teach her assertiveness, and she uses it against me.* But the more I thought about it, the less okay with it I was. I hit redial, figuring I'd give her a second chance to confess. That wasn't exactly what transpired.

"Hello?"

"Donna, listen, we need to talk about the visit to my house and the dead rat. That's--"

Listen, Cortman, you can go fuck yourself! And don't forget to say hello to your parents for me. Don't fuckin' call me again, got it?"

"Lucinda, wait!"

Click!

Any fear I had originally felt had vanished. My compassion for Donna's dilemma took a back seat to that sense of violation. But calling her a third time was certainly pointless. Time had come to appeal to a higher authority.

Lieutenant Robert Mitchell of the Sarasota Police Department arrived promptly after my phone call. I was embarrassed by my report of a crime and even more so when he asked to see the evidence. I had to retrieve the corpse from the garbage can in the garage.

Mitchell was cool about it, respecting my decision to not press charges. I had only two agendas, I explained to the man in blue: First and foremost, I was invested in helping Donna, not punishing her. Secondly, I needed to establish some firm boundaries with her. I could not enable her to violate my person, family, or property as a function of her working through her past. I would not tolerate it. Unbeknownst to me at the time, this proved to be a critical decision in our therapy at a most crucial juncture.

Mitchell would file a report but no charges. The police would inform her of our meeting and warn her that any subsequent harassment on her part would culminate in an arrest. Lieutenant Mitchell chose not to keep the evidence. The murder victim, he decided, was mine to dispose of.

With an hour to spare before heading to the airport to pick up Laura, I ran into Jerry, the condo maintenance supervisor. He was working on the beach, hosing down the pool chairs. Without prompting, he offered that a woman had stopped by the condo office with a package for me. Jerry described Donna/Lucinda perfectly, then added," I hope it was okay that I used the master key to put the packagein your foyer. The black balloons made me wonder if you were celebrating a birthday or mourning the end of your bachelor days."

"Not quite," I replied, and chose not to explainwhat really had happened.

Relieved that Lucinda had no access to my home, I simultaneously felt guilty for having accused her of breaking into my home.

After coming in from the beach I checked my office answering machine. Peter Carrington, Donna's recently estranged husband, had phoned in and requested a return call. Peter was aware of the limitations of confidentiality; I was not free to tell him anything about Donna. Instead, he wanted to provide me with some information.

"I was with Donna when you called her before and heard her end of the conversation," he explained. "First, I want to thank you. Your discovery of the different personalities has helped me make sense of the past twenty years." He paused a moment. "In the interest of helping her therapy, I wanted you to know something that Donna probably hasn't told you: Near her vagina she has a pentagram branded into her skin. I know it's some kind of satanic symbol. Her gynecologist also inquired about it, saying he'd never seen anything like it."

Peter went on to say that she would never talk about it to him or her doctor.

Peter's information served an important purpose--to underscore how real Donna's torment was, both physically and emotionally. I seemed to require the reminder to regain my perspective and my composure. My anger toward Donna/Lucinda melted, which was a good thing; my weekends with Laura were too precious to let a bad moodinterfere.

Done with my detective work for the night, I had a plane to meet.

Chapter 19

A Day at Disney

As any guy courting a beautiful woman knows, few places offer romance and fun as readily as the amusement park. And the granddaddy of all such parks, of course, is Disney World in Orlando, Florida. Just in case any of the original magic was disappearing from the relationship with Laura, I figured I'd take her to the Kingdom with the endless supply of it.

We did the mandatory exhibits: Country Bear Jamboree, Jungle River Cruise, and Space Mountain. We were also stuck in a room for twenty minutes while dozens of international puppets convinced us that it's "A Small World After All." Still, in all, we had a great time, especially when fiveof the seven dwarfs wanted to have their picture taken with Laura. I didn't mind, except that four of them were taller than I was.

Laura almost always falls asleep in the passengerseat when I drive home from anywhere, including the local supermarket. (Her idea of insomnia is staying awake for an entire television program.) On this two-hour trip,however, she was unable to doze off. So, my nonsleeping beauty opted to use this as an opportunity to talk.

"Honey?"

"Hey, look who's awake! Is the music too loud?"

"You didn't wake me up. I'm just not that sleepy tonight." She motioned to the radio. "Did you write this one?"

"Yes, I did. Shortly after I left Van Halen, andjust prior to my comeback with the Rolling Stones, I wrote several songs for Steely Dan. This one I wrote when I was having an affair with Jaclyn Smith back in the late seventies. You probably read about it."

"You know what really worries me, honey?" sheasked with all the sincerity that her wrinkled forehead could muster.

"What's that?" said I, playing the part of the straight man.

"People come to you for help with their problems." "That is disconcerting, isn't it?" I agreed.

Quiet minutes passed like innumerable white lines down the center of Interstate Four. There were too many other cars for me to consider using cruise control. I found myself feeling excited each time I was able to shift my Z car into fifth gear.

"Do you mind if I ask you anotherquestion?"

This one sounded serious. My insides muttered Uh-oh while my words rang out a confident, "Not at all."

"Well, I don't know how to say this to you, but you seem different lately distant. Not as interested in me as you were. Today while we were in line, you stood far away from me, as if you wanted to be somewhere else. Are you seeing someone else?"

"No, of course not. Don't be silly," I answered accurately, hoping, but knowing full well that the inquisition would not end here.

"Are you sure?" she asked again.

"I'm sure. There's nobody else, Laura." "*There, that ought to do it.*" "Then what is it?" Her persistence left me only two viable options, and although I didn't want to drive head-on into a tractor trailer, I figured it'd be less painful than getting serious and addressing Laura's questions.

"Okay. You're right. It's time to talk." I exhaled until my lungs were devoid of oxygen and noticed how damp my grip had become on the gray steering wheel. "I know you are upset, and that's important to me. You have a right to know what's up with me.

"Good. But if you break up with me, there's no changing your mind when you get over this thing you're going through."

I paused and reflected on just where I should start, then chickened out completely. "You see, I'm beginning to feel that I'm really a woman trapped in a man's body and—"

"C'mon, Chris, can't you be serious?"

Her words cut painfully. "I'm sorry. This is very hard for me." I found a crack in the traffic and went for it.

This served as a metaphor for my opening up to Laura. "For some reason I have had a number of different patients lately, maybe six or seven of them, who are beginning to tell me some shocking and scary things." I proceeded to tell my lady of the unconscionable accounts of the survivors of satanic abuse. Up to that point, I had elected to protect her from the topics of infant sacrifice and the consumption of blood.

"That's gross," she said after my recitation. "Aren't they worried about AIDS?"

"I guess not. I have had the same thought myself. I can't seem to understand how they do this stuff. I don't even get *why* they do it. There's just so much about this that has me mystified!"

"I don't mean to be rude, but what does this have to do with us? What, are you blaming your behavior on the devil now? Not even Scott used that excuse."

I didn't like being compared unfavorably to her ex-boyfriend, but I laughed anyway and tried again. "It's just that I'm starting to... I don't know, take things a little personally." I introduced her to the story of Charles Evans. After catching her up to speed on my interesting new friend, I provided her with the latest developments in my elementary understanding of the underworld.

"And truthfully, Laura, that's been on my mind a lot lately. I'm not sure what I've gotten myself into, you know?"

"So, let me get this straight," she said, folding her arms across her chest. "The government is messing up our relationship?"

I took my eyes off the Honda Civic with the Pennsylvania license plates that had set the pace forthe past thirty miles. It was a necessary move in order to stare incredulously at my unsympathetic sweetheart.

"There's more. You sure you wanna hear it?"

"I can hardly wait," uttered my little skeptic.

"I have several multiple personality clients whoare not only sharing cult stuff with me, they're alsotelling me about demons."

"Demons?"

I knew this wouldn't go over well. "Yeah, you know. evil spirits. One client suggested that she may have had contact with demonic entities--some in the past, some recently. Last week in my office she appeared to be possessed. I've never seen anyone's eyes light up so evil like hers did. Her voice deepened to that of a man! She glared right at me and said, 'You're scared!' I'll never forget it as long as I live. I was petrified and completely unsure as to how to handle her. I can't begin to describe the eerie feeling that filled the room. Evil definitely has a distinct feel toit."

I spent the next several minutes vividly remembering an experience that had seemed entirely different from talking to an alter personality. I could almost recall the sensation in my stomach. Suddenly my office had become disturbingly quiet, and a sense of doom permeated the room. It felt as if all oxygen had been sucked from the air. My insides vibrated with a low-voltage current.

"You'll never find all of us,"' the demonic voice had taunted me. "We don't intend to go. We will hold on to this woman. Don't think we can't, for I hold the keys to the gates of hell."

I shivered now, remembering the taste of fear and how panicky I had felt.

"So, what happened?" Laura prompted, bringing me back to our conversation.

"I remembered a Bible verse that goes, 'Greater is He that is in you, than he that is in the world (I John 4:4)." My understanding of the verse--that God's spirit is superior to any evil spirit--helped me stay calm. I clung to that promise, telling the evil voice that it couldn't have this woman anymore, that she was choosing to pursue God instead of Satan. What amazed me was that this voice--I don't know what else to call it because I can't be sure if it was a spirit or an alter personality--quoted Scripture to me. It said, 'The devil walks about as a roaring lion, seeking whom he may devour (I Peter 5:8).' I respondedwith the verse about God being greater, and much to mysurprise, there was silence. Nothing. Not a word. Then within seconds, the woman's whole countenance changed again, and the evil eyes were gone! All she said was,

'He left. It's okay now.' Then she wanted some reassurance from me. She did not want to talk about it anymore."

"So now you're the exorcist?"

The more I shared my story with Laura, the more hostile she became. She was not hearing what she was hoping for, but she was getting the truth--at least as I understood it. I decided to respond to the content of the question rather than process the disappointment that lurked behind her inquiries.

"No, I didn't attempt to cast out any demons. Again,I wasn't sure what I was dealing with. But I told my client that if she was certain she was confronting a spirit and not an alter personality, then she might want to seek out some spiritual help--maybe talk to a clergy person of her choice. It was either that, or I was gonna burn her at the stake."

My attempt to lighten the mood with humor struck out with my stone-faced girlfriend. That was it! I realized in a flash of insight that we both had needs, conflicting needs to be certain, and neither one of us was getting them met.

She needed reassurance that she was cared for, that I wasn't going to abandon her physically or emotionally. She didn't need the long-winded explanation as to why I was different. She needed to believe that I wouldn't use my struggles as an excuse to create distance between us.

What did I need? I needed to share some of this craziness with someone other than Richard because although he was bright and objective, he could not provide the nurturing support that a woman could. That someone who loved me could. That *Laura* could, if she felt secure with me! I decided to use the chivalrous "ladies first" method and address her needs.

I began with the single most difficult sentence a guy

ever has to utter: "Look, sweetie, I know you're right. I'm sure I've changed. I'm more serious since all this has happened. But it's not you, and it's not going to break us up. I'll get through this all right, and so will you and I. I love you, Laura. Nothing has changed as far as that goes. I'm just wrestling with a lot now." I squeezed her hand as I reached across the console. "Please believe in me now and be patient 'cause I really need your support more nowthan I ever have." I meant every word of it.

For the first time since we left Disney, I saw the loving brown eyes that I had come to treasure. Thisallowed me to continue with my pursuit of her support.

"I feel weird saying this, but I feel as if God is dealing directly with me. I haven't given Him the time of day for nearly eight years but ... I don't know, I just sense that a lot of this stuff is not just about helping other people but also bringing me back to Him."

My tone grew more serious, as I considered the possibility that God was somehow involved in all of the unusual events of the last several months of my life. I wondered if He might not only be allowing butorchestrating the situations for His purpose. But what might thatpurpose be? And what did He expect from me?

My musings were aborted once again by that same sweet voice from across the car. It seemed that Laura couldn't resist one last jab: "So it's not only the devil and the government, it's also God that's messing up our relationship?"

"'Yeah, honey, but if you really loved me, you'd fight for us 'Against All Odds?' (the song that was nowplaying on the radio). Did I ever tell you that I wrote that song for Phil Collins?"

Chapter 20

The Wedding

Undoubtedly every successful organization has a prescribed way of doing things. Social scientists contend that the individual family unit--even the dysfunctional ones-- abide by an unspoken code of behavior. Family members play specific roles: hero martyr, persecutor, black sheep, overfunctioner, screwup, and so on. Unknowingly we rehearse and perform our specific scripts, for each person's behavior feeds off the others. That is, the screw up makes his customary mess of things, thus drawing to himself the attention he so desperately craves. Then the overfunctioner may step in to save the day. Meanwhile, the persecutor criticizes, and the martyr laments. Pleasant or not, the systems are often quite rigid and resistant to change.

As Shirley's clinician, I learned that dissociative people have similar systems in their inner world. Certain of these alters communicate with others; some stand alone. Some protect; some cry out for healing; some persecute the children. It's not unlike a dysfunctional family system.

(This arrangement was subsequently confirmed by many other clients with this diagnosis. One woman's alters, for example, resided in separate rooms of a dark and dreary cave, where she reportedly was chained as a child during satanic rituals.)

Shirley's system appeared at first to be rather straightforward. Every alter had a story to tell, albeit a gruesome one. Our modus operandi began with Shirley's presenting a bizarre set of symptoms. We would follow the symptoms like breadcrumbs upon a forest trail, until at last they led to the painful memory. Shirley would own the story as real, feel the concomitant pain, and eventually say good-bye to that alter personality.

The steps worked without fail and provided me with a degree of hope and confidence that we would soon realize the goal of oneness for Shirley. In fact, I foolishly began to forecast that her complete integration would take place before the end of our second year together. My prediction faltered miserably. Just when it seemed that every last alter had joined forces with Shirley in her quest for wholeness and unity, I learned that her system was made up of more than one level! We had indeed been successful in our efforts to heal and integrate Shirley's poisonous past, but that was only the first level of her innersystem.

She broke the news to me during her Tuesday morning session on a tepid winter day in early January. Without a word she set down her small, charcoal gray journal on the cluttered desktop in front of me, then plopped into the recliner. Twice her eyes darted from my gaze to her writings on my desk, as if to say, *Forget the smalltalk. You need to read the journal now!*

"Shall I read this out loud? I asked. She shook her head. If she couldn't bear the thought of hearing her entry read back to her, then I concluded its content was painful, if not humiliating for her. I snatched up the notebook and commenced my journey:

Don't be mad at us. The others didn't know we were here. You don't know us. We are not like them.

Please don't be angry. We need to tell you about the wedding. It was very scary and very bad. We are not with the others. They were on the first level. They are all gone. They liked you, Chris, because they could trust you. Can we trust you, too? Will you believe us, too? Please tell Shirley we will be listening, okay? Thank you. (Signed) All of us on Level II.

To admit I was disappointed would be an understatement. I was angry. Maybe I felt duped by Shirley--I thought we were so close to the finish line. Maybe I was embarrassed by my lack of awareness that Shirley's system contained another level of alters. Maybe I hadn't understood her system as well as I wanted to believe I had.

Maybe we weren't close to the finish line after all. And maybe I wasn't succeeding as therapist extraordinaire. And then I had a sobering thought: *This isn't about you, Chris. Get over yourself and treat your patient. You're not done yet, but you're making progress. Stay with it!*

Shirley's discussion about the second level and the so-called wedding dominated our therapy for at least ten sessions over two months. But she did little to resolve anything. For me--and I assume for most therapists--one of the most frustrating aspects of the profession is dealing with patients who talk about problems but do nothing about them. I had never thought of Shirley as anything lessthan sincere and hardworking, but I wondered if she might be running scared now and avoiding her issues.

Again, I was wrong. The sessions seemed necessary due to the incredible fear and the sheer power of her experience at the wedding. Ironically, two years to the very day of our initial session, Shirley announced herself ready to finally discuss the story and its relevance to level two.

Presenting in well-worn jeans and a plain white T-shirt with a pocket on the left side for her smokes, Shirley arrived on time for a two-hour appointment. Nothing about her seemed extraordinary--no overt signs of anxiety, no sense of urgency--so I had no reason to suspect that anything special would be happening that day.

"How are you? she began, already one withthe recliner. "Good, Shirley, thanks. What's up with you today?" "I am in for a double session, right? My nod invited her tocontinue.

She reached into a beat-up black purse the size of a Buick and pulled out a notebook with permanently bound pages.

"I need to read the entire story to you today. We all expect we can handle it. But it won't be easy. She expressed herself in the familiar manner of changing her pronouns from first-person singular to first-person plural. Her expression conveyed a warning to me.
Is there anything I need to do besides listen?" I asked.

"No, she reassured, there isn't anything anyone can do. I just need to know that you're here for us and that you believe. It may be hard to believe what I'm gonna read you, but we didn't make any of this up, okay?"

"Okay."

She bent her head to the book and began to read.

I was a little older, probably twelve years old. I'm sure it was before our pregnancy. We had been told repeatedly that we were the "chosen one" in our group, and that meant that we were to bear the seed of our lord. I remember it was a Saturday morning, because I was relieved to be off from school but afraid to be home if my father wasn't off working somewhere.

My mother announced to me, "This is your special day, honey. Tonight, you will be joined together with our master and lord. Everyone will be proud of you. Some of the ladies from the group will be coming over later to help me prepare you for tonight. So run off now and get yourself cleaned up. We'll be having lunch in an hour or so."

I remember being surprised that Mom was talking to me about the group's activities. Prior to that, I can't remember a single instance of Mom saying anything at all about the group. It was always Dad. And he was never nice about it.

I fought all day with anxiety--that would be the word that you would use, Chris--I tried to give way to a person that I created on that day to help me make it through whatever it was that was planned for me. But I would need more than one imaginary helper on this day.

The ladies came over--the same ones you may remember that induced labor upon me when I was pregnant. They curled my hair and did my makeup and eye shadow. I found that particularly upsetting because my father forbade me to wear any makeup whatsoever. But I knew better than to say anything. I would only be punished. I went far away in my head as much as I could and went through the motions as the women paid all this attention to me.

My mother said to me in front of the others, "We need to get going soon. We'll be meeting your father later at the church for tonight's ceremony. That is where we will be putting on your dress. Tonight will be very special. Again, she said that. I had no idea what was in store for me. It was better that way.

Later on at the church, I remember being placed in a room at the end of the hallway in the part of the building known as Fellowship Hall. Ours was a Lutheran church, and my parents didn't often attend. My brother and I were sometimes sent to Sunday school with one of the neighbor ladies who was probably a true Christian. "Anyway, there was a contact in the church. I think it was the local undertaker, truthfully. He had access to the church along with the groundskeeper, who I'm pretty sure was his brother. So, we often had our meetings and ceremonies in the church.

I interrupted Shirley to ask a question. "Why are cult ceremonies held so often in churches?"

Because Satan worship is the exact opposite of Christianity, it requires so many of the same tools of worship that churches contain: altars, goblets, statues, bibles, what not. We could use all of their stuff for our ceremonies. Besides, it gives great pleasure to Satan and his demons to make a mockery of God like that. I nodded my understanding, and she continued.

I remained in that room for what seemed like hours, initially to try on the wedding dress that the ladies had brought me. It was far from a perfect fit, but a nip here and a tuck there, and they had it looking like it was tailor-made for me. I might have enjoyed all the attention and the pretty dress, were it not for the fact I knew that something had been planned for me. And while I didn't know what it was,I knew one thing--it wasn't going to be pleasurable for me. It never was.

When I was completely made over from head totoe, the ladies quickly removed all positive attention from me. They returned to their typical way of treating me with insults, harsh words, and especially threats!

Don't even think of doing anything to mess up your hair or your dress, or you can easily be sacrificed tonight.

My mother added, "Not a peep out of you now, you understand, Shirley?"

The door was closed behind them and locked, leaving me alone in a small room on one of those folding metal chairs that they always seemed to have for Sunday school. The walls were plain and bare except for a familiar picture of Jesus knocking on the door of a house. I stared at that picture and kinda got lost in it until, at last, I fell asleep.

I have no idea how long I was in that room sleeping, but looking back, I can see that drifting off to sleep was another defense against experiencing the dread in the pit of my stomach.

I was awakened by a combination of loud voices and the rattling of keys unlocking the door. My heart raced as the same small group of women entered, now dressed in ceremonial black robes and dark makeup.

They were rushing about as if something urgent was driving them. Perhaps the group leader had ordered them to hurry and fetch me. My mother grabbed me on one side and Winnie on the other. Winnie squeezed my arm a lot tighter than she needed to--per way of inflicting pain on me unnecessarily. That's how she always got her jollies.

More cautions were issued and more threats in case I screwed up. Then Mom handed me a Dixie cup of water and two blue pills and said, "Take these now." The pills were probably Valium, definitely some type of sedative. Mom looked as if she needed them more than I did. I could see by her unsettled expression that she was upset. Lord knows by what.

She handed me a pack of stale crackers, to make sure I had something besides the pills in my stomach.

The women led me down a brightly lit hallway and into

the adjoining building to the main sanctuary.

The exterior doors were always locked, with a guard stationed to fend off intruders.

The sanctuary was dark with the exception of a smattering of candlelight. My eyes needed to adjust to the darkness. The women led me past the circle of robed adults to the other altar in front of the great room. The men had relocated the pews to one side of the sanctuary to make space for the circle in the center of the room.

I was forced to kneel in front of the inverted cross and recite an evil prayer that I will not repeat. Never again will those words pass my lips. Organ music filled the room as the chanting began--softly at first, then more and more loudly until reaching a feverish pitch.

A man with a white robe silenced the crowd and greeted everyone in the name of the great lord and master, Satan. "The purpose of our gathering tonight is the wedding of the divine one to the chosen one of our group, Miss Shirley McIntyre. I expect that the great master himself will make his presence felt by honoring us with an appearance to condone and bless us for our faith.

The people applauded wildly, and excitement filled the room. I'm sure I was the only one who felt an almost overwhelming sense of dread, then terror.

I realized that I might never leave this room alive. At that moment I switched into another alter.

The high priest then signaled a couple of the men.

"Present the bride for the lord's visit," he instructed them.

They grabbed and lifted me off my feet and set me atop the altar, then joined the priest on the platform. I remember feeling relieved to be able to lie down; my knees were beginning to wobble now that the drugs were kicking in.

Again, my perception of time was distorted by the drugs, my apprehension, and even the switching, but what happened next was real! My memories have no cloudy moments, no vague images. They are all crystal clear to me, and I can see it today exactly as it happened then. And since remembering it, I have watched it play nonstop in my head like a horror movie.

He did appear! He was huge! Probably eight feet tall, although I'm aware of how difficult it is to judge based on my age at the time and the fact that I was on my back on the altar. His face was stern, handsome, and as crazy as this might sound to you, he had a goatee and horns! He did, I swear it! The horns were not the type depicted in cartoons. They were more like ram horns. He was completely naked down to his hoofed feet. He was unusually muscular, and yes, his penis was disproportionately large. There was not a trace of hair anywhere on his body except for his face. Even his head was completely without hair.

The people were awed by his presence. I gather most of them had never seen him before. When they found their voices, they shouted out in praiseand exaltation, and some people burst into song. It was truly their god appearing before them.

Then a very unusual thing happened. Several of the members groped each other, initiating a sexual orgy. But he did not approve. "Stop! he shouted in a very loud voice. In fact, it was the loudest voice I have ever heard. "You can have sex after I'm gone! You are to attend to me while I'm here!"

The people stopped immediately and turned their attention to their lord. More organ music followed, and the high priest pronounced the wedding vows in a nontraditional fashion. He stated that I was indeed the eternal bride of Satan, forever to honor, obey, and worship him as the one true god of the universe. I would be the chosen one, the one selected to carry his seed and bear his name on earth and in the hereafter.

After praising the bridegroom once more, the priest turned to me. "And now for the final act of preparation of the bride!" He produced a dagger, raised it high above his head, and brought it to a full stop inches from my heart. He whispered to me, "Behave if you wish to live," and then slit the dress down the middle and yanked it apart, leaving me fully exposed for--well, I'm not even sure how to address him--the evil one.

He came forward and placed his hand upon my chest. I was not developed at age twelve, but that didn't matter--he pulled and yanked at my nipples. The remarkable thing, however, was his touch. His fingers produced intense heat! I was actually startled and had the impression that he was searing my skin!

I know I heard more of Shirley's account, though only a portion of it registered with me. She told of the forced penetration that caused her to bleed profusely. I learned of how his tongue was forked on the end and darted from his mouth like the serpent he once inhabited in the Garden of Eden.

I caught the part of Shirley's story wherein she proved herself worthy to the evil one by demonstrating no discernable signs of weakness--no fear, no tears, nosounds of distress or pleading. Shirley claimed to have developed the capacity to dissociate from the entire horror through the creation of no fewer than twenty-one different alters who did everything from absorb the physical pain to stare without flinching into the eyes of the beast. She seemedto understand that in recounting the incident, the terrorand pain she had farmed out to the alters were now hers to reclaim in order to heal.

I admit my attention to some of the remaining details was less than absolute. I was hung up on one aspect of her supposed encounter with the evil one--his burning touch.

Imagining Satan's touch to be red-hot doesn't sound far-fetched if we assume that he resides amid the scorching fires of hell. What bothered me was that I had heard this very same complaint only the week before from another patient: "Satan's touch was burning hot," the other had said.

Could it be more than a projection of the troubled patient's mind? Is it possible that Satan or some spiritual entity really appears at ceremonies that seek to praise and arouse evil forces? I could no longer answer my own questions objectively. I was certain that I had been in the presence of evil spirits at least once, so I couldn't rule out the possibility that Shirley's account was valid.

But Satan himself appearing at some local gathering in a small-town church? If he is indeed real, wouldn't he function behind the scenes in some official capacity, like a general or a president? Or was he so egotistical as to solicit face-to-face adulation from his believers? The Bible, I remembered, mentions that the devil was capable of taking on many forms, even an angel of light (Cor II, 11:14). *Hell if I know,* I thought, half smiling at my own silly pun and half resigned to my inability to decipherthe truth.

But did I have to know the truth to help Shirley?

Probably not. I just needed to validate her beliefs and her version of the truth. I knew she wasn't lying. But was it possible that her memory was tainted or distorted in some way by the drugs she was given to enhance docility and cooperation? Again, I couldn't answer that.

Was it possible that Shirley had never met Satan at all? Possibly a man in costume had been selected to play the role of the devil. That seemed plausible, even likely to me, although I couldn't rule out the presence of the supernatural, as much as I wanted to. Despite my willingness once again to endorse that Satan was aliveand well, I preferred not to believe that he was capable of visiting cult meetings or raping and marrying my patients. I wanted him to return to a distant hell with apitchfork, a tail, and a snowball's chance of making it out of his imprisonment.

Regardless of Satan's reality, Shirley had successfully taken me through the wedding and the purpose of her level-two alters. Once she could make peacewith this memory, I assumed that she would be fully integrated into one person and done at last with visiting and remembering her past.

This time, I was partially correct. We *were* virtually finished with the childhood abuse. But even after she resolved level two, she was still not fully integrated or able to function as one person.

Again, I was shocked to learn why our work together was still far from over.

Chapter 21

The Devil Herself

One of my all-time dearest clients was an eight-year-old survivor of a vicious dog attack. She was thrice bitten by two Dalmatians, and as a result, this precious childhad lost her confidence, her focus in school, and her illuminating smile. Her understandable fear of dogs, especially big ones, had become more than a nuisance to her in her canine-filled neighborhood.

Treatment had been quite successful, very quickly.Her premorbid personality had returned. She had an infectious way of taking over the whole office with herquestions about becoming a psychologist. After our work together, she was certain she knew how to be one. I believed she was well on her way; she sure knew how to make me feel better.

The last item left on our list to fix was her dog phobia. I was using some behavioral techniques to help her gradually overcome her fear. One such technique, called in vivo (real life), required exposing the child to dogs in the safety of my office. She had passed the little-dog test, but the big-dog session proved more trying.

I enlisted the help of the K-9 unit of the local police department, which brought over a monster of a German Shepherd. I figured if she could learn to relax in the company of this creature, then no neighborhood dog would scare her. It was a great plan and worked magically--that is, until the building's maintenance man trudged through the shrubbery bordering the parking lot, to wash my office's exterior windows. (In the five years of renting in that office, I had never ever seen anyone clean the windows.)

The Shepherd, alerted to a potential intruder, exchanged his relaxed sprawl for an attack stance--tail erect, teeth fully exposed. His explosive barks and angry growls prompted me to check my boxers for moisture and, more importantly, terrified my patient. My little princess huddled herself in a ball behind a pillow on thecouch peering out with eyes the size ofhubcaps.

The K-9 plan temporarily backfired. If anything, the dog phobia infected me like a contagious virus. Happily, my little beauty and the beast regained composure, and the child managed to renew her relationship with dogs, great and small.

Donna was still reeling from the horror of havingthe Sheriff's Department show up at her door to issue her a warning. She still had no recollection of either thevisit to my house or to my parents; but she accepted that Lucinda was capable of anything. In fact, that once- secretive part of Donna's psyche called me to cancel our appointment, as she had to prepare for a cultmeeting.

"Oh, didn't we tell you we're still involved, Christopher?" she asked breezily. "Please excuse the oversight. Sometimes things get confusing, with so many of us attempting to share one body. But do understand that *I have the power,* and nothing anyone can do will stop me from attending that meeting."

"Donna wants to attend this meeting, Lucinda?" I asked, knowing full well that Donna would never approveof any such thing.

"Do you think I give a shit about what Donna wants and

doesn't want? She's so weak, it doesn't much matter if she wants to stop me, does it, Christopher? Say, why don't you join me for the meeting? I'm sure they'd welcome you. We just love having Christians attend."

Rather than be intimidated, I chose a sarcastic tone designed to communicate that I would not back down. "Thanks, Lucinda, but I'm certain I have to work that night. You may need to find another sacrifice."

"Oh, that's a shame. You'll miss the rededication service. We're rededicating our lives to the group and to the master."

"Lucinda, I don't think missing our session this week is a good idea. I'd like a commitment that you'll be here.

We can talk more when face to face in session, okay? "Fuck off! We won't be seeing you anytime soon, but don't think we're done with you. We have only just gotten started." Lucinda laughed with what can only be construed as the stereotypical evil laugh, then hung up on me.

She was pushing my buttons--or maybe I was allowing her to--and she knew it. Either way, I wasn't going to allow this to go on. But how could I stop it? I checked my artillery for any weapon that might prove useful in protecting Donna from herself. Fortunately, I still had the most powerful tool in my arsenal at the ready—the Baker Act, or BA52.

A Florida state law, the Baker Act empowers mental health professionals to commit people to an involuntary, mandatory seventy-two-hour confinement in an appropriate mental-health facility. The patients are observed and often clinically treated before being released or brought before the judge to assess the appropriateness of an extension of confinement. The Baker Act is generally utilized in cases of potential harm to self or others, or in situationswhere people are deemed to be bizarre and/or psychotic enough in their behavior to warrant involuntary help.

Did Donna fit into one of these categories? I wasn't sure. But I was fairly certain that Lucinda did, and I concluded that if she didn't reconsider her stance on the session, it was time for a return visit to thepsychiatric unit--an involuntary trip this time, to becertain. We were going to have our session one way or another.

After outlining for the police the details leading up to my decision, I convinced them of Donna's appropriateness for involuntary commitment. They picked her up peacefully on Tuesday morning before work; the re-dedication ceremony was scheduled for Wednesday evening.

Donna was confined in the locked-door unit, where precautions could be taken to prevent suicide attempts.

I made a special evening appearance to see her in the lockup ward. I made arrangements to have one-on-one time with her.

Because several staff members were privy to the police report and because of Donna's unusual diagnosis, she had quickly become the talk of the staff.

I walked into her room and was genuinely happy to see her and relieved she was safe after the events of the past week.

"Hi, Dr. C. I'm glad to see a familiar face." She was quiet, sad almost to the point of defeat. I had never seen her without makeup, and her pale complexion may have contributed to her downcast appearance. Dressed casually in blue jeans, Donna was transformed from the businesswoman I had become accustomed to seeing, and she was certainly a far cry from the seductress of a week before.

"Are they treating you okay?" I wanted to break the ice and alleviate some of the inevitable awkwardness in this, our first session since Lucinda's hostile activities.

"Yes, fine. Everyone is nice."

Cold silence followed, with a fidgety Donna avoiding eye contact.

"You're not happy with me, are you?" I violated the no-mind-reading rule, figuring I would save some time by getting right to the obvious tension.

"No, I guess I'm not. It's just that… well, I don't know."

"Tell me what it is you need to say.

"I just wonder if this was really, you know… if this was necessary to lock me up. That's all. I don't know. I just feel so ashamed and"--on came the tears--"Dr. Cortman, I don't want to lose my job. What do I tell my boss? I was in the hospital last year, and now this! If management knew why I was here, I'd be out on the street. I'm just a mess. Please help me get out of here. Please! I didn't mean to hurt or scare your family. I would never hurt anyone. I'm so sorry."

The sobs increased in volume and intensity, but in the primitive confines of the locked ward, tissues were a luxury we were not afforded. I reached into the pocket of my blazer to furnish a clean hanky when Donna looked up from her hands to fire a visual missile at me.

"You must get a real thrill from **all** this power you have to reduce a woman to tears. What a turn-on for you, Doc, huh?"

"Lucinda? I felt a churning in my belly, thinking the devil herself had returned. But I had missed the clue about reducing 'a woman' to tears.

"No! I'm no devil worshipper. It's Mary, in case you've

forgotten me. How could you do this to her? She has placed so much trust in you, and you lock her up like a convict. Are you going to buy us groceries when we lose our job? Pay the mortgage? No, I'm sure the problems you're creating didn't even occur to you when you decided to imprison us like this. We hate it here, Cortman, and most of us are not so crazy about you anymore."

This last remark was designed to express her fear and rage and also to retaliate. Mary's job description contained two important functions: to protect Donna from abusive men and assert thoughts and feelings that Donna was not comfortable expressing herself.

"I'm sorry this is so upsetting to all of you. I didn't mean it to cause harm; I intended to protect you from Lucinda. Her behavior has become too dangerous for you and possibly for others, too. As far as your job goes, I will personally see to it that your employer understands that you are under severe stress right now. I don't believe that your job is in jeopardy."

"Oh, Dr. Cortman, would you do that for us?" Her words dripped with sarcasm. But the tone was not Mary's. "You are sooo kind. How can we ever thank you enough?"

"Lucinda, is it you? I asked awkwardly, wishing my multiples would change colors every time they switched.

"My, how perceptive you've become, Christopher. I'm so impressed."

"I'm glad you came, Lucinda. I was hoping to see you tonight."

"Don't give me that bullshit. You are no more glad to see me than I am to be in here. You had no right to stop us from attending our meeting."

Lucinda's icy demeanor was gone, along with the

sarcasm. She was now ablaze with rage, seemingly from the moment I had said I was glad to see her. A second observation quickly followed: Lucinda appeared very *hurt* by her inability to attend the ceremony. Anger, I believe, is merely a cover for emotional pain. What made the ceremony so important to her? I'd have to inquire in a nonthreatening manner.

As I had learned from dealing with Shirley's alter Colleen, getting into a power struggle with an alter personality is a no-win battle. Better toestablish boundaries and allow her to take me to the pain. I had a plan, but I needed to be subtle.

"So, tell me about this ceremony, Lucinda."

"What would you like to know?" She seemed to perk up in her chair. I took that to mean that the interest in the topic outweighed her need to oppose me.

"Your part. What exactly do you do?"

"I am the master's high priestess. I hold the most exalted position of all the women in the group. I see to it that the elements are presented properly. I make sure that the men are entertained and satisfied. They all like me and are always happy to see me."

"What do they like so much about you?" The time had come to allow Lucinda to take me into her private domain. I needed to establish what empowered Lucinda to be the mightiest of all of Donna's alters.

Her chin tilted up proudly. "They like what I can do. I dance for them. I know how to prepare a sacrifice and to carry it through. I know how and where to make the incisions. I can remove the bowels from the body. I am not afraid of anyone. I am always obedient to the master."

"So, everyone in the group loves you for what you can do. Is that it?"

"They *respect* me for what I have accomplished,"she corrected me.

I had accidentally stumbled upon something. I went with my hunch. "You differentiate between their lovingyou and respecting you. Tell me about that, please." I attempted to convey respect in the manner in which Iasked the question. I would like to think that I do this uniformly with all of my clients, but Lucinda's situation required an exaggerated effort.

"I am respected for the position I hold, as I already told you. I have earned my status within the group. The women look up to me. Themen-"

"Excuse me for interrupting. They respect you. That's clear. But do they love you, Lucinda? Do they really care about you?"

Her frigid disposition had all but been defrosted by the question about love. She stammered and looked nervously about the room, as if looking for a place she could hide. She was exposed, emotionally naked in front of the opposition! And a Christian, no less. Beads ofperspiration intruded upon her now-twitching face; the eyes began to blink rapidly. Too fragile to remain another moment, she appeared on the verge of switching to another alter. But I would not allow that switch just yet.

If I intercede right now, I thought, maybe she won't vanish into the darkness. "Lucinda, wait!", I hoped she would need to stay another moment if addressed by name. "Did your father love you?"

Lucinda stayed only long enough to absorb the blow of the question. My once-formidable foe appeared as defeated as a helpless boxer staggering against the ropes. She looked once more at me, a desperate, pathetic look, and then she was gone.

My question had not been intended to destroy her or to hurl parental rejection in her face, but to help Donna heal. I had to expose the root of Lucinda's pain in order to champion the deleterious effects of the abuse.

I'm sure I spoke to other alters during that session. (One even handed me a fingernail clipper with a sharpened point, which Lucinda had smuggled into the locked unit to harm the others.) But nothing registered as powerfully as Lucinda's demonstration of vulnerability. I knew her weakness now; suddenly I held the power as far as she was concerned. I hadn't caved into the attempted intimidation or the seduction, the rodent, or the card to my parents. I wouldn't stand for her canceling our appointment in favor of her cult meeting, and I wouldn't hesitate to use my newfound information with her in the future--not in a cruel way, not to hurt or destroy Lucinda.

No, my strategy was to require her to take me to the source of her pain, the absence of love in her life. Its expression and release would, I believed, render Lucinda powerless and permit Donna to heal from the parental rejection. Finally, it would allow Donna, Lucinda, and all the others to become one person.

I couldn't help but continue my musings as I made my way home from the hospital. Why did Lucinda wield the most power of any of the alters? *Because she carries the most pain,* I realized. Lucinda rose to the occasion when it was time to pull out the heart of a child. Lucinda danced for the men and appeased their pedophiliac desires. And it was Lucinda who served as hostess--the alter in control--when the ceremonies were held in the woods on cold December nights.

Petrified on the inside yet maintaining a placid facade,

Lucinda had witnessed unspeakably severe child abuse, and she kept the pain and the terror to herself so that Donna could rise in the morning as usual, the obedient child on time for grade school.

If a child--heck, if *anyone--were* repeatedly exposed to abominations without the opportunity to turn away, wouldn't it make sense to try to like the experience?

Wouldn't it be the wisest thing an individual could do, to *embrace* the bloody rituals? If Lucinda could convince herself that she truly *enjoyed* the sacrifices, *reveled* in pleasing the men, and *coveted* the approval of the master, wouldn't that attitude be far superior to trembling helplessly during the ceremonies? Yes, of course it would, I concluded, continuing my internal dialogue.

My car headed home on automatic pilot. My mind was light years away from my body at that point, registering nothing consciously. I was completely focused on my theories regarding Lucinda.

I considered one such psychological theory--it's called *cognitive dissonance--when* people resolve conflict and make internal peace by convincing themselves of something not quite true. For example, if I need to exercise to stay in shape, why not convince myself that I really enjoy working out? Again, if Lucinda could convince herself that she enjoyed the practice of satanic worship, that would be construed as *psychologically healthy.* Perhaps one might consider it to be a survival response.

Moreover, didn't Lucinda claim to command respect for her diverse talents? Respect evidently meant a lot to her, especially in the absence of love. Like any child, Donna/Lucinda hungered for love and attention. Like every little girl, she desired affection from her father. With none forthcoming, the respect she earned from the cult members would have to suffice. They filled the role of surrogate father. Secretly she still craved love and affection like the dieter craves carbohydrates. For in either case, this is the fuel that sustains life.

Chapter 22

God's Firefly

Donna was released from the hospital after the Baker Act's three-day-minimum confinement had elapsed. Her admitting psychiatrist was convinced that she was not an immediate threat to herself, to me, or to the rodent population of Southwest Florida. He held the unenviable position of assessing Donna's mental status and, if his determination proved inaccurate, accepting full responsibility for her behavior. This was true despite the fact that he spent so little time with her, especially when compared to me. He consulted my office to ask if I thought she would be ready to return to the real world of work, bills, and adult responsibilities, including her intensive therapy.

After meeting with her for a second time in the hospital, I was able to offer him my blessings for her release. In the form of Dianna, she had made two statements that swayed me in that direction: First, Lucinda promised no more shenanigans, as she hated confinement and would never subject herself to that again. Second, Dianna claimed to be speaking for the entire group when she asserted, "Okay, Dr. C, we're ready. Whatever it takes to get better, we'll do it. We are tired of hurting."

I suggested twice weekly sessions and dropped my rate to accommodate the increase in session time. Donna and I both knew that there was no turning back, now that she had promised to invest her all. I believed her and was invigorated by the promise of what lay in store.

Indeed, several weeks passed without a peep from Lucinda. The other alters didn't even mention her. I didn't consider that to be a bad thing--merely an indication that therapy was a very dangerous place for therejection-phobic Lucinda.

But one thing was certain--sooner or later shewould return. I wouldn't allow her absence to be anything buta temporary break from treatment and an opportunity for some of the other alters to finish their stories, share their feelings with Donna, and begin the process of integration.

One of the first alters to attempt integration was Mary, the former man-hater. Mary confessed somewhat unwillingly that she had chosen to trust me and believed that I would not do anything to hurt Donna. This was quite a concession for the hypervigilant Mary.

If I did integrate--and I'm not saying that I'm ready for that--how do I know that Donna will be able to protect herself from men?"

I stroked my imaginary beard. "Excellent question, Mary. I'm glad that you're considering integration. That tells me that Donna is ready to own all the memories and feelings that she once gave to you. It also indicates that she's preparing to do for herself the things that you've always done for her. Are you concerned that she may not be able to handle it without you?"

Mary nodded, which I read as encouragement to continue my didactic--educational--psychotherapy. "When an alter integrates, Mary, she becomes one and the same with the core person. There's no distinction between the two. In the future she'll protect herself against men. You don't abandon her; you become her, and she gets to keep your skills. But she'll assert herself with men without hostility or verbal aggression because she has skills beyond your behaviors."

I told her the analogy of the snowman that I had shared once with Shirley, then concluded, "You have done so much for Donna for so long. I believe it's time now to help her to do it for herself. I was certain that I caught a welling up of tears in her eyes--clearly an atypical expression of emotion for the hard-boiled, defensive Mary. To me, this was indicative of the fact that the boundary line between Donna and Mary had become paper thin.

"I'm ready, announced Mary, who shut her eyes as if she knew exactly what to do and where to do it without any prompting from me. This was just as well, because I had learned by now that every multiple developed his/her own unique and personal style to integrate the alteredself.

But before she departed, Mary opened her eyes to bid me adieu. "We haven't always gotten along, but I needed to make sure that you were really different from the othermen who have hurt Donna. By now I know that you are as safe a person as she'll ever meet. I have chosen to trust you."

Again, she closed her eyes. One final time they opened. She hesitated, then uttered three words that were uncharacteristic of the Mary with whom I had so often sparred: "And thank you."

Before I could respond, she reached for the lever of the recliner with her right hand and closed her eyes. Some ten minutes later, Donna emerged and shared the fantasy through which Mary affected her integration:

"I envisioned myself on a baseball field, and I stood in as the batter. The bases were empty. Don't ask me about the score or who the opponent might have been. None of that seemed important. I was completely absorbed by my own at-bat. It seemed as if the pitcher, who was definitely a man, was throwing a lot of pitches to me. But none of them was right for me to swing at. I waited patiently until I saw one coming right down the middle, and I tell you, Dr. Cortman, I just whacked it good!"

Donna's eyes shone brightly, and her voice was filled with excitement. "The ball sailed over the centerfielder's head and kept rolling away from him. I took off around the bases, running as fast as my legs would carry me. Past second and still going strong, I found myself heading for third. I don't remember a third-base coach--" hesitating, she looked up to the right as if peeking back into her fantasy for confirmation "--but somehow I knew to keep running and running. So, I rounded third and made my way for home. The last ninety feet--that is how long abaseball field is between the base paths, right?"

I nodded, secure in the fact that I knew baseball better than I knew psychology.

“Well, the last ninety feet home seemed to take forever, with me laboring and chugging slowly all the way, until at last, the ball and I arrived at almost the same, exact time! The catcher turned to tag me with the ball,and I slid underneath him in a great cloud of dust andchalk.”

She paused incredulously, contributing to a sense of drama that now accompanied her story. "But there was no call from the umpire, who stared at the catcher and me, both ofus frozen in our respective positions awaiting the call.

"Finally, the catcher broke the silence, asking, 'Well, is she out?' I paused only for a brief moment in responding, 'No,

I was safe!' At this point, the umpire shed the protective facemask and exclaimed, 'Yes, youwere, young lady!'

"And you know what, Dr. C?" asked Donna, exuberant. "That umpire was Mary! I got onto my feet to celebrate my homerun with her, but she was gone. I didn't need long to realize that she wasn't really missing. She had become me, and I, her. There is no more Mary, Dr. Cortman, but I no longer feel a need to have her protection. I have to admit, instead of feeling sad, I feel elated. Maybe I can. Well, let me change that... I *know* I can fight my own battles now.

"That's terrific, Donna! My excitement spilled over like boiling water from a pot. And that's how it's supposed to work.

Donna had, after a year and a half of weekly therapy, successfully integrated her first alter personality. The painful remembering and telling of the stories were at last bearing fruit! Treatment was working.

I had been getting somewhere with Shirley, but until Mary and Donna were united on that afternoon, I wasn't entirely certain that Donna would be made whole. But now, as far as I was concerned, nothing could stop us--not a lack of courage, time, or commitment on Donna's part; not a lack of knowledge or faith on mine, either. And certainly not Lucinda. She still had to be dealt with, but this time we would focus on helping her, not grappling with her. At least that's what I figured at the time.

Before long, several of Donna's alters finished their healing work and integrated with her: Amy, the alter in charge of Donna's sexuality; Sally, the flirtatious teen; and Stephanie, the wise old woman. All joined forces with Donna within weeks of Mary's pilgrim voyage.

The two remaining major players, Dianna, thespiritual

fortress, and Lucinda, the cult princess, had yet to fulfill their integrative missions.

I have known few alters as consistently positive, encouraging, and helpful as Dianna. In fact, I had good reason to daydream about integrating the other alters and leaving Dianna as the sole remaining person. After all, she was kind, patient, and always spoke as if she had a direct word of hope from the Big Man upstairs.

But integration does not allow for killing off the undesirable alters in favor of keeping the pleasant and helpful ones. The goal was ending up with one normal, healthy person who could survive challenges without switching to an internal helper and losing the time. The key, it seemed, was to be comfortable enough to feel all of one's emotions and deal with them appropriately, rather than farm them out. When Dianna integrated, she would provide hope and spirituality for Donna, and that would be as it should be.

Dianna announced her desire to integrate with Donna at the end of a Friday afternoon session, virtually assuring herself of one more weekend as a separate personality. She promised to tell me the story of her creation in Donna's mind during our next session. Without sharing her tale, she said, there could be no final healing.

And so, Donna appeared the following Tuesday, in the alter of Dianna, eager to begin. Never before had Donna arrived at any session as Dianna. I noticed another deviation from the norm: Donna was not dressed in an elegant, businesslike manner. Instead, she wore the blue jeans and casual blouse that had surprised me during her first hospitalization. I had no idea why she presented in jeans, although I told myself that her clothing reflected increasing comfort with me and all aspects of herself.

Dianna was all business. She immediately launched into her story. "I was seven years old. That is, *we* were seven, but you know, we are not one. I'll keep it in the third person just to make it easier. It was the day of Donna's first communion--a big event in the Catholic church--and only four girls were being honored. She had a beautiful white dress purchased especially for the occasion. She was so proud about publicly displaying her dedication to Jesus Christ. It was a formal event and attended by virtually the entire church congregation. Flowers were everywhere-- carnations, roses, lilies.

"I don't remember every detail, but that's because I wasn't created until later in the day. I'll explain that eventually. You were told about Father Delvecchio?"

"Yes."

"Well, he and a few of the faithful followers of the dark side, including her father, met in the church cathedral later the night of the first communion. It wasn't a black mass or a formal ceremony of any sort. The purpose was to dispel that which had been celebrated earlier in the day--Donna's soul being promised to the Lord Jesus and her life dedicated to God--and to prevent her from reveling in personal glory."

"They wasted little time in sending her a clear message. Her devotion to God would not be tolerated. It was strange for Donna, since virtually all the people in attendance that evening had also been present at the morning ceremony. The same people who provided her with the accolades and the dress were back to convince her that everything that she had experienced that morning was a lie, a cruel joke or, worse yet, a mockery."

"Again wearing her dress, shoes, and frilly socks and

carrying her white Bible, she was paraded down the center aisle to the platform area where the priest stands to lead the service."

I nodded my understanding and asked her to continue. "Father Delvecchio, alone on the platform, extended an invitation to anyone desirous of joining Donna in her celebration. Immediately all the attendees descended upon her to share in her moment, or so she thought.

Suddenly the smiling faces were transformed into angry scowls and menacing stares. She was caught completely off-guard when the first hand grabbed at her dress. Delvecchio ripped the Bible from her hand and promptly--uh--well, I'd prefer not to say what he did to it. It makes me feel so ashamed." Her watery eyes confessed to the depth of that shame.

"It's okay, Dianna, the shame is understandable, but it doesn't belong to you. You are not responsible for the choices the cult people made." I reached across the desk to hand the box of tissues to her.

Dianna blew her nose, then continued. "Okay. Well, he urinated on her Bible. Then he began to curse the same Jesus he seemed to extol that morning. He mocked not only God and Jesus, but he ridiculed Donna, too. The priest spat in her face and told her that Christians were worthless and weak. Meanwhile, the others tore her new dress into rags, leaving her in her white underpants."

"Instead of switching into an alter, Donna fought the adults in an all-out attempt to salvage the dress that she loved. Her defiance enraged her father. He yanked her by her ponytail, snapping her head back. 'Where is your Jesus now?'" he taunted.

"Donna clutched a little gold cross that her mother had given her to wear for the occasion. That was all her father needed to see. He ripped the necklace from her neck, grabbed her again by the hair, and bent her over. He awkwardly tried to pull off her underpants, and the longer it took, the angrier he became with her. Finally, he pulled them down around her ankles and pierced her anus with the cross. 'Here's where your Jesus belongs!' He laughed. 'He's always been a pain in the ass anyway.'"

"Donna resisted her father's attack and made a stand for her Jesus. She also remained as Donna. I really don't know why. But maybe it was her way of making sure that she didn't give in to the group."

"In taking a stand, she enraged her father further. Even back then, Donna's religion was important to her. Her faith in God was paramount, possibly because she was told that God loved her. And the Sunday school teachers at Our Lady of Lourdes referred to God as her Heavenly Father. *Any* father who loved Donna was worthy of her devotion, even if He was in heaven. She would never admit to her father that she loved God, because she didn't want to hurt her father's feelings!"

"As far as Jesus went, Donna really didn't understand his sacrifice or that he was one with God. What kid does? But what did register with her was that he loved her enough to die for her. She felt sad that he suffered and died--she hated looking at him hanging upon the crucifix--but she always loved hearing how much he loved her. She memorized songs like 'Jesus Loves the Little Children' and 'Jesus Loves Me, This I Know.' She even derived a little pleasure from watching her father wince when she used to sing these songs in the car on the way home from church."

"Why was she allowed to attend church in the first place?" I asked. This had always puzzled me, and Dianna was the alter who held the answer.

"Because church attendance and being called practicing Christians presented an excellent front for all of the people of this secret society."

"Back to that evening," Dianna continued. "There were other attempts to disgrace her. She was hung upside-down with rope tied around her little ankles. She was spat on, slapped, and hailed as the Little Queen of the Jews. While upside down, she was forced to perform fellatio upon both Delvecchio and her father. Delvecchio suggested that if she were indeed Christlike, perhaps she could turn his semen into wine."

"As much as Donna attempted to oppose the group, she was too frightened to remain as herself once they hoisted her from the rafters. She switched several times during their punishment, most notably when she had such difficulty breathing with her father's penis in her mouth. Had she not switched then, she likely would have passed out. She--"

"Hold on a second," I interrupted. Before Dianna integrated, I wanted to learn from her whatever I could to help Donna. "Why didn't she just become Lucinda at that time and just go with it?"

"That's a good question. Lucinda had already been created by age seven, but she was not so pronounced in Donna's system as she grew to be. At that time, she was reserved for formal ceremonies and did not have the power to emerge unless summoned to perform the rituals that none of the other alters was capable or willing to perform."

"I see. And where were you at this time?"

"I was not yet a separate part of Donna. That happened a little later." She paused, thinking. "Let me take you right to that point now. The remainder of the time spent in church after she was returned to her feet was minimal--maybe another fifteen minutes. Their point had been made, and Donna was deeply wounded and confused. Why had they dressed her like a princess and made a fuss over her first communion with Jesus, if their plan was to blame and abuse her for it that very evening?"

Shirley's pseudopregnancy came to mind. She had been impregnated by the group's men, then taunted and ridiculed by the women. I understood a little better now how the cult's mind control takes hold during the formative years: Teach a child to distrust what she perceives to be true, thereby rendering her incapable of relying upon her own beliefs, thoughts, and feelings. The result is her mind is no longer her own.

Dianna continued. "For the ride home from the church that night, Donna wore a raggedy old dress that was too small and most unflattering. I gather that her mother selected it on purpose, knowing in advance the white dress would be destroyed."

"Her father launched into an abusive verbal tirade, but with Donna's now-advanced capacity to dissociate, she didn't absorb much of what he said."

"'But he was not done doling out the abuse--or what the group referred to as 'discipline.' He took her to the backyard and told her to sit quietly while he fetched a small wooden crate from his shed. The crate was no bigger than that of an average sized microwave and had a hinged lid. He commanded her to get into it. 'Girl, you are gonna learn to obey your father one way or another--the easyway or the hard way. If you want to keep pickin' the hardway, well, have at it. But don't think for even one fuckin' minute that you will ever defy me and get away with it.Do you understand? Do you?'"

"She just nodded obediently, partially relieved that the lecture was apparently over, and partially terrified at the prospect of climbing into that tiny crate. You see, Donna was now claustrophobic, probably as a result of having her father bury her in the dirt. I'm sure we've told you about that."

"Yes."

"Well, she could barely fit in the box without having to crunch up into a tiny ball, her knees below her chin."

Dianna lifted her feet from the carpet and folded them under her as she continued to relive the story. I didn't think she was aware of her change of position.

"Her father closed the lid and locked it, sealing her fate for the evening. He spoke one more time before retiring to the house. 'Don't even think about trying to escape from there, girl, or you'll wish you had never been born. If you have any fuckin' brains at all, you'll learn something tonight. I'll see you in the mornin'. And there better be no cryin' out here. You understand?'

'Yes, Daddy' was all he needed to hear to signal his return inside. She briefly wondered if her mother might rescue her sometime soon, but reality quickly overruled that fantasy. Her mother chose to ignore whatever she might find disturbing. This was likely something that would fit that description."

"Donna attempted to position her legs in such a way that she might be capable of kicking the top of the box open. If that meant defying her father, so be it. Anything was better than spending the night inside the crate! But by moving her legs in such a manner, she succeeded only in worsening her contortion. Her knees were stuck inches from her nose, and she could not move."

"Donna panicked. Her heart raced, pounding like a bass drum in her little chest. Her head spun in circles, her stomach swarmed with butterflies. At first, she thought she would die; soon after, she wished that she would because then she would never be disciplined by her father again. If she were dead, he'd never hurt her. He'd never yell at her. He'd never call her names. He'd never touch her private areas. He'd never put his penis inside her mouth. Best of all, if she could die, maybe she could meet the Jesus who supposedly loved her so much and have a heavenly Father who would be happy to have her for a daughter. Yes, that was the answer. She would die right here, right now."

"In the tiny wooden crate under that starry summer sky in her small Illinois town, she began to ask God to take her home. She closed her eyes and tried to bow her head just like she was taught to in Sunday school. Donna prayed for the darkness to set in, for her breathing to cease,for her Jesus to take her."

"It has been said that God works in mysterious ways, and we believe that. He heard Donna's prayer, and He answered her. He didn't take her home. It wasn't her time. But His Spirit met with Donna right then and formed a part of her that would always commune with Him. That, Dr. C.,is I, Dianna. I am borne out of God's own Spirit, designed to provide a limitless source of hope and a promise of restoration and wholeness."

"I was called to accompany Donna through the worst of

times, to comfort her in loneliness, to assist her in moments of desperation. Were it not for God's presence made manifest in me, Donna would have taken her life by now. On that evening, I took over for Donna and removed her fear and calmed her spirit."

"And God provided a small token of His great love for her. Through a crack in the box, a small lightning bug crawled into our space. We watched as he walked about the crate--an uninvited but not unwelcome visitor. He settled upon our nose and lit up, causing our nose to glow like our favorite Christmas cartoon of Rudolph, the Red Nosed Reindeer. We laughed and laughed and played with the firefly for what seemed like hours. We imagined the bug lighting up our box and turning it into a playhouse. We saw images of beautiful things--flowers, birds, dogs, and even Jesus--all through the illuminating presence of our new friend."

"Donna experienced a joy through her capturing God's loving Spirit and her heightened capacity to imagine and create beauty. And she did so from even the least significant stimulus, a tiny firefly sent to her from the Almighty. She fell asleep in that box, surviving the night in extraordinary style. And she never feared enclosed spaces again, for I was with her and would not leave her. She would never be alone again!"

I realized I was not breathing, so stunned was I by the beauty of Dianna's tale. We sat immobilized, just staring at each other. I didn't know if I had ever heard anything so beautiful as the story of the firefly.

"And now," Dianna said, "Donna is ready at last to rely upon me no more as her guardian spirit. She must now incorporate me as one with her. She must be courageous, so as not to disappear into the darkness and hide from her fear. She must embrace her past and grieve the horrible injustices of her childhood. I will always be with her, even as God's Spirit will never leave her nor forsake her. But she was intended by Him to be one and be one she must. It is my time now to go. God be with you, Dr. C. And thank you!"

In the blink of an eye Dianna was no more. Sure, I understood that she was always there, just one with Donna. But I've never stopped missing her.

Chapter 23

Snake Boys and Superheroes

My clinical supervisor, Dr. Robert Nay, had taught me that the key to effective treatment is an accurate assessment. That is, until you know what the problem is, you can't fix it. Unfortunately, the clinician's accuracy and completeness are dependent upon how fully and honestly the client unveils him/herself in therapy.

Multiple Personality Disorder patients commonly participate in treatment for six or more years--not necessarily continuous--before they are accurately diagnosed. During that time, they typically compile an impressive array of therapists, diagnoses, medications,and healthcare bills. Eventually many multiples connect with a therapist they choose to trust when they are prepared to begin their necessary journey. These explorations include uncharted territory in their mind and long repressed traumas from a miserable childhood.

From the beginning of our relationship Shirley chose to trust me and repeatedly led me places that never stopped amazing either one of us. Accounts of unparalleled torture and abuse regularly invaded my office, twisting Shirley's prematurely aging face into masks of pain.

There was the story of her father walking in on her mother and a lover. Shirley recounted in chilling detail the single bullet lodged in the head of the man with the plaid shirt and how he was locked in a basement freezer.(A subsequent memory revealed Shirley's stumbling upon the frozen corpse in an attempt to sneak ice cream from the freezer.)

There was also the unfathomable story of Shirley's return from a delightful walk with her German Shepherd.Her father, reportedly incensed by anything that brought his daughter pleasure (besides him), forced sexual relations between the dog and the eight-year-old. Shirley, unable to endure the shamer could not care for the animal and loaded its food with rat poison and put an end to him.

I wanted to disbelieve her. I really did. So many times, I wanted to classify her as a *histrionic personality*, prone to exaggeration, attention seeking, and superficial relations, or a psychopathic liar with unparalleled imagination. But then, she'd sit on the carpet, happily involved with a box of crayons and a coloring book-- obviously a child alter--until a loud sound from outside the office would prompt a look of pure terror. And then, unexpectedly, the rapid submergence of several crayons into her mouth to consume the evidence of enjoyment from her father.

And, then there was the reported memory of Shirley's father and his best friend's method of dealing with a young woman who wanted to leave the cult after witnessing some gruesome activities. The men took her and Shirley for a ride that culminated in a brutally fatal rape with a broom handle. Shirley was forced to watch, to reinforce the lesson of faithfulness and devotion to the group.

The accounts seemed to spring from a bottomless reservoir of horror that eclipsed the imaginings of Alfred Hitchcock or Stephen King. There was the time a man was overheard indicating his desire to be an organ donor and was tricked into attending a "party" where he was mocked, butchered, and disemboweled to "grant him his wish."

And let me not forget the remarkable series of sessions when Shirley reportedly remembered the process of her "rebirthing," a takeoff on the "born-again" concept that Jesus discusses in John 3:3-7, and dedication to Satan. She told of how a goat was sacrificed and disemboweled, then how she was forced inside the carcass, which was sewn shut. Shirley always needed to share her recollection in vivid detail; this time, however, she requested that the office lights remain off as she reenacted her birthing sequence on the recliner.

As we continued to work on the integration of her memories, an episode as bizarre as her false pregnancy played out in my Sarasota office. She was, per usual, casually dressed for her regularly scheduled Tuesday morning session--a clean, pressed T-shirt and heavy blue jeans. A halter top and shorts would have been more suitable for Florida's heat and humidity, but the jeans and T-shirt hid her outlandish butterfly tattoos.

Despite her numerous alter personalities, Shirley was transparent and straightforward in regard to her mood. Today her eyes appeared dark with misery. "How ya doin'?" I began.

"We're disgusted!" She paused long enough to yank several tissues from the box on my desk. Her lips quivered. "Why does this shit keep happening to me?" she said, then burst into tears.

Eventually her crying subsided long enough to answer my obvious question: "What happened, Shirley?"
"Look at this!" She thrust her arms in front of me.

I stared at huge blotches of peeling skin on both forearms.

"My whole body is peeling away!"

I'm not sure what type of reaction she anticipated, but I must have worn the look of a confused man. "What do you mean?"

The question didn't seem stupid as it was leaving my lips, but Shirley was incensed at my lack of understanding. "Can't you see? Look! Look!"

She frantically rolled up the sleeves of her T-shirt, exposing more and more blotches and peeling skin, all the way to her shoulder. She leapt to her feet and pulled up the legs of her jeans--still more splotching and peeling. I had never seen anything like it, and there was more. She pulled the shirt out from where it was tucked in her waistband and exposed yet more discoloration. "It's like this all over my fucking body! And I haven't even been in the sun at all! This will go on until my entire body peels from the tip of my fingers to the bottom of myfeet!"

Surely this was a dermatological condition. "What is it, Shirley? Has your doctor checked it out for you?" My role, I figured, would be to help her cope with whateverit was that was upsetting her.

"No, I haven't seen a doctor," she answered sternly. "And I don't need to. I went to that neurologist you sent me to, and he said it was all 'stress.' And remember when I looked pregnant?" (As if I could forget.) "Well, that was in my head, too. This is the same thing. I knowit.
Something about my childhood, that's all I know."

I wanted to ask how she knew that but decided itwas pointless. Sometimes patients--especially multiples--have an awareness of something that escapes their capacity to understand its origins. I have learned to trust that awareness. Call it intuition, unconscious thought, or whatever you will.

To my knowledge, that awareness has never let me down.

"Is it painful?" I asked. She shook her head. "Dangerous?" Negative.

"So, what do we need to do?" Again, I thought it was a fair question. She didn't.

"Why are you taking this so lightly, Chris? Do you think this is some kind of joke?"

This was not a time to become defensive, not if my goal was to help her through her suffering. Instead, I attempted to gain a better understanding of what I was doing (or not doing) to upset her. "Is there something that I'm doing to convey to you that I'm not caring about this, or that I think it's funny?"

"Yeah, you're not reacting. You don't seem overly concerned or scared--like it's no big deal. This is a big deal to *me.*" More tears. More tissues.

I attempted to validate her pain and her perceptions without suggesting that I didn't care. "I suppose you're right, Shirley. I can see how painful this is to you, and I'm not quite sure why. Maybe it seems like I'm underreacting because I don't yet understand why this is so upsetting to you. You have lived probably the worst childhood I have ever been exposed to and dealt with so many unimaginable horrors, that--I don't know--your skin peeling off doesn't seem to measure up to the degree of pain that you've experienced. I mean, my skin has peeled numerous times from sunburn, but I've never been locked in a cage or raped by a dog. I guess I just don't understand why it's so upsetting. Do you?"

Shirley quietly shook her head, then softly offered a thought. "Maybe it's not the skin peeling. Maybe it's something else."

"Like what?"

"I don't know. It's just that I can't stop it. I feel so helpless." She shook her head in frustration and grabbed another tissue.

"If the condition is so very upsetting to you, then undoubtedly it represents something else that you need to know about that contains some degree of pain or trauma. Everything you suffered seems to manifest itself in some here-and-now symptoms. Does that seem correct to you?"

She nodded her head twice. The excess energy must have been drained from her body, because she sat motionless.

I did have a direction--the same treatment plan that had repeatedly proven successful with Shirley to this point. I wanted her to "take me to the pain, either by speaking to the Teller or by inducing a hypnotic trance. Then I would accompany Shirley--or more accurately, one of her alters--on a journey to some unresolved, emotionally charged incident.

Disappointed in our attempt to locate the Teller, we utilized a brief hypnotic induction, and within minutes, Shirley signaled me (by raising her right index finger) that she was prepared to go to the next level of responding to questions.

"Okay, Shirley. Thanks for your signal. I'd like to ask you now to place me in touch with any part of you that understands what is happening with your peeling skin. When you are in touch with that part, please give me the same signal with your finger."

I waited with increasing impatience as more than a minute of silence and immobility cued me that the hypnosis attempt had been a failure. (My frustration suggested that I might have been taking the failure a bit too personally.) Just as I was about to bring her back to the here and now, her index finger hesitantly rose. She had located something!

"If you have in fact found someone who is prepared to speak to me regarding your skin, you may open your eyes and join me in the room. If not--"

Shirley's eyes opened rapidly. She turned her head and looked about the room as if visiting for the first time. She reached her right arm for the lever that releases the footrest on the recliner and brought the chair to a forty-five-degree angle. "Cool," was the only word she utteredas the chair responded. Her monosyllabic expression was my first clue as to what type of alter I might be dealing with. Then came the second.

"Ya wanted to talk to me," she said with a shrug."So, talk."

"Yeah, thanks for coming. I appreciate your being here. Do you mind if I ask for your name?"

'Why do ya want to know my name? How is that important?" Her face evolved from a cool nonchalance toa distressed annoyance, with a mere wrinkle of the brow.

"Well, I suppose it's not vital. I just like toknow who I am speaking to. But we can skip it."

"John."

By not engaging in a power struggle, I got the requested information. (Parents, take note.)

"Oh, hey, John. What's up?" I assumed I was addressing a young male and immediately I attempted to speak his language.

"Nothing, man. Ya want to talk to me, right?" "Yeah, that'd be great."

"So, talk."

Shirley's voice was deeper than average for awoman. But if I weren't staring straight into her face, I would swear that I was speaking to an adolescent boy. "Let me get right to the point. Do you know something about Shirley's skin peeling off?"

"Yeah." He answered with more than a hint of defensiveness in his tone.

Must be a teenager, I surmised.

"Okay. How about if I ask you to tell me everything you know about her skin condition." I thought I was clever, avoiding the yes-or-no answers.

"Like what?"

"Like everything that might help me to understand why her skin is falling off in huge patches." I remained calm despite wishing that I could ground him to his room for a week without MTV.

"Well, I'm getting ready to leave, and, uh, like I wanted everyone to know."

"Know what, John?"

"I dunno. About the snakes, I guess."

"What about the snakes?"

"They, uh, they used to lock us in a room sometimes, ya know, with a lot of snakes. A hell of a lot of snakes."

"Uh-huh."

"And, like, no one wanted to be with them. Ya probably know how scared girls are of snakes."

"Sure."

"Well, *I'm* not. So, I would come out and be withthem. I mean, shit, there must have been like, fiftyfuck--I'm sorry. I shouldn't swear."

"It's okay. Go ahead."

"Anyway, there were tons of 'em, especially black snakes. They're not poisonous, ya know. They don't like to use poisonous snakes, 'cause all they really want to do is scare ya, not kill ya or anything. So, it's mostly black snakes that they use. And I'd be in there for like hoursat a time, ya know, cause they'd be punishing her for somethin', and we'd get put in the room with thesnakes. Oh, and she'd be real scared, so her asshole father would think it was such a great punishment. But I didn't care, I kinda liked the snakes. Ya know what was really cool?"

"Hm?"

"Well, like the snakes would watch me, and shit. I mean, they'd be totally aware of everything that I did and if I moved a lot of times, they would move, too. But they didn't, ya know, bother me or anything. But as long as I was in the room, they wouldn't sleep. Always watching me. It was pretty cool."

"So, you were the snake boy, John. Huh?" "Yeah."

"And so, tell me about her skin now."

"Oh, yeah, well, it's pretty simple. Snakes can shed their skin, ya know? Well, I just wanted everyone to know that I could, too. Like I said before, everybody is telling what happened to them, and I wanted to tell my story."

"So, you figured that you needed to do something that would get her attention. And what better way to get noticed if you're a snake boy, than to have someone shed their skin. Is that right?"

"Yeah, ya got it, Doc"

"Well, that makes sense. You don't eat mice, do you?" He thought that was funny. It was the first time that I'd seen her/him smile since the beginning of the session. It was an excellent point to put some closure to the session and bid farewell to John, the Snake Boy.

But it wasn't quite the last time that I heard from him. In the very next session, Shirley handed me the following letter:

"Hey, Dr. Kortmen! Thanks for talking to me the other day. I liked it. I think your a pretty cool guy and I know your helpin all of us a lot. She's not gonna pele anymore skin. Don't worry about that. And don't think that I'll eat any mice cause that will never happen. But I do like to scare her cat. I'm going away now. Thanks agen for all your help.

Your friend,

John (The Snake Boy)"

Attempting to suppress my tears after reading the note, I chided myself for crying over losing someone who wasn't really a person in the first place. But I knew I was wrong. Any sentiment I felt was certainly appropriate.

There was no boy, true, but instead a terrified little girl, brilliant enough to escape her terror by forging a different identity that could rise to the occasion with skills specific to any situation.

I recalled watching cartoons as a child, where superheroes were a predominant theme. Whenever evil forces created a crisis, the superhero with the appropriate skills would be called upon to save the day. Sometimes it was the muscular guy to stop a speeding asteroid, or the elastic guy when they needed to catch a criminal with his extended arms.

Hadn't Shirley done the very same thing? She produced

an alter specific to any given situation, then added a wonderful twist to ensure her survival: She'd learnedto think that she was enjoying the experience! Not only aren't we afraid of snakes, we like the slithery creatures! (And we become self-taught experts on them.)

Okay, maybe John was no superhero. But then again, how did he make her skin peel off like that?

Chapter 24

The Bus Boys

Donna was developing a sense of self and taking tentative steps toward establishing boundaries and responding to her own her needs. For example, she calledto ask if she had to see her parents during her annual visit home. She would be visiting "old college friends" but "I don't need to face my father right now. I may choose never to see that man again." Frightened, perhaps, by too much assertiveness, she hedged a bit and asked, "Is that okay to do?"

I assured her that the decision was not only okay, it seemed necessary. We agreed that she would drop them a note to let them know that she'd be coming home but wasn't ready to get together.

Shirley was also making outstanding progress, doing well with her kid, setting much better boundaries with her ex-husband's abuse, working successfully at her job, and continuing to uncover trauma. She had already integrated quite a few of her alters, and she and I were both hopeful that we could be done processing her childhood in the not-too-distant future.

My friend Dr. Richard Levine needed my attention, also. As I offered a sympathetic ear during his divorce negotiations, our relationship had moved from his mentoring me to our being on a more equalfooting.

I was just coming home from a particularly painful Thursday night at the softball field--one for three, including flying out to end the game--when he called.

"Catch you at a bad time?" he asked.

"Well, actually, yes. Cindy's spent a couple of days here, and she's just leaving."

"Oh, sorry. I'll let you go. Just call me back when you're-- Hey, wait, who's Cindy? That's not Ms. Ohio's name."

"Cindy Crawford. I told you she's been stalking me, no? Oh, hold on a second." I called over my shoulder, "No, you can't stay any longer, Cindy. C'mon, good-night already. I'll call **you** next time. I opened and closed the front door, then returned to the phone. "Okay, sorry, Richard."

"You know you're a delusional narcissistic asshole, Cortman, don't you?"

"Flattery is useless. So, what's up with you?"

For almost an hour he filled me in on the bitter divorce negotiations, then said, "It's like she castrated me. I feel like that John Wayne Bobbitt guy."

"Hey, don't go blaming your lack of masculinity on your wife. You've had that problem since birth." I went for the cheap emasculation shot, a favorite among guys, in an effort to lighten the mood. I could tell it was somewhat successful by his sarcastic response.

"I'm so glad I can call you--long distance, noless-- for support. I can see why you have such a busy practice." I

I laughed, much to his delight. "Don't worry, buddy, I may not even bill you for my services."

Once the laughter subsided, I expressed my heartfelt sentiments and support. "Listen, I'm truly flattered that you would call me to talk. It means a lot to me. I hear how much pain you're in. It's gotta be awful to feel so helpless in court, to be bombarded by false accusations and have the judge buying them. It sounds terrible, especially when it translates into being barred from seeing your little ones. I feel for ya, man. I wish there was something I could do to help."

"Thanks, Chris. I appreciate your understanding. And that is all you need to do tohelp."

It was getting too mushy. Like most guys, I can't handle it with another guy for too long. I attempted to set him up for another ribbing, but he spoke next.

"I didn't mean to dominate the conversation with my tales of woe. How's the Ohio hairdresser?"

Laura had issued me an ultimatum during her last visit, and I could hardly blame her, after more than two years of long-distance dating. *Defecate or dethrone thyself* was the message when translated in the polite vernacular.

If I wasn't about to marry her, it was time to set her free. It was the biggest decision I'd ever make, save the choice of what to believe about God. After all, marriage was the Super Bowl of relationship issues. I didn't feel like sharing the dilemma with Richard, though. It was a decision I'd have to make myself, in my own way.

"Laura's good, thanks. She was just here a couple of weeks ago. I took her to a Bucs game. I tried to explain football to her, and she attempted to uncover themysteries of male-pattern baldness, using the man sitting in front of us as a diagram. It was quite educational,actually."
"And the game?"

"Well, naturally the Bucs got shellacked. But we had fun."

"Good. What's going on with Shirley?" "You wouldn't believe it if I told you."

"Why not? I'm sure even you have a success in

treatment once in a while."

"Well, that wasn't the unbelievable part," I said, chuckling. "It's what happened this week. Shirley told me that one of the evil alters--she's not sure which one--had been secretly bringing satanic books into the house and engaging in rituals in the backyard at night. She says she finds remnants around the house and in the yard. Anyway, she claims that she was hearing demonic growls coming from her refrigerator."

"I have that, too," Richard interjected. "But that's just my teenage son at feeding time."

"But get this: Lately she's been seeing diabolic, piercing eyes at night, just staring at her. And then she wakes up feeling as if she just had sex. She believes that this spirit was raping her! So, the following night, when the eyes appeared, she decided to stay awake so she wouldn't get raped. And this thing said to her, 'It doesn't matter if you're awake or not.' And it attacks her, holds her down, and penetrates her violently!"

Richard snorted in disbelief. "C'mon, man. I mean if this is true, don't you think I would've ordered a female spirit to come and visit me at night? It would have to be an improvement on the demon I married."

I ignored the joke to make my point. "But she came into the office with great big bruises in the folds of both arms and claims to have even worse bruises on the insides of both legs! The next session she wore shorts and showed me what she could of these bruises without dropping her pants. They were the nastiest bruises I've ever seen!

"'I'm sorry, pal, but I can't buy a demon rape. She's multiple. She loses time, right? So why can't we conclude that she was raped by someone else--most likely a human male-- and the bruises are the result. Or maybe it was her ex-husband.

Hey, any explanation is more likely than some spirit has moved in, raiding her refrigerator, and bangin' her at night. Shit!"

"I know exactly what you're saying. I could come up with any number of explanations for the bruises, believe me." Shirley had already exhibited an uncanny ability to create *somatic,* or bodily, phenomena to express her inner conflicts. "But I can't seem to get past one important factor--her credibility. After more than two years of in-depth therapy, everything this lady shares seems toturn out to be real."

I paused to consider, then plunged ahead. "I did a little research on the topic and found that there are reportedly two types of demons that have been known to rape women and men. Their names are Incubus, which visits women, and Succubus, which preys upon men. I call them the Bus Boys. Anyway, there are reports of sexual visitations with humans for thousands of years!"

"Lose that subscription to the *National Enquirer,* man. Sorry, I guess I'm too skeptical, or a tad on the scientific side, to believe this really happened to her. Maybe I don't want to. It challenges all that I think I know about the world. I can't make this information make sense with my world view. Know what I mean?"

"Tell me about it! That's exactly what I've been wrestling with since meeting Shirley. I used to think I was a regular guy with a good practice. Now I've got Satan worshippers in high places screwing with children's minds and bodies; I've got multiple personality patients coming out of the woodwork; I've got a government guy telling me that I'm a threat to the cult powers because I know too much; and I got reports of demons by a handful of people. I don't know what to think anymore. Maybe I need a vacation."

It felt good to vent, in spite of Richard's understandable skepticism. I didn't need him to believe in the existence of demons any more than he needed me to fix his problems with his ex-wife. We both just needed a little validation from someone we trusted.

My right hand was moist with sweat from the phone, my ear was flattened beyond recognition, and both Richard and I sounded exhausted. It was time to end the conversation and call it a night.

"Hey, thanks for being there. It was good talking to you." He was sincere this time. "And don't forget, okay?"

"Forget what? I've already forgotten."

"Tell Shirley to summon me up some Bus Girls. Or better yet, give Cindy Crawford my address. I'm a little more tolerant of being stalked than you are."

"Yeah, yeah. Good-night, Richard. Stay in touch, okay? I care."

"Me, too. See ya."

*   *   *

I had a history of making life-changing decisions ina matter of minutes: I had selected my college and graduate schools sight unseen, based on catalogues and acceptance letters; I bought a beachfront townhouse condo after a brief walk-through and despite a nasty headache. Not one to "sweat the small stuff," I had the good fortune of sidestepping worry, even in regard to life's greatest challenges and so far had no regrets.

But what to do about Laura? I wondered as I carried my blue canvas chair and a bottle of water onto the sand, to think under the stars. The warm night, unusual for early January, required only my denim jacket, jeans, and mygood- luck New York Giant's hat. Barefoot, I sifted through the cool, deep sand and set up the chair some fifteen feet from the water's edge. I hoped that the tide wouldn't change, now that I was parked. *Where do I even begin in making such a decision?* I stared at the heavens. I was the only unmarried member of the family. *How had my siblings done it?*

I knew I was good for her. Laura, I figured, was subconsciously looking for everything she needed in a father figure but had never pursued to thispoint: stability, softness, consistency. I flattered myself with that one.

Next, I confronted my own idiosyncratic characteristics--what attracted me to Laura and not to some other woman. *Here goes,* I thought as a group of sandpipers scurried along the shoreline like ladies hunting for sale items at Filene's Basement. *Okay, I like beautiful women. So, sue me. I mean, what man doesn't?* I thought defensively.

But beyond sexual attraction, why did I need a beautiful woman on my arm? Was I so insecure that I needed to marry an attractive woman to add value to my esteem?

That very hypothesis stabbed through layers of defense and pierced my fragile ego. *Ouch!* I rocked back and forth in my little beach chair in an effort to soothe my soul from its fresh wound. Yes. Guilty as charged! But so what? I was sure I loved Laura.

All right, what if she got older (I figured she might), wrinkled, or God forbid, wasn't the prettiest girl wherever she went?

I was better prepared for question. I would undoubtedly prefer my lady to remain beautiful, slim, and wrinkle free until middle-age struck her in her mid-eighties, but I would go on loving her even if that were not the case.

Relieved by my noble yet honest responses, I threwmy arms back behind my head and clasped my hands.

"Next," I challenged myself. "Why her?"

Well, she had come along at the right time. She is good hearted, honest, and loyal. I felt satisfied withthat answer. But why had I repeatedly chosen attractive women who were needy and plagued with problems, rather than the beautiful, high-functioning ones? Although I didn't know all the intrapsychic reasons, I guessed I had a need to be needed as a core personality trait. I needed to be the higher functioning person in the relationship--the stable one. That probably accounted for becoming a healthcare professional as well.

Was that an adequate foundation for a healthy marital union? I didn't know. I didn't know if it would have been better to marry someone less attractive, more together, or more Christian, for that matter. Dammit, I didn't even know if we could stand living in the same town, let alone share a name, a life, and a family. But I did know that I loved her.

I looked up at the stars, then out at the sea. The decision was made. Laura would be the one. I stood up, folded my chair, and headed inside. The time had come to create an unforgettable marriage proposal.

Chapter 25

Reaching The Child

The publisher of the *St. Petersburg Times,* I've been told, offered a free newspaper to patrons on days the sun doesn't shine. Few things in life are as reliable as sunny days in the Sunshine State.

Thus, when Donna appeared sporting a new pair of French sunglasses on a rain-soaked Tuesday, I had reason to be alerted. Silent, unsmiling, she trudged into myoffice and seemed oblivious to my greeting.

"So how are you doing, Donna?" No response.

This was hardly what I expected, given the success of the last several sessions. But then again, I wondered, was that the purpose of backing off--too much vulnerability too quickly? I waited for some sign of Donna's present condition in order to formulate a tentative plan ofaction.

Eventually she spoke. "This is our last session.We just came today to say good-bye."

"Who am I speaking to?"

"Why is that important? Can't you just accept what I'm saying without all the detective work?"

Her response was a clear attempt to steer me away from the real issue--whatever that was. "I guess I just don't understand. You seem to be making wonderful progress--making peace with your past, integrating many of your alters, and well on your way to becoming one person. And now you'd like to quit therapy. Maybe you can help mesolve this riddle."

"There's nothing to solve. We're just tired of it, that's all. Did you expect us to work with you forever? Surely you have other patients who need you."

We both knew she was avoiding something. My job was to help her figure out what and face it. "You know the idea of dropping out of treatment isn't new. Dianna called me to stop therapy when Lucinda was threatening everyone. I can't help but wonder what the threat is this time. Is it Lucinda again?"

"No, I'm not the threat, Christopher. You are the threat."

Now we're getting somewhere, I figured. Regardless of who walked into my office, Lucinda was here now.

"Oh, hey, Lucinda. I'm pleased to have you here. It's been weeks since we've spoken." I paused to afford her the opportunity to respond. When she sat motionless behind her protective eyewear, I continued. "How am I a threat to you, Lucinda?"

"Nasty is here. He's telling me that you're dangerous, that you want to get rid of me, kill me. He says I should never trust you, Christopher. He knows that you killed Mary, too."

This left me with two potential places to go with her: identification of Nasty or reclarification of the process of integration. I opted for the former. "Who is Nasty, Lucinda?"

"He's a guardian spirit of mine. He has been with me since the…" She backed off from continuing her sentence and shifted her weight on the recliner. I wished I could see her eyes.

"Is Nasty an alter, Lucinda?"

"No, I already told you he is a guardian spirit!" "So, he's not inside Donna like you are, or Dianna, or Mary?"

"No. He's on the outside. He doesn't like you." She

paused and looked to the right as if to listen to someone or something. "He wants us to leave now."

"Please don't, Lucinda. I'd really like to talk to you, if at all possible. I don't have any desire to hurt you, I promise." I was deliberately putting myself in a one-down position in an attempt to empower her. I considered the irony of my attempt to strengthen the alter who only weeks before had enough potency to intimidate Donna, my parents, and, yes, me.

But things were different now. Her power appeared to be waning in the wake of the most recent hospitalization. With my locating and identifying two of her greatest areas of vulnerability--confinement and an unrealized desire to be loved--Lucinda was obviously fearful of beingdestroyed. This was most definitely the impetus behind her unconvincing attempt to terminate therapy and the reason she hid behind the shades. Perhaps her fear also explained her decision to bring a companion with her to thesession.

But what to make of Nasty? If Lucinda claimed he was a guardian spirit, to me that translated into evil spirit. How good could a spirit named Nasty be?

Or maybe he wasn't a spirit at all. Maybe he was an imaginary friend created to provide support and companionship or perhaps to blame for things Lucinda had done. Then there was the possibility that he was an alter that had splintered off from Lucinda during some overwhelming experience. Obviously, I didn't have enough information yet to explain Nasty.

Lucinda responded well to my request that she remain with me. "What is it that you want from me, Christopher?" Her tone suggested earnestness, not the biting sarcasm that I had grown accustomed to hearing from her.

"I suppose I'd like to hear all about you, your beginning with Donna… and Nasty." I did my best to convey interest and concern as opposed to judgment or disdain.

Lucinda sat quietly for a moment, then tilted her head toward the right, in the same manner she had previously used when "listening to Nasty." Evidently having heard what she needed, she ripped the glasses from her face and shot me a glare designed to penetrate my defenses. She sprang to her feet and, pointing at me, declared, "You will never defeat us. We belong to the Prince of Darkness. Helays claim to our soul. It is to him that we have sworn our undying allegiance."

Oh, this again, I thought in disgust. A hint of annoyance no doubt colored my carefully worded response. "No one has claim to your soul. It's your decision where you place your trust. You can believe in yourself if you want, or you can believe in a god bent on evil and destruction. Or you can believe in a God who loves you more than you can even imagine."

I may have crossed over the line where psychologist becomes preacher, but my intention was to exploit theword *love,* which had so effectively broken Lucinda in the hospital session.

It was no less successful this time. She looked in my direction as if to respond with some defiant message or diabolical curse. But not a single word flowed from her lips. In fact, she underwent a total metamorphosis before my eyes. The evil gaze melted into a confused countenance; this in turn wilted into a weakened, pathetic expression with fallen eyes and sunken cheeks. Suddenly she turnedand collapsed onto the floor. Her head fell forward, just missing the bookcase that was jutted out from the wall.

I rushed over to find her crumpled on the carpet, her face buried in her hands. She sobbed the tears of a helpless child and was no more a danger to me than a wounded five-year-old. I placed my right hand gently upon her shoulder and knelt beside her as her sobs diminished to whimpers.

"It's okay," I reassured her. "You're gonna be all right."

I honestly believed that, even though I could not know for sure. I didn't even know exactly what had just happened. A low-blood-sugar reaction, a seizure, spiritual deliverance? Or was it a stress-induced psychological reaction as Donna reexperienced the pain of childhood rejection? I preferred to believe the latter, although I was open to any information that she might provide me with.

I didn't even know how to address her. Was this still Lucinda, or some unknown child alter? Was Donna back? I hoped it wasn't Nasty, now that I believed in the existence of demons.

"Are you all right?" I asked, poised to call 911 if necessary.

"Yes." The tears had slowed. "I think he's gone, Dr. Cortman." I helped her to a sitting position, from which she scanned the room for someone or something. "Yes," she concluded. "Nasty's gone."

I recognized Donna from her respectful manner, but I hadn't realized that she knew Nasty. I had many questions, but first I had to get her off the floor and back to the recliner. She refused my offer of assistance. She was steady and lucid in her conversation. I could relax. Donna would be fine.

"So, what do you remember about our session so far?" I asked, returning to my desk.

"Dr. C., Lucinda is so threatened by you now. She thinks

of you as an enemy who has the power to destroy her. Funny thing is, she seems to be smaller or--no, what Imean is she is less intimidating to the children inside than she once was. She doesn't scare me so much anymore, either. But because she's so afraid, she has been moreactive."

Pausing, she brushed her blond hair from her facewith her right hand and stared past me. Then she elected to share something else that was on her mind: "If I told you something illegal that Lucinda may have participated in, would you have to report me?"

I explained again the rules of confidentiality, which afforded Donna the privilege to share with me virtually anything short of murder, child/elder abuse, and suicide plans. I couldn't imagine what she was about to tell me.

She dug into her purse and pulled out her journal, opened to a particular page, and pushed it across the desk at me. I read a few paragraphs, all written in backward satanic code. I didn't think I could be surprised anymore by anything Donna could do. I was wrong. I read and then reread the journal, half hoping I had missed something. No such luck. Donna, or rather Lucinda, had snorted cocaine over the weekend with the cult member who would sponsor Lucinda when she returned to active participation in a local group.

Cocaine? Donna? The sweet and polite woman, with a straw up her nose and a line of powder on the table? I tried to hide my disappointment; after all, Lucinda, not Donna, was snorting the coke.

I never failed to be awestruck by the diversity possible in one person's behavior: soft-spoken CPA by day, coke-snorting Satan worshipper by night!

One more item of note in her journal: Lucinda had met

her contact at a tattoo parlor in Manatee County. There she danced with him in a drug-induced frenzy, all the while chanting, "Natas, Natas, Natas!"

Our time all but gone, I expressed appreciation to Donna for all she had shared with me this day and shared a word of encouragement that we were indeed getting closerto understanding and healing her past. I also reminded her that I was her teammate. I cared for her and wouldcontinue to help her in her quest to be whole. Finally, I assuredher that I would not be contacting the authorities about her cocaine use.

Where to go from here? I wondered after she had left. Would I need to monitor Lucinda's cocaine consumption, or would that take care of itself? Donna had told me several times that she had never experimented with drugs of any kind; was she hiding a pattern of recreational drug abuse?

I remembered her horror in finding herself smokinga cigarette with her little sister at the mall, contending that she had never smoked. I believed her then, and I believed her now. I would keep an eye out for subsequent drug use but not yet consider it an issue.

And what about Nasty? I would ask Donna/Lucinda about him in future sessions and, if need be, suggest she get spiritual help and guidance. As for Lucinda, I needed to show considerable interest in her, especially in the wake of her admission to feeling unloved by her father. Ineeded to win her over myself and perhaps provide her witha father figure who could offer unconditional support. If I could take the power that Lucinda was convinced that I held, then use it in promoting her rather than attempting to overpower her, she might become an asset in Donna's healing.

I still believed we were close to finishing with her past

and that an all-out effort to help Lucinda was the last great hurdle.

One thing was abundantly clear: Neither Donna nor I would stop until we had successfully cleared that hurdle.

In our next session, I assessed for cocaine use and believed Donna's denials.

I asked a couple of other questions pertaining to her estranged husband, Peter. Evidently reconciliation was impossible; she would be filing for divorce once she felt strong enough to do so. I felt some sorrow for her and Peter, as I'd always liked him. Even more powerfully, I experienced guilt and failure. *Wasn't that the reason they had come to me in the first place?* I tried to silence my inner critics with my version of the truth: *Donna was in no shape to do successful marital therapy.* Then I let go of the justifications, deciding it was okay to feel a little bad. *I don't have to be perfect.*

In keeping with my strategy, I brought up my desireto work directly with Lucinda, if Donna and Lucinda would accommodate my request. Donna had no problem with it, so I asked to speak directly to Lucinda. Donna closed her eyes, and within seconds, my wish was granted.

"Why do you ask for me, Christopher?" Her tone was not nearly as defensive or combative as I'd come to expect. "What could I possibly do for you?"

I liked her question and answered it directly. "I'm hoping that you would consider becoming Donna's ally."

"Donna wouldn't want me! She thinks I'm a wicked,evil person."

I was tempted to reply, "Well, I wonder why!" But I knew sarcasm would be counterproductive. Instead, I focused on Lucinda's assertion that "Donna wouldn't want me"--the fear of rejection again. Now that I was sensitive to her problem with it, I could hear it in virtually all of our communications. Exploiting that fear was no longer necessary; more helpful would be an attempt to heal it. I aimed to make her feel wanted.

"I'm not sure of that, Lucinda. Donna needs you very much. She has always feared you, but that does not mean that you aren't needed."

"Needed for what?" The tone grew harsher, but the question was fair.

"She needs you to help her heal. Don't you know that you have always had more power than any of Donna's alters because you contain the most pain? You have done so much for her, Lucinda. Without your help, she would've died or gone crazy in some of those ceremonies! You always call her weak, right?"

Lucinda nodded. "Well, you have been a big part of her strength. Now she needs you to share that pain with her and let her experience it. That way the two of you could be as one!"

"Yeah, we become her, and then I'm gone. Nasty was right--I shouldn't trust you. You really do want to kill me! I'm gonna go."

Before she could even close her eyes, I excitedly yelled, "No! Don't go anywhere. I don't want to talk to any of the others. I want to talk to you! I'm not going to kill you or anyone, no matter what Nasty or anyone else says. I didn't kill Mary. She is as alive as ever. But she is not a separate part of Donna anymore. And neither is Dianna. In fact, Donna is now a lot stronger because they and the others who have integrated are all a united front--a powerful team. But it's incomplete without your participation. Am I making myself clear,

Lucinda? Or did I lose you in my babbling?" I chose this verbiage to appear as unintimidating as possible.

"No, I understand what you're saying, and I was listening when you told Mary about the snowman. I get it. I'm not stupid. But I do have a problem with joining Donna's team."

"I'm listening."

"You see, in the cult I had a job. I knew what was expected of me, and I learned to do it toperfection.
Everyone was proud of me and the work that I did." She paused reflectively and stared at the carpet. "That was the only place where anyone ever approved of us."

The once-mighty Lucinda was now the hostess with the quivering lips and the moistening eyes, as she was bravely confronting the truth of her past: No one loved her or believed in her unless she was killing babies or dancing for perverted men.

I decided to say exactly that and risk inciting her with the inflammatory truth. To my surprise, she was not angered. Instead, she sustained a break in the waterlineand succumbed to tears--just a few drops at first, and then a waterfall. She went through a dozen tissues, many of them stained with mascara.

"Dr. Cortman?"

I took immediate notice of the change in the manner in which I was addressed. A gentle, if not fragile woman peeked up from the tissue. "I know I wasn't loved. I can't tell you how much that hurt. But worshipping the master is all I know. What would I do if I left the group? What good could I be to anyone?"

Lucinda's pain, the result of years of rejection and

abuse, had never been more evident to me. I wanted to grin from ear to ear, not because she was hurting or because I was gloating in victory. No, my desire to celebrate stemmed from the obvious conclusion that Donna/Lucinda was healing from what reportedly was one of the saddest, most horrific childhoods I had ever heard of.

But we were not yet there. Surfacing alongside her hurt was fear, which was equally powerful. She was confessing that she needed to change and wanted very much to do so. But the notion of switching teams and submitting to the unknown world of risk and potential failure was terrifying.

I understood her completely at that moment, for she was totally human--that is, emotionally naked and vulnerable. She stood in the humble position we all must face in our striving for healing and wholeness--powerlessness. She needed restoration from the power that only love can afford the soul.

Could she embrace that reality? I wondered. I would soon find out, for the first taste of that love had to be extended from the therapist before Lucinda could ever consider accepting it from Donna. Ultimately, she would need to experience love from the highest and most important source of all. She would need to feel the gentle cleansing of her spirit from the divine power of God.

I addressed her question of what good she couldbe with a simple but thoughtful response: "Well, I have an idea, Lucinda, and you can tell me what you think.

Supposing you were placed in charge of caring for and protecting the remaining children inside Donna? They have always been so afraid of you. Maybe now they would all look to you for safety and protection. I don't know, what doyou think?"

I had never seen Lucinda smile before. Of course, it was the same smile I had seen dozens of times before from Donna (after all, they were sharing the same face), but somehow it seemed brighter, fuller, more convincing. For the first time I saw a genuine flicker of hope in hereyes.

"I could do that!" she exclaimed excitedly. "I could care for those children! I would make sure that noone hurt them ever again. I would treat them like they were my own kids!"

Although this might seem that the fox was being appointed to guard the hen house, I was convinced of the sincerity of Lucinda's metamorphosis and expected the children would sense the same thing. First, though, I had to make certain that Donna was at ease with the idea.
Regardless of Donna's response, I knew we had made monumental progress with Lucinda today.

"Well, why don't we give that a shot, Lucinda, and see what happens?"

I caught a change in Lucinda's facial expression. She was not switching; she was merely evidencing a look of concern.

"What's on your mind?" I didn't yet understand the change.

"Oh, I don't know. Nothing."

"C'mon, there's *something*. You can share it with me. You know by now that I won't judge you."

"It's just, it's--well, it's Nasty. He's been with me my whole life. I don't really like what he says to me--he's the one who told me to visit your house with the rat--but I guess I'm not sure what to do with him now. He'll need to leave me, and hers not going to like it. I don't knowwhat he'll do."

"Is he talking to you now?" I asked.

"Oh no! He won't come here again after last time. You aren't his favorite person. He doesn't like that you believe in God and know the Bible. He wants me to stayaway from you because he says that you can't be trusted."

"Do you believe that?"

"No. I know you're trying to help us. I'm justa little scared, that's all."

I was impressed by her childlike choice of words and tender facial expression. I couldn't help but inquire about this. "Lucinda, do you mind if I ask you a personal question?"

"No, what?"

"How old are you, really?"

"Why?"

"I don't know. I'm just wondering, that's all."

"I'm not supposed to tell you."

"Why not?"

"Because maybe you wouldn't be very afraid of me if you knew that I was only eleven."

I could sense her embarrassment and immediately recollected the false bravado that underscored all her defiance with me. I suppose she was saying that itwas all an act — I'm really just a scared little kid with an evil guardian spirit who was trying to run you off.

I expressed my gratitude to Lucinda for revealing so much to me in such short order and praised her for all the courage that she had to muster to be so open with me.

Predictably, she ate up the compliments like a starving child would a piece of chocolate. Finally, I reassured her that Donna and I would address the Nasty issue, so all she needed to do was prepare herself to be without him. If she really wanted him to be gone, God would make him leave her alone. At last, I said good-bye for now to my new friend and asked her to come back to see me again soon, because I wanted to make sure that it was Donna who left my office.

Secretly I wished that Lucinda was a separate person, an eleven-year-old whom I could befriend and maybe even spoil a little bit. I felt sorry for that little girl. I hoped she would learn that not all men are hurtful and exploitative. Someday soon that little girl would be one with Donna.

Chapter 26

More Surprises

"What happened to your eye, Shirley?" I asked, making certain I sounded more caring than nosy or disgusted.

"I don't know," she mumbled.

After more than two years of work together, I knew to believe Shirley if she claimed not to know what produced the shiner. I would do well to tread lightly; the losttime and black eye undoubtedly created a profound shame within my patient. One thought lingered painfully, causing me to wince: Shirley was not fully integrated yet. If shewere, she would not suffer amnesiac periods. She was still dissociating. The thought reverberated in my mind.

What do we need to recover the account of the bruised face? I wondered.

"I don't know what happened to my eye," she began. Tears fell from behind her sunglasses. "I'm so depressed, I just want to die!" She angrily ripped at the tissue box twice, then dabbed carefully at the tears on her left eye.

I felt terribly sorry for her. "What do we need to do, Shirley?" I hoped she could point me in the right direction.

All she could muster, however, was a defeated shrug. "I don't know."

If depression could be quantified as units of liquid, gallons of it were spilling onto the floor. I needed to take some action before she drowned in her hopelessness.

"Is there someone I can talk to who can help us

understand what we need to know?" More shrugging.

"Okay. Let me ask you to close your eyes and concentrate. Focus on something peaceful inside and relax. You know the routine."

She responded in short order. No matter how many times I had seen her do this, I still marveled at the abruptness of her change in countenance and attitude.

"My name is Amber. You don't know me. Neither does Shirley. I am not supposed to be here. I was told never to talk to you. I am here because you need to know more ifyou are going to help her. Chris, she is not out of the cult."

Butterflies gathered by the thousands in the pit ofmy stomach. "What do you mean, Amber?"

"Shirley is still a member of the cult in Sarasotaand Bradenton. She doesn't know that she still participates, and she does so unwillingly. Her parents are still in, andthey would never let her out alive--it would be humiliating to her father. She really does have a new faith in God, Chris. She credits you for helping her with that. But the cult still controls her with certain codes and signals, and she responds to their every command."

Amber stated all of this in the most matter-of-fact style, as if recalling what she had ordered for lunch the previous day. "What do you mean 'codes' or 'signals'?"

"They call her and hang up. She is alerted to pickup the phone when they call back ten seconds later. By that time, she is already in a trance and can be told where and when to report for duty."

I struggled to ignore any emotional reactions that might be brewing inside of me. "Please continue, Amber. I'd like to know whatever information you're willing to share."

"She's been told not to talk to you about group matters. They know she comes to you--they know everything she does--but they don't know how much she tells you about them or about her past. They think she is working on staying sober. They don't think treatment has gotten into her past issues or that we have integrated so many alter personalities."

I didn't understand. "Why wouldn't they know that, too, if they ask her while in a trance?"

"Because I'm in charge of informing them about Shirley's sessions with you. They don't know about me; they didn't create me. They've created several others who report to them or respond to them at their meetings and ceremonies. But when they ask to speak to an alter named Cynthia, they end up talking to me. I won't tell them what's really happening in here, because they wouldn't allow her to continue seeing you. They might even kill her. They don't like that she sees you. You are not their favorite psychologist, you know."

"So, I hear," I muttered under my breath.

She ignored my response. "Although they can control many of her behaviors, Shirley is different since being with you. They sense that. Because she is still rebellious, they demoted her to cleaning up after the ceremonies. You know, wiping up the blood and tossing the remaining body parts of the people and animals into the fire. There must be no trace of anything that might make people suspicious."

"So, what about the eye?" I was conscious ofchanging the subject.

"Because they're not happy with her attitude lately, they pulled her off the road yesterday and 'disciplined' her. She was punched in the face, kicked in the stomach, then buried in a ditch they dug in a wooded area. I don't know how long they left her in the ground--severalhours, anyway. They told her to shape up if she hoped to seeher next birthday. They aren't willing to tolerate more rebellion. I thought it was time you knew what was happening--she's in big trouble, Chris."

Again, I expressed my gratitude that Amber had taken the risk of coming forward. I couldn't remember ever feeling so frustrated about a case. We were stuck in a vicious cycle. "I'm at a loss," I admitted. "What can I do to help her? What can I do if they're threatening her life?

I can't get her out of the cult, but she can't heal if they continue to subject her to new abuse and trauma all the time! I feel like my hands are tied, Amber!"

I should have contained my frustration. In retrospect, I know I should not have expressed the powerful sense of futility that pervaded my being. If Shirley had felt suicidal earlier in the session, my declaration of hopelessness was not exactly what the doctor ordered.

"I don't know what else to tell you," Amber continued. "I will continue to tell them as little as possible about our sessions. You must help Shirley to deal with this to the best of your ability. Then maybe we can figure a way to get out of the group."

"Anything else I should know?" I asked, trying hard to not convey any more of my disgust.

She shook her head and closed her eyes as if to communicate that she would be returning me to headquarters in short order. Before she vacated the premises, I requested that she pass the information shared with me on to Shirley, so I wouldn't have to. I found this to be a great time saver as well as a more valid method of transmitting information within. In a way, we'd be "cutting out the middleman."

Upon returning, Shirley reacted to the informationin a
nner that I could only characterize asappropriate. Through
more tears and loud sobs, I heard her ask, "What am I gonna
do? Maybe I should just take my life, so they won't have the
satisfaction of murdering me. What's the point? I thought I
was almost done with therapy, and now this! I'll never be any
better! They'll never let me go!"

As a therapist, one steers away from phrases like, "I
know how you feel"; unless we walk in the shoes of another,
we rarely do know how they feel. But this time, this one time,
while I didn't share her feelings of suicidal depression, I did
experience the most profound sense of despair I had ever
known in a session. And no doubt she could sense that the one
earthly guy upon whom she was hinging her entire recovery
was out of answers.

I stared blankly at her for what felt like an eternity,
before the first intelligent thought surfaced-- the Hanky Man!
Whoever the guy was, he could probably verify Shirley's cult
participation and maybe have enough influence to pull her
out. It was a long shot, but what else did we have?

I relayed all of this to Shirley, and predictably, she
shrugged and granted me permission to contact him. Once
again, she was entrusting her safety, if not her future, to me.
And at this moment, it was more responsibility than I cared to
have.

As I reflected on the remainder of the session--
assessing Shirley's potential for suicide, coaxing a verbal
commitment to refrain from such an act, agreeing to her
request of a phone call if I had anything to report from my
contact--I felt myself sinking into despair once again.

Nothing in my training had prepared me for this. If a

patient were suicidal, I knew what to do. If she were homicidal, or fearful of danger from the hands of a companion, I could handle that, too. But if Amber/Shirley were accurate, I could do nothing. No one would believe her, and I didn't know the name of a single group member--I preferred it that way. Besides, if it were indeed the truth, then law-enforcement officials, judges, and district attorneys were, from what I had been told, members of the cult.

And if, by chance, this was all a product of Shirley's fertile imagination, then obviously no danger existed from any cult. That would mean she was profoundly psychotic and would benefit more from an antipsychotic medication than from talk therapy. I didn't like my options.

*   *   *

At home, my dinner consisted of what could only be a typical bachelorhood feast: a large tuna sandwich from a takeout place called Sub Conscious (a psychologist couldn't help but like that name) and a Diet 7-Up. Drained from an exhausting day, I opted for some light "reading" from the Victoria's Secret catalogue.

And with the last of the giant sub finally consumed, I decided to take my chances and call Charles Evans. My watch read 9:15, and I told myself he wouldn't be at the number he had given me.

I was wrong. Charles answered by saying "Yeah." As we conversed, I couldn't tell how he felt about my initiating contact with him. He didn't sound surprised, disappointed, pleased, or angry. And for the first time, I couldn't even tell if he was perspiring. My inability to detect any emotional reaction whatsoever from him amused me.

He heard me out and took down the pertinent information about Shirley. He told me he'd find out what he could and get back to me within a couple of days. Then he told me one more thing: "Don't mention the cult from your home telephone anymore. I'm pretty sure your line is tapped."

His words struck like a punch to an unprotected abdomen. "But what about this call?" I asked.

"I've got it covered tonight."

After we hung up, I heard the clicking sound that a wiretap makes at the disengagement of the call--yet another personal invasion to address, one more unsettling evening alone in the condo. I decided to tune out the preceding conversation and the events of the day in favor of a phone call to Laura. Maybe she could lift my spirits with that giggle I'd grown to love. Perhaps she could restore me to some semblance of joviality.

But nothing Laura or anyone could do could prepare me for my next contact with the Hanky Man.

<h1 style="text-align:center">Chapter 27</h1>

<h2 style="text-align:center">The Bug in the Office</h2>

The Hanky Man rarely called me, and to the best of my recollection, he'd never contacted me at work. But as I emerged from my first session on a Thursday morning, anote in my message tray read: *Call Charles. He wouldn't leave a last name. He said he was a personal friend.*

From what little I knew about Charles, I seriously doubted he had any personal friends." He was far too private and abrupt; he didn't appear to have the time or the interest in inconsequential matters like affiliation with people. His call had to be business only, and I hoped it pertained to Shirley.

This time, he didn't say "hello" or even "yeah." Instead, it was, "Chris, I need to see you. Let me in the back door of your office after your next session. I'll only need a minute, okay?"

"Yeah, sure." I didn't know what else to say.

He appeared at the designated time and place, dressed as if on official business--midnight blue double-breasted pin-striped suit, red power tie, leather wing-tipped shoes. Of course, he was wearing shades.

He walked into the office without a greeting. He briefly glanced at me before scanning the room as if searching for something. Wrinkling his brow, he stated, "Your office is bugged. It's under the black chair."

Shocked, I watched him stride over to the recliner, kneel on the floor by its left side, and turn it over to expose

291

the underside. "See anything?", heasked.

I didn't. Needless to say, I was relieved. He lowered the chair and went to *my* desk chair. With one hand, he lifted it to reveal its dusty underside. There it was, in plain view--an object about the size and shape of a hockey puck, duct-taped to the bottom! I stood speechless, rigid.

Charles tore the device from the chair as if he'd done this routinely for years. "Ever see one of these before, Chris?" he asked without so much as a glance in my direction. He destroyed it before handing it to me.

"Nope, can't say that I see a lot of those in my line of work," I wisecracked. My sarcasm was a reassurance that I was okay.

Charles grabbed the bug back from me and headed toward the door. "Shirley's still in the cult. She reports to a physician who's a bigwig in the local group. It's not looking good." He went to let himself out, as if his mission for the day had been accomplished.

"Wait, Charles!" I followed him out the door. "Can you do anything for her? I mean can you, uh, is there a way to get her out?" I felt like a child, begging for a video game.

"I dunno. I'll see what I can do. She has a kid, right?"
"Yeah, why?"
"It makes a difference to me, that's all. Gotta go.
I'll call you. And I'll see to it that your office is swept from now on."

"'Swept'?" I asked, doubting that he was alluding to vacuuming the carpet.

"Yeah, it'll be checked for bugs. I'll be in touch."
"Thanks, Charles. I really appreciate everything you're doing. Especially for Shirley."

"Yeah."

I watched as he walked through the parking lot. I hoped to see his car for the first time. I was curious as to what he drove and wondered if it had a government license plate. But he disappeared around the corner.

Figures, I thought, disappointed.

Returning my body to the office was easy, but getting my mind there was something else entirely. Once again, I was overwhelmed by questions: Who was bugging my office? What were they interested in learning about my sessions? Were they targeting one patient, or were they assessing how much I seemed to know about the cult? That last question hit home in light of the fact that the bug was placed under my chair and not the patient's recliner. Would that indicate their desire to zero in on me? I didn't know if that was a fair conclusion; my knowledge of technology was too limited for me to determine whether the bug could record the sounds of the entire office or not. I could ask Charles about that.

Is it ethical to ignore what occurred in the office this morning, or do I have an obligation to tell my patients about it? I wondered. Again, I struggled with an issue not included in the A.P.A. Ethical Guidelines. I had never read the heading "Office Bugging--see Cult Tampering."

As for informing my patients, that would be impossible. No one would confide in me, knowing the office had been bugged by the underworld. No, I would keep my mouth shut, and I would mention nothing on the phone about the cult.

Meanwhile, back on the couch sat my next client, a dear little lady in her eighties with a diagnosis of obsessive-compulsive disorder (OCD). She suffered from an obsessive concern over contracting the AIDS virus. Although her psychiatrist was treating the disorder appropriately with medication, Milda needed psychological counsel tohelp her fend off the incessant, unwanted thoughts.

I figured I'd challenge her worries with a littlequiz on risk-taking behaviors and AIDS. "Are you sleeping witha lot of bisexual men lately, Milda?"

"One or two a week, tops," shequipped.

"Do you inject your drugs intravenously, or areyou content to smoke your dope?"

"I enjoy a variety of methods, actually," she claimed, suppressing any outward display of emotion.

"Okay, well, when you do inject your drugs, are you inclined to share your needles with anyone?"

"Why, of course," she continued. "Do you know how expensive needles are? It's not like when I was a kid!" She returned every volley with an ace of her own. I couldn't keep a straight face any longer. I burst out laughing.

In an attempt to be helpful, I concluded, "Milda, in all due respect to the nature of OCD and how easy it is to obsess about things, I'd say you have a better chance of being drafted in the first round by the Cowboys than you do of contracting AIDS."

From what I could determine, Milda's session probably benefited me more than it did her. Somewhere in our lighthearted examination, I rediscovered a perspective I'd lost since Shirley's alter, Amber, admitted that she was still active in the cult. I realized that I had a job to do. People were investing their time, money, and emotional vulnerabilities in my services. I owed them the best of my clinical skills and undivided attention, no matter who might be listening in or why.

That being true, I was still admittedly upset thatall of my sessions' confidentiality had been compromised by the listening device. But what to do? Contacting the FBI seemed foolish, especially since Charles knew about the bugging and he was a government intelligence agent.

He never showed me a badge, I thought. I simply accepted that he had told me the truth about himself. If I asked him for a business card, that would convey a lack of trust on my part, and my relationship with him was too tenuous to risk alienating him. But I needed to keep my eyes open until I could verify who in the world he was. After all, if he alone knew of the bug, there was a chance that he had planted it.

I decided to stop that train of thought without viewing the full complement of boxcars. It was too scaryto pursue at that point. I wanted to believe that he was a good guy. I **needed** to trust him right then. My renewed faith in God was still too fragile to place all my hope in the Almighty. I needed to believe in an earthly source of support and protection from the evil forces that I had often heard of but could not see.

After Amber's appearance, my worst fear in treating Shirley was that if she didn't extricate herself fromthe cult, she would lose all hope. It didn't take very long for that fear to materialize. At her next appointment, I revealed Charles's confirmation of her continued involvement, in an effort to reassure her of two things: First, she was not crazy, and second, to provide her with an inkling of hope that through Charles, she might be freed from the cult's grasp.

But my plan backfired. Shirley reminded me of something I had been told repeatedly since I began treating people with this problem: "Once a member of a satanic cult, it's next to impossible to get out alive."

Consequently, treatment with Shirley regressed to suicide prevention and weekly efforts to unravel the mysteries of that week's cult programming. I learned that Shirley received special attention from the cult's psychiatrist, who reportedly took delight in refining his hypnotic skills and brainwashing techniques at her expense. This was designed to punish Shirley for lack of compliance with the group's plan for her and to frustrate my efforts to restore her sanity. It became a game of cat-and-mouse, and the rodent continually thwarted my efforts.

One example of the malicious strategies of her cult shrink: Tenants of the Sarasota city Center, a magnificent downtown edifice that housed my Sarasota office, were often exposed to the sound of ringing bells during the day, lasting as they did for only four- to five-second intervals. On the Friday morning after learning my office was bugged, the bells rang some ten minutes into mysession with Shirley. At the sound, Shirley froze, motionless,like a victim of Mr. Freeze's gun on the old *Batman* television series.

But this was not an act. I tried everything from calling Shirley's name, to snapping my fingers, to attempting to induce a trance, to whatever else I could muster in the way of a desperate measure to bring herback. Nothing worked. She remained in a startled expression, her body rigid as though preserved in wax.

Once again, I was clueless as to how to help her. The spell broke and Shirley returned to the land of the conscious and functioning when the bell rang again after ten eternal minutes. Shirley was back as though she had never left, with the same stream of consciousness that she had entertained prior to the freezing over. Mercifully, the City Center bells did not toll again for Shirley that day, so we were spared another trance.

She came prepared for the next session with a little message for me from the unidentified evil shrink: "Ask Cortman how he liked the hell's bells game."

For me it was personal now, and humiliating. Through Shirley, they were deliberately exerting their power over me. We all knew that I was incapable of stopping them, and the feelings of helplessness and frustration scorched my soul. The world became a different place for me. Like the rape victim who suddenly feels unsafe in even the most familiar of settings, I found myself ill at ease in my own office. I had been violated--a nonphysical form of rape. And would the cult's power plays escalate to include violence? Was Laura safe in visiting me? *Your imagination is getting out of control,* I told myself. *Time to reel it back in and reassume that there was nothing to fear.* Denial? Maybe, but preferable to living in fear.

Chapter 28

The Deadly Tape

"Yeah," came the now customary greeting as he picked up the phone.

"Charles, good morning. Listen, sorry to bother you so early, but I need you to hear this tape. It's on my office answering machine."

I played it back for him: "We know about your meeting with Mister Evans."

That was it. No further explanation, no identification. A woman's voice I didn't recognize. No detectable accent, an obvious lisp. The answeringmachine had recorded the message at 10:56 P.M. Perplexed, I didn't bother to listen to the two remaining messages before calling Charles.

"You know the woman?" "Nope, you?"

"Nah, I *don't* know who the hell she is." He exhaled as though disgusted. "Awright, if there's anything else on the *tape* erase it. I don't want the other messages to identify who you are. I'm coming over. Have the tape ready for me. I'll have it examined in a government lab and see what's going on."

He hung up.

Less than a week after I turned the tape-recorded message over to Charles, he left a message of his own on my home machine. "Chris, it's Charles. I need to see you Saturday morning, seven-thirty, at the McDonald's on Bee Ridge Road. If you can't make it, let me know."

I found my heart rate increasing, like it used to before I

stepped into the batter's box in Little League. Back then, my fear had been of striking out or, in a word, failing. Now it was the fear of the unknown. Anxiety had rocked my life since the report of the evil underground and its members' interest in my working with its people.

Quickly I turned my attention to the meeting withthe Hanky Man and looked for an excuse to postpone it till later in the day. Just because he didn't sleep didn'tmean I shouldn't, I griped silently. But my grumbling soon ended. The meeting was important enough for me to get up early on the weekend.

I was surprised to see how crowded Mickey D's was at such an ungodly hour. Charles sat at a corner booth near the exit. Coffee steamed in a paper cup between his hands. He was dressed for a business meeting, in a navy double- breasted sport coat and a starched white shirt monogrammed in maroon thread on the left sleeve. The maroon tie was particularly handsome. I wondered if he might be willingto trade wardrobes with me.

He motioned for me to join him. I could see my reflection in his sunglasses as he said, "I know you don't drink coffee, so I got you an orange juice. If you want breakfast, why don't you head up to the line and grab something?"

I elected to forego breakfast in favor of listening to what Charles had to share.

"We searched for days to locate the woman who made that call. The lisp helped to narrow down the possibilities. We were able to determine that she was from the Midwest, most likely Iowa, and is in her early thirties. She called from Sarasota, but it was impossible to determine where, except that it was a phone booth. She also called to harass me about seeing you."

My mouth dropped. "What'd she say?"

"She left a message on my machine that virtually said the same things as on yours--just that her group knew about you. Then she made the mistake of calling a third time, and we managed to trace it. My people were on her like flies on shit." He paused to gulp down a few ounces of his no-nonsense black coffee. "Where did you nab her?"

"Never mind that. We tried to get her to talk. I'll tell you man, she was tough. Cursed like a sailor. Not just curse words. She was praying to Satan in some foreign tongue--I don't know what the hell she was saying."

He lowered his voice as one of the early bird senior citizens turned her silver head in our direction. Charles looked over his sunglasses to make eye contact with the eavesdropper. Embarrassed, she glanced away.

Charles peeled off the glasses and continued. "She told me to mind my own business if I value my life.I'm pissing off some of their big people."

"Is it that you know too much?"

"No, it's more than that." He paused, looked around, then lowered his head and his voice. "I've gotten involved in preventing the annihilation of children. I'm finding out more and more about how these people operate, and specifically how they breed and even import children to sacrifice. If I can help it, that's gonna stop. I've already intervened once this past Halloween; managed to save a couple of kids."

"How?" I felt a surge of adrenaline firing throughmy system.

"That's not important. Just know that you are a part of all this."

"Me? How?" I asked defensively.

"They blame you for turning me into their nemesis. That's partially why they're interested in bugging your office and your phone. They're aware that your patients talk to you and that you talk to me, so obviously theywant to know what you know."

My head spun. "So would it be better if we didn't speak anymore?"

He tightened his lips as if suppressing a smile. "Try not to worry. They can't touch you. I've got--"

"What do you mean they can't touch me?" I had spoken too loudly, and the woman turned to look at me. I lowered my voice. I'm a sitting duck! I do the same things and go to the same places everyday!"

"Yeah, you can be taken out in a heartbeat," he agreed. "But that's not what I mean. You're untouchable because I got my hands on a list of people in this area who are in their group. They know that. If they mess with you, I can do some serious whistle-blowing on them. So essentially you're on a no-hit list."

"Well, if that's the case, why--don't I just blow the whistle on them now?" I nodded.

"It's not that easy. Exposing their organization has to be done in an intelligent and thoughtful manner. A lot of government officials are involved. Others know about their cult and are sworn to secrecy. If anything is revealed, heads will roll--some literally, some figuratively. But if they ever mess with you or my family, man, I swear to Christ I'll use everything this fuckin' government has ever taught me to expose those freaks. I'll make it my only mission in life!"

His face was now beet red. The cool, calm man inthe beautiful jacket was perspiring. Out came the trusty handkerchief to mop his brow.

My appetite was gone. I sure couldn't qualify for a Happy Meal. I just sat in silence; my circuits overloaded with too much information. I knew he'd bounce back in a moment.

"There's a little girl in my neighborhood," he continued. "She's probably eight years old. Beautiful kid. Sits on the swing in her backyard for hours. Her parents are in the cult, and I understand she's to be sacrificed. I'll do whatever I can to stop it. I watch her from my bedroom with my binoculars sometimes, just to make sure she's okay."

I wondered how the cults could get away with these murders. Wouldn't the schools inquire about a student's whereabouts if the child suddenly stopped showing up? How about aunts, uncles, grandparents? I wanted to ask Charles, but I detected a trace of tears around the rim of hiseyes. If it were a therapy session, I would have pursued the emerging emotion. But this was no place for therapy. I changed the subject back to the original topic, still unclear about why we were meeting in the first place.

"So, what about the woman with the lisp?"

"She won't be bothering you anymore." "Hmm?"

"She wouldn't reveal a thing. Kicked me in the fucking ribs, man. I swear she cracked a couple of 'em. She was a tough soldier. I mean it. But she threatened me too many times, so she won't be threatening anybody ever again."

"You killed her?" I asked, probably a bit too loudly. Fortunately, the booth adjacent to us was empty.

He smiled wryly, reaching down to his left and pulling a large McDonald's cup from the seat next to him. He tipped it to a forty-five degree angle in my direction, revealing a blood-soaked slice of meat, no more than a few inches in diameter. "Like I said, she won't be threatening anyone again."

"Her tongue?!" My stomach dropped, as it does on the first chilling descent of a roller-coaster ride.

"She won't be needing it where she's going. My buddies and I shoved a cross up through the roof of her mouth and tossed her in a swamp somewhere, where not even the devil will find her."

I have learned to keep a calm demeanor and a stoic face when patients reveal shocking material. I reached for that face, ignoring the war that had been waged in my soul.

"They hate having a cross in the mouth," Charles said smirking. "They think their fucking master won't touch them if they're buried in that condition."

"Was it necessary to kill her?" I asked, sounding like a squeamish twelve-year-old on a deer hunt.

"No way we could release her, Chris. No way. Try to understand that there's more going on than I am at liberty to reveal. She needed to die, that's all I can tell you.

You don't have to trust me, but it's the best option you have. I won't let 'em hurt you 'cause I know your heart's in the right place. You're trying to help your patients. They need you."

Possibly feeling himself softening in an uncharacteristic manner, he re-erected his wall. "If you think it's your duty to turn me in, remember I'm not your patient. You don't even know who got whacked. And there's no body. No body, no crime. Besides," he said with a smile, "I am the fucking government."

My whole world was tilting crazily. How had I gotten involved in all this crap, with murders and mutilations? And if Charles was really the government, then how was I supposed to tell the good guys from the bad? What had given him the right to kill that woman? What will happen next? More bloodshed?

Panic encased me, spawning a new line of questions: What if Charles was really a mobster? Wasn't the Mafia known for removing body parts from their victims? Surely the U.S. government doesn't operate this way, no matter how corrupt Charles' supervisor.

Or maybe he was an imposter. Maybe that "tongue" was just a piece of meat purchased at a local market and dressed up to evoke a response from me. But why? Who would do such a thing?

Who the hell was this guy?

I have a right to ask these questions! I told myself.

I have a right to ask for some identification. I needed something to prove that this violent man was a government official and not a psychopathic killer. And I had a right to excuse myself from the table and tell Charles that I never wanted to see him or hear from him again.

But I froze.

Charles got up, said he had to attend some "official business," and hurried out the door, while I sat in a lump of self-betrayal, nursing my orange juice and my wounds. I had done nothing! Maybe I was too cowardly. Or maybe I was in so far over my head, I didn't know where to turnor where to start.

I cringed, again appalled that I had gotten stuckin such a mess. More importantly, could I ever get out?

Chapter 29

Baby Ginny

As much as I love it, my vocation can be a thankless job. I'm thinking of the initial session wherein a married couple of thirteen years decided to call it quits. The ugly remarks born out of hurt, rejection, and fear began the verbal free-for-all. Then came the threats. Predictably this grew into financial warfare He was incensed not only because she wanted out but because she had waited until he sprung for a three-thousand dollar breast implant. (I assume he meant for the whole job-- not per breast.) She was embarrassed and insulted that he would bring this up at such a time, and so grew her fury. But I still did not anticipate her threat to hand them back to him right there in my office! She had already begun to pull her T-shirtout of her jeans when I intervened (I was concerned that the saline would stain my carpet). She was able to restrain herself enough to cancel her self-surgery but was far too embarrassed and distraught to remain in the office. She stormed out, and he followed. It was the briefest of all of my career therapy sessions. Naturally, neither onepaid. I wonder if the surgeon had been wise enough to secure payment in advance.

With Donna in therapy twice a week, we had the time to deal with here-and-now issues as well as make peace with the past. She was correct in saying that her employers had come close to terminating her, especially when one of the partners caught wind of police involvement in her involuntary hospitalization.

On a cold January afternoon, I picked up the phonein my Sarasota office and made good on my promise to speakto her superior in the conservative accounting firm. The senior partner was not about to risk twenty-seven years of maintaining an excellent reputation in Sarasota County for the unbecoming behaviors of an unstable psychiatric patient." Although I could not guarantee that Donna would never embarrass him or his firm, I could assure him that she was beyond the crisis that had prompted hospitalization and not inclined to stumble upon legal or extreme psychiatric difficulties again. My presentation must have been convincing, for the senior partner elected to spare Donna her job.

When we had completed the call, I sat back and looked out the window at downtown Sarasota, where a new judicial center was being built. I had a few minutes between patients, so I dug a bag of peanuts from my desk drawer and relaxed, munching, and thought about how happy Donna would be with the outcome of the phone conversation. Why had I made such bold assertions about her mental health and stability? Because I knew she was a good and reliable employee. Besides, a termination in her employment would prove detrimental to the fine work she had been doing in therapy. More than that, however, I honestly believed that she was very close to making peace with her unresolved past and would soon be functioning as one united person.

Donna had a new attitude toward Lucinda. She was now referring to her eleven-year-old alter personality as "Lucy." Ever since Lucy had agreed to serve as Donna's ally, the name *Lucinda* was never uttered in session.This change reflected a new found affinity that had been building within. Donna spoke of Lucy in such endearing terms that I needed to remind myself that she was referring to an imaginary aspect of self and not a separate being.

She even purchased a stuffed animal for Lucy, which she carried to every session. "Woofie" was no bigger thana miniature Schnauzer and possessed the floppy ears of a Beagle and the please-love-me face of a Maltese. The three of them-- Donna, Lucy, and Woofie--slept together inPeter's absence, reportedly on one oversized pillow on the left side of the bed. Donna seemed content to revel in her new relationship with Lucy, who was now construed as an almost angelic being. Naturally there was more than a hint of irony in this belief in Lucy, the sainted.

This domestic bliss bothered me. Although I enjoyed success with at least ten multiple-personality patients at this point in my career, not one of them had reached the goal of complete integration--not *yet*. And so, I was understandably motivated to escort Donna past the goalline and into the end zone.

But for some unknown reason, she wasn't. Where had her anger gone? Who was now considered the enemy? Why was she resisting integration? My frustration culminated in a half-eaten bag of peanuts.

As the weeks went by, I told myself that Donna was merely enjoying her newfound motherhood and unwilling to part with her Lucy. But when the weeks of avoiding the inevitable integrative work totaled six, I found myself harboring a secret grudge against Lucy--or what she represented as a stall to the healing process. But when I caught myself resenting Woofie's presence in the office, I knew something was wrong. As far as I knew, I had never before held ill feelings toward a stuffed animal. The time had arrived to get to the bottom ofthis.

Wanting to devise a strategy, I reflected on all of this while driving my car, running on the beach, and watching NFL playoff games. At last, a powerful thought occurred to me as I was unlocking my front door at the end of a long day's work: *It's about fear. Donna is not merely enamored with Lucy; she is afraid to integrate her. She fears something.* But what? Was it loneliness? Did she fear releasing Lucy because she'd be living all alone?

Maybe, I thought, setting down my briefcase and searching the kitchen for food. *But wait a minute. If my assumption is true that every alter tells a story, and every alter is a container for emotions and memory, then isn't Lucy's lingering suggestive of some unfinished business?* My reaction was less a celebration of insight than "How could I be so dumb as to miss that?" She and I had an appointment the following day. I resolved tobring it up to her then.

Donna reacted to my conclusion--that she might have to take us to some unresolved area of pain--with a rim of water surrounding her eyes. I knew I was right. She reluctantly agreed that Lucy had a story to tell, but then added, "I believe it has to do with Lucy's birth."

I could see by her face that we were dealing witha delicate topic.

"Is it absolutely necessary to integrate her?" Donna asked. "Isn't there some way to keep her? I mean, is it written somewhere that a person has to be one in order to be healthy? Couldn't I just have one part of me that survives integration? Is it some kind of sin? Can't I just keep Lucy?"

I felt as if I were being a cold-hearted authority who was denying a mother access to her only child. I had no "right words" to offer her, so I settled for: "I'm only asking you to take me to whatever pain is still unresolved. It's the same process that you've been engaged in since the beginning. Why don't we take the focus off Lucy's integration for the time being and return it to the healing process? As long as you have some painful material lurking inside, it holds power over you. I'm just asking you to take me there so we can work through it." I concluded my mini-exhortation with a request for input. "What do you think?"

Donna rubbed her eyes tiredly. At last, she raised her gaze. "I know what I have to do, Dr. C. I would just prefer not to do it because I know how much it's going to hurt. Do you realize this is the best I've felt in years?"

Her voice sounded constricted. "The prospect of leaving my little oasis to return to the blistering desert heat doesn't hold much appeal. Can you understand?"

"Of course, I understand that. And that's an excellent analogy. But I promise there will be another oasis at the end of this journey with Lucy. I know you can do it."

She nodded and glanced at her watch. Our time had not elapsed, but Donna had had enough. She bade me farewell and made a beeline for the door.

I didn't like playing the heavy, but we had a job to do. Donna would not benefit from weakening and backing down from what she must face. I didn't want to be the enabler.

And I was getting tired of that little Woofie staring at me each session.

*　　*　　*

Two weeks after Donna admitted her reluctance to integrate Lucy, she dropped off her personal journal formy perusal. I had no time to read between sessions, and I found myself wishing the day would end so I could read her entry-- a clear indicator of how invested I had become in Donna's case.

Why? I wondered. Why was her case more important than anyone else's? After some self-examination, I realized that I was more drawn to the clients who had suffered an extraordinarily abusive childhood. But there was more to it; Donna and I had a special connection founded on having gone through so much together. Truthfully, I had a personal stake in Donna's complete integration. I wanted to participate in the process of healing a shattered mind and a fragmented soul. Watching her cross the finish linewould be important for me, after enduring such a grueling marathon.

And if we could do it, then my other multiples could do it, too. I would have a success story, to encourageand give hope to the others who trusted me with their ravaged life.

A final thought cemented my convictions: My jobwas not worth doing if there was no hope for healing. If the Donnas of the world could not ever make peace with the horrors of yesteryear, then I would not be happy in this career. She needed to get well to move on with her life. I needed her to get well to go on with my career.

I had no plans for the evening, and the miserable winter rain easily convinced me to steer away from a jog on the beach. An intimate dinner out with Donna's journal seemed like a good idea, but after an extended bachelorhood in a small town--even a resort community with dozens of eateries--I was bored with the same old restaurants.

I got into my car and considered my options--Outback Steakhouse? No, I didn't feel like waiting in line for three and a half hours. Red Lobster? Nah, I wasn't in the mood for fish. Hooters? Sounded like fun, but I never seemed to get any work done there for some reason. I decided to head home, where an unopened box of Special K and a half-gallon of lactose-reduced milk awaited me. I was ready to party.

Stopped at a red light, I peeked at the journal, where a protruding bookmark opened to the most recent entry. The bookmark featured the Twenty-third Psalm, "The Lord is my shepherd…" For the rest of the ride home, I thought about Donna/Lucy, the lost sheep in need of a divine shepherd. I felt reassured to know that she and I weren't alone on this case. Home, I changed into a sweatshirt, a pair of jeans, and warm socks, then sank into my reading chair. I was readyto begin what I'd hope would be the last battle of the war.

> *Dr. C., I am so terrified to begin. I know Ineed to process something that may wound me so deeply, I may never recover. I don't know how much more pain I can stand. But I am learning to trust God, and I trust you. And I need to trust the healing process. OhLord, help me!*
>
> *I must have been six years old at the time. As you know I had an older brother but always longed for a sister. I used to sit and play in my room for hours and hours with a tiny doll. She was an adorablelittle girl with long blond hair and a cute pug nose. I fantasized that she was my little sister. How I dreamed of one day having a sister of my own! When I could manage my*

fear of my father's rejection, I would plead and beg with him to bring me home a sister. I didn't yet understand where babies came from. I thought if my parents wanted to have a baby, somehow they could. (It's interesting that I never asked my mom for a sister. I guess I already knew who was the leader of the household.)

I remember a day when my daddy announced that Mommy was pregnant--I didn't know what that meant either at the time--and that in several months I would be having a little brother or sister. I was thrilled, but I didn't want a brother and couldn't understand why Daddy couldn't just make me a sister forsure.

The months passed, and Mommy's belly grew. I repeatedly asked her, "Could you make it a sister? Please make me a sister!"

She evidently thought this was cute, because she would always smile and say, "I'll do what I can, Donna, but I'm sure God would want you to love whatever He gives to us."

The child was indeed a girl. My mother went away to have her--I'm not sure where--and returned after a couple of days. My parents named her Virginia, and we called her Baby Ginny. I can remember being instructed to keep her birth a secret. "It's nobody else's damn business," my father told me, and I never talked about Baby Ginny to anyone, even though I wanted to tell the whole world about her.

My sister's infancy was undoubtedly the happiest part of my entire childhood, if not my whole life! I played with her every chance I could, spending hours touching, kissing, and loving her. She was my little doll come to life. My fantasy had come true. I couldn't imagine that anyone could ever love their baby sister as much as I did. And so, every day I thanked the Lord Jesus and my mommy and daddy forthis little gift of love.

My mother was okay about my spending so much time with Baby Ginny, but for some reason my daddy would always tell me, "Leave the damn baby alone! She can't sleep with you always smothering her!"

I didn't understand why he said that. I would never smother her or hurt her in any way. I lovedher so much, and when she was sleeping, I wouldn'tdisturb her. I would just lie there and watch her sleep, sometimes for hours at a time.

I noted that the handwriting switched from an adult's cursive--Donna's own penmanship--to a bold printing at this point. Some alter personality had taken over.

On a cold, dark and foggy evening, my daddy shook me on my left shoulder and commanded me, "Get up and get dressed, Donna. We're going out!"

I knew better than to ask why. I put on the clothes that I had worn that day to school. Within minutes, his voice bellowed from downstairs. "Get down here!"

I flew down the stairs without latching my shoes properly and noted that my entire family was congregated in the living room waiting on me. Baby Ginny was wrapped tightly in a blanket in my mother's arms. Everyone wore overcoats. It was the middle of the night. We climbed into the car, which was not parked in the garage as usual but was out on the street in front of the house. I tried to fall asleep leaning against the door of the back seat, but I couldn't. I sensed trouble. I can remember the anxiety brewing within me. Mom saw me shivering and offered me a blanket.

We drove into the night as the heat finally reached the back seat. But before I ever became warm enough to remove the blanket, we drove into what appeared to be a state park, then down some twisting dirt roads into almost total darkness. Dad seemed to know exactly where we were going. Eventually we came upon a police car, with its parking lights on. Outside the cruiser, a familiar site: the Rat Man leaned up against the side door, smoking. He recognized our car and waved us through to a clearing where eight to ten other cars were already parked. About fifty yards from the parking area, well into the clearing, was a brilliant bonfire. Adults were clad in long black robes and hoods.

My heart dropped as I began to anticipate something horrible transpiring. I didn't want to think about it. I didn't want to feel. I switched often, as I had already learned to do quiteproficiently.

Dad ordered us out of the car and went aroundto the trunk. There he fetched the robes for each oneof us. We dressed quickly, ignoring the biting cold.

The handwriting again switched, this time back to a soft cursive; still, it was not Donna's typical penmanship.

My memory becomes blotchy here. I think I was given something to drink, with a tranquilizer. I'm cloudy. I feel very drugged. There is a gap of time missing. I can't say how long. An altar stands just beyond the great fire. Father Delvecchio stands over it to one side. My father stands proudly to the other side. I squint to focus on the altar. There is movement on top of it. It's a baby. What baby? Oh, God, what baby? Where is Baby Ginny?

I look to my left, and there silently stands my mother. Where is Ginny? Where is my sister? I ignore the groggy feelings and nausea and scramble to the foot of the altar. I notice my helpless little sister bound to the altar with rope on her tiny feet and hands. She is breathing, but her movement has slowed. I realize with one look in her eyes that she, too, is drugged.

My father calmly walks over and grabs my hand firmly, leading me to his side of the altar. He bends down as if to kiss me and says in a menacing tone, "Not a word out of you, or I will cut your throat and drink your blood until you die. Understand?"

I try to whisper, "Can't I take Ginny?" He places his hand over my mouth very hard and repeats, "Not a word!" He then makes a concerted effort to cover up our encounter as if part of a smooth-running program: "My daughter Donna has just volunteered to help me make the sacrifice to our master and lord!"

The people applaud. Daddy smiles triumphantly. Father Delvecchio raises his hands toward the heavens and summons "the Prince of Darkness and a legion of his worthy soldiers to descend upon our humble gathering; and accept the sacrifice of our anointed little one."

He honors my father and speaks of what sounds like his promotion to second in command of the Luciferians. He asks for the group to pray as one that "the evil one" would "honor master Dale Thompson (my maiden name) and bless his remaining family members with joy and prosperity."

The people chant and pray their dark words. Daddy accepts the diamond-studded dagger from Father Delvecchio. Baby Ginny lies motionless upon the cold stone altar.

Daddy commands me to come forward with a one-word instruction and a stern glare. Despite numerous attempts at switching to other parts of me in an effort to not feel, my anxiety burns inside like the bonfire behind me. Though a child of only six, I have learned enough of the ways of the cult to know what is next. The idea of anyone or anything hurting my baby Ginny is unthinkable. I can't stand for it, and yet what am I to do? Surely, I can't stop all these people from doing what they are intent on doing. And to show weakness, as I learned repeatedly in their instructions and disciplining of the children, will only incite them to destroy me. In an instant I know that Daddy will allow that if it means saving face for him.

The intense emotions--especially fear--get the best of me. My head spins like a top, and my knees wobble uncontrollably. I am about to pass out and fall headfirst to the ground. I don't know.

The paragraph ended there, leaving half a page of empty space to the bottom of the page. On the top of the following page, however, the writing began anew, with yet another different style of handwriting, a cursive with a more pronounced slant, and misspellings.

> *It's me, Christopher--Lucy. I have written to you before, but always in the code of the evil one. I will tell you what happened next. Donna was very weak. She was about to pass out. I knew for sure that they would kill her for deminstrating such weakness. I came to be at that moment. I was strong, powerful and confadent. I felt no fear, no doubts. I cared only about doing whatever it took to keep Donna alive. I did not feel for the baby. There was no place for that. I had a job to do, Christopher, and I needed to make sure that it was completed. None of us had ever killed anything to that point, let alone a child. But we had been to enough of these ceramonys to know how to killsomeone the right way.*
>
> *Daddy's hand was steady and sure as he held the knife and my hand firmly in his grasp. I did not flinch for even a second as we slit the throat ofthe sackrafise. The incision was made from left toright. The chest was split...*

I had heard and read enough of the how-to-sacrifice-a-baby crap, and at that moment I was angry. But atwhom?

Where could I direct my fury? Her father? Sure, but that didn't seem like enough of an outlet to satisfy my rage. All abusive parents? Satan? Sin? I didn't know what to do with all that hatred I felt, and for a moment thatfeeling brought me closer to Donna and all my suffering patients, especially those who had survived helpless agony during their tender years. Where could they direct their anger, and what good would it do even if they had a person to blame and hate?

I wanted to destroy her journal, but I've never been one to aggress physically when angry. I'm not a smasher.I don't throw or break things. I've never punched a wall. But my indignation at the needless abuse and suffering of children seemed too powerful to be contained by words.

I clenched my teeth and chose to read on past the gory details of the sharing of the child's flesh and blood. I also skimmed past the part wherein Donna's vaginal area was branded with the pentagram on this night.

Lucy continued a couple of paragraphs later:

> *It was here, at the sackrafise of Baby Ginny, that I was born. I didn't want to kill her. I didn't hate that baby. I only wanted to keep Donna alive! That was my only purpose! No one else inside would come forward to save Donna, and so I did. I didn't enjoy killing Baby Ginny. I didn't like the taste of the blood or the chewy texture of the heart. But I did what was necessary, without question, so we would be able to live another day.*
>
> *But the people were so nice to me! And they said things that made me feel special inside. Things that we never heard before from my mommy or daddy. So, I learned to do whatever they told me to 'cause I wanted them to keep saying nice things. And they did. So, I did*

my best for them and learned not to care who or what was laying on top of the altar. And I didkill others, too. I continued with the group off and on even after Donna and Peter were married.

When we moved to Florida, my father hooked me up with someone from this area's group. I had to kill someone down here (in Florida) in order to prove my worthiness to this group. It was an old man this time, who had been in the group for years and was willing to be a sackrafise since the time was short before he would probably die. I also partisipated in thekilling of several animals, especially cats.

These people became my real family. They seemed to love me, and that was very important to me. But noone else inside Donna ever knew any of this. Not until they started working with you. You enkaraged them to remember everything that I tried so hard to keep from them. And that's part of the reason why I hated you, Christopher. But I don't anymore. I now realise that you care about us and really want tohelp.

But now we have another problem. It was not only my job to obey the leaders of the group, it was also important to hide all of the truth from Donna. If she knew about this, espeshally about Baby Ginny, itwould destroy her. So, I have tried all these years tohide in the darkness with all of these secrets. And now you are asking us to become one. This can only be done when Donna is ready to know all that I know. Then she must feel the pain that I have buried from her in a deep pool of dirty water. I don't know if she can ever do this. Please help us, Christopher. That's all I have to say right now.

I chose not to stop for a water break, because this material was far too compelling. This was what we had been working toward for a couple of years now. I read on.

>*Oh, Dr. C., (it was Donna's handwriting again) I am in utter disbelief over what I've just read. Can this really be so? God help me if I am truly responsible for taking the life of my precious sister!*
>
>*I cannot live with that. I believed you when you told me that remembering this would lead to healing.*
>
>*…but how can I ever heal from this? I never even knew I had a sister, and now this! Please, please God! No! No! No! Don't let this be true! Oh why? Why? Why?!!! How could I be so guilty of cowardice? Why didn't I just let them take me? What have I ever amounted to? They should have spared Ginny's life and taken mine instead. God help me!*
>
>*Maybe I should gain vengeance for Baby Ginny's life by taking my own. Maybe that would appease God for killing his precious gift. I don't deserve to live. I want to die, Dr. C! I WANT TO DIE!!!*

The journal entry ended at this point. But there was another one a couple of pages later in the book. It was again Donna's legible cursive but dated three days after the last entry. (And three days before she dropped it off at my office.)

>*I called your office Friday night after I wrote in the journal. Of course, the answering machine was on.*

I wanted to talk to you so badly but elected not to leave a message. I decided that suicide was a noble thing to do after what I read about Baby Ginny. So, I gathered up all of the old medication that I could find in the medicine cabinet--there were quite a few of them, Elavil, Xanax, Prozac, Asendin--who knows how many others I have stored away for such a time as this? I got a glass of water and brought it all to bed. I wanted to write you a note to thank you for everything. For trying so hard and sticking with me when I couldn't believe anymore. I tried to convey all of my heartfelt gratitude in a letter to seal and mail to you so you would understand. But I couldn't do it! Every time I started, I would just sob and sob a thousand tears of sorrow. It hurt so much to think about Baby Ginny, and here I was writing to say goodbye to you. I just couldn't! I tore up three sheets of paper that fell short of expressing my sentiments. Somewhere in my grieving,

I must have fallen asleep.

In my slumber, Dr. C., the strangest thing happened. I saw Baby Ginny again! She was not mutilated anymore. She was in Jesus' arms! We walked together for a while, along the beach--don't worry, Dr. C, it wasn't by your house--and talked. All the time, Ginny was cooing and smiling, and then he let me hold her! It was the most beautiful feeling I've ever had to touch that child again!

And then Jesus said something like this to me: "Donna, don't be afraid. Ginny, like all the children in this world, belongs to me. Don't ever be deceived. The evil that men do to children is not forgotten. I will bring judgment to them one day. It is not for you to worry over. You are not to blame for Ginny'sdeath. I know that you loved and still love your sister. But she is safe with me and happy. And no one can ever take her from my hands. You will be with her again someday. But not now. Now you are to continue in your healing. And know that I won't ever leave you, nor turn my back on you. I will always be with you."

I don't remember Him leaving or what, if anything, transpired at that point. I don't know if this was a dream or a true spiritual encounter with the Lord! (I'm curious as to what you would say.) But truthfully, I'm not sure that it matters. Whatever it was, I have attained such a peace that I can't even begin to describe it! I'm just so grateful to God for his presence in time of need!

That is not to say that I have no sadness. The losses that I have experienced, especially Ginny, may always cause me to tear when I think about them. But I feel a freedom now because I know, I truly know that God has a hand in everything and will ultimately have His will done in all things. And that, I'm sure, includes my life.

As for Lucy, my precious, brave little Lucy. I now understand that she did what she had to, to save my life. I can't ever repay her for that. I also have come to understand her/our need for approval. That's only normal. I can also appreciate how much pain I allowed her (and the others) to hold on to for me, because I simply wasn't ready to feel it myself.

But that has changed! I have felt the horrible

pain that was buried in that cesspool of Lucy's, but I know that Jesus has taken it from me with the hope that He affords me. I can't tell you how much different an outlook I have right now!

Lucy asked if she could take Woofie and the remaining children to an island where they could walk the beaches with Jesus and be safe from the evil one and all of his followers. He promised that they would never be troubled by Nasty again! So, they set sail this morning in her imaginary sailboat with her and Woofie at the helm.

I expect that the island will be her last stop before becoming one with me. I understand what that means now, Dr. C.--I've got to own all that I've remembered and feel the numerous losses. Among them, of course, is the loss of my baby sister. I'd be lying if I told you I was over that or could ever be. But I feel the restoration of hope--hope that my past is finally over, hope that I can be a whole person again, and hope that I will one day be reunited with Baby Ginny. I need to stop writing now. I need to cry again. I feel so many things. And I need to rest. This has been the toughest and most draining weekend of my adult life.

I thank you, Dr. C., for seeing me through this.

And I thank God for the promise of wholeness, healing, and forgiveness. And I thank God for the promise of wholeness, healing, and forgiveness.

I'm not certain if I was touched by Lucy's gratitude, moved by her courage, or overwhelmed by her suffering. I only knew that the characteristically stoic Dr. Cortman fought hard against a growing urge to weep uncontrollably. Alone I sat on the living room couch, clutching the journal that represented the triumphant striving of a wounded little girl.

Then in a second of heart-melting thanksgiving, I praised God for choosing me to facilitate in Donna's deliverance. For in that same fleeting moment, I knew that I was right where He wanted me to be.

Chapter 30

The Kid in the Closet

"So, what are you doing tomorrow night?" I asked Laura, as if I didn't know. I had been planning this surprise for weeks. I was thankful we were talking long distance. If she had seen my face, she'd have known something fishy was going on.

"Oh, we'll be going out--all the girls--to a real nice club in Youngstown. They've got a dance floor, a restaurant, and a comedy club, all under one roof. I'm so excited!"

"Sounds like fun," said I, suppressing a chuckle.I had set up the stupid girls' night out.

"How 'bout you?" she asked. "What are you doing tomorrow?"

"I, uh--I'm going out with Marc. I don't knowwhat we're doing."

Silence. Then, "You have a date, don't you? I know when you're lying to me, Chris. Listen, if you can't be honest, why don't we forget the whole thing? If you wantto see other people, just say so." She was very upset, and her voice held an edge of threat.

No, *I don't want to date anyone else, Laura,* I thought. *As a matter of fact, I'm flying up to Cleveland tomorrow night with an engagement ring in my pocket to propose to you in Youngstown, in front of your friends.*

"No, honey, I'm not going out on a date. I promise. Let's not fight, okay?" Those were the real words I offered to my jealous princess.

"Yeah, whatever. I'm gonna go--have fun on your date."

Click!

Frustrated, I muttered a curse under my breath. Why was she so bloody insecure? I hated her jealousy! Was I being smart, really going to propose to a woman who couldn't trust me? What was I getting myself into?

Ever since Laura had issued me the ultimatum to get married or stop wasting her time, I had sidestepped all discussions about our future. My decision to marry her hadn't taken long; planning an innovative proposal and implementing the scheme, selecting a stone and setting, and having the ring made up had taken weeks, though. As each day passed, my beloved became a little less tolerant and a bit more hostile.

I had settled on a size-three band and a diamond big enough for Laura to hide behind. I hoped she would say yes, because the only other females with Laura's ring size were in second grade, and there were so few of them I wanted to marry. Well, I would find out the next night.

"Hello?" I mumbled into the receiver, completely disoriented. The clock radio read 11:45 P.M., but I had been so deeply asleep, I expected it to be the middle of the night.

"Chris, it's Charles. Sorry to awaken you."

"Don't worry about it. What's up?" My heart thumped against my ribs. Charles never called just to say hello, and whatever he had to tell me, I was certain I didn't want to know about it.

"I need to meet with you again. It's important."

"Uh, yeah, okay," I said with all the enthusiasm of scheduling a day at the Division of Motor Vehicles. My inclination was to rid myself of this relationshipforever.

"Good. Let's meet at your office at seven sharp tomorrow."

"Wait, Charles--," Too late. We were already disengaged. I just wanted a little something to reassureme that I wasn't in imminent danger, and neither was Laura, my family, Shirley... My list, I decided, was too long for any guarantee of protection. Besides, what could Charles do? I wrestled with his call for the better part of the night, often replaying his haunting words, "It's important."

Morning could not arrive soon enough, as Iexperienced the same anxious anticipation that had followed me into my licensing examination: "Let's hurry up and get this over with already, but, oh God, don't let it be too awful."

I pulled my car into the abandoned parking lot at7:02. Late, but not bad, I figured. Charles was nowhere in sight, which struck me as unusual for my uptight, anal-retentive acquaintance. I smiled to myself, fantasizing what his homelife was like.

A gentle tap at my window startled me. I jumped, then felt embarrassed by my reaction; I have never been inclined to demonstrate hypervigilance. Before I could collect myself, Charles walked around the front of the car to the passenger side, motioning for me to let him in. I obliged, and he climbed into my portable office, relocating journals and papers from the seat to the floor in front of him. He set his briefcase on his lap.

Before I had a chance to ask him where he had come from or how he had managed to hide his car, he immediately took charge. "Do you know where Caspersen's Beach is?"

"Yeah." I raised my voice as if to say, "So?" "Please take me there," he asked politely while rearranging his briefcase upon his lap for comfort. Heading out to Albee Farm Road, I stole a glance at the silver- haired gentleman. He was not dressed for a day at the beach: starched, multihued Polo shirt, perfectly creased khaki trousers, argyle socks, dockside shoes, and of course, the shades.

Ironically, I sported my New York Giants' cap and had sneakers somewhere in the back of my car--both suitable for a beach walk, even though I had been ignorant of our destination.

Charles attempted small talk with me, asking about the year and make of my car as well as fuel consumption. He was as incapable of making casual conversation as my mother was of discussing sports. I found myself feeling his awkwardness. Or maybe my anxiety was the byproduct of an emerging line of thinking: Why are we going to an all-but-deserted beach? Is he planning to dispose of me there and make it seem like an accident?

I still had no proof that he was a government agent. *Maybe it'll be my body parts featured in a McDonald's cup next week at some meeting.*

Pulling into the beach parking lot brought me back to my senses, temporarily. I told myself I was just being paranoid and that broad daylight at a public beach--however unpopulated--was not an ideal location to "whack" me. But my moistened palms on the steering wheel suggested that I was not completely convinced. I deliberately parked next to an old midnight-blue pickup truck--one of three vehicles in the entire parking lot--with hopes of being as conspicuous as possible, just in case I was on my way to meet my Maker.

I found an old sandy beach blanket in the hatchback, and Charles agreed that it was better than sitting directly in the sand. But I gathered that it didn't make a lot of difference to him either way.

*   *   *

The Hanky Man led the way past the sea oats and manmade fences to a desolate spot south of the parking lot. Not surprisingly, he was the only person in sight carrying a briefcase. I told myself that it contained suntan lotion.

"How was your conference last weekend?" he asked, exhibiting personal information about my life.

"You mean the week before last?" I wasn't so much correcting him as attempting to clarify. I had attended a conference on dissociative disorders for continuing education.

"Yeah, whatever. The one you went to in D.C." He sounded disgusted about being corrected.

"It was informative," I offered cautiously. "Why do you ask?"

"Because you ran into a big shot from the cult there." He paused, as if anticipating a reaction. I didn't bite. "A federal agent. He spoke on cults, and you went up to him afterwards to ask a question."

I wanted to ask, "How did you know?" But the question likely would have contributed more to my embarrassment than my understanding of the Hanky Man's surveillance of my life.

"I remember. I asked him about alleged reports of

331

satanic ritual abuse in my area. He gave me his name and phone number."

"Yeah. And he took down your name. Just as you were walking away, he glanced up at your name tag--it was hanging from a string looped around your neck--and scratched it on a piece of paper."

For a moment I lost his words somewhere in my feelings of shock. He could not have made that up. At most of the conferences I've attended, nametags stick or clip to the clothing. But this conference was different; all the courses for which we registered were written on cards that were encased in plastic behind our nametag and hung from a string looped around the neck! I swallowed hard to contain my sense of violation, a feeling I was becoming all too familiar with since meeting Charles.

I was not permitted to wallow too long in my discomfort; Charles was just warming up. "I am acquainted with Mr. Alexander--you know, the federal agent you're referring to?" he asked rhetorically. "He called me after meeting you last week. Says he's aware that you and I talk and have been supplying each other with information about their group. He doesn't like the fact that you are attempting to liberate some of 'their people' from the cult. He's also less than thrilled about my interference with some of their plans to sacrifice children. Worst of all for you, they blame you, Chris, for getting me involved. It's not that I pose a tremendous threat--I'm a minor irritant, like a pain in the ass. But like I've told you before, I have enough information on who they are and what they are up to, to keep them on their toes."

Despite the early hour, the April sun bore down upon us with an intensity that matched the information already revealed. Charles dug deep into his right pants pocket and produced the first hanky of theday.

"Anyway," he continued between dabs on the furrowed forehead, Mr. Alexander is interested in changing our perceptions of his group and would like it very much if we would consider switching our allegiances. In other words, they want to recruit us."

"What? Worship the devil? I don't think so!"

"Of course, they don't talk about the devil per se. Instead, they emphasize their ever-growing membership and point to the power they wield, especially in government and finance. And speaking of finance, Mr. Alexander wanted to make it worth your while to consider his offer." He popped open the briefcase, revealing huge stacks of cash bound with rubber bands. A closer inspection of the bills landed me face-to-face with Benjamin Franklin, the proud man who stared up at me from the hundred-dollar bills. I began to calculate the dollar value of the stash when Charles, right on cue, relieved me of my accounting chores.

There's more than forty thousand dollars here. Mr. Alexander wants you to know that there is plenty more where that came from. Oh, I almost forgot. He claims that his group has already established a bank account in your name in the Bahamas. It's supposed to be worth more than seven figures. I gather they see you as a potentially valuable asset if they can successfully solicit your participation."

Why would Alexander entrust Charles with the cash? I wondered. Whose money was it, anyway? Was Charles setting me up to take a bribe? And again, I wondered, was he inthe cult? God forbid! But seven figures? My heart raced as if already halfway to the Bahamas! A million dollars could really come in handy: pay off the condo, do someinvesting, take some much-needed vacations. A million dollars would certainly lighten my load come October, when I'd be paying for an expensive wedding and a Hawaiian honeymoon. But at what price? Betrayal of God? My ethics? The law? Just how does one explain a windfall emanating from a federal agent on behalf of a satanic cult?

I thought of sharing that information with my mother and almost laughed out loud. There was just not enough money in Charles's briefcase, nor Mr. Alexander's bribe. There couldn't be. Despite enjoying money as much as the next guy, I figured there were more important things to me. A Bible verse, Mark 8:36, memorized in childhood rang out in my head as if by design: "For what shall it profit a man to gain the whole world and lose his own soul?"

"No, Charles, I don't want the money. You keep it or send it back to them. Whatever. I'm not interested in the Bahamian account, either. Is that the sole purpose of today's visit?"

"I wish it were that simple." He removed the RayBans and wiped the perspiration from his eyes. He seemed to shrivel in the sunshine, like one of Hollywood's vampires. But he recaptured his confidence and mysterious demeanor merely by returning the shades to his face. It's more complicated than that. Whether or not we join them, they want us out of their business. The truth is, they can find ways to break you."

"What do you mean?"

"Chris, they know you. They know your family. They know who and what matters to you. They know about nieces and nephews and your girlfriend. It wouldn't take much to cause an accident or make someone disappear. It happens all

.he time."

He popped open the briefcase again; reached into a side pouch and produced a single sheet of whitepaper--a copy of a receipt from my office. *How did--?*

"Read the name on it. Know the patient?"

"I never heard of the guy. I don't think he was evera patient." Suddenly the relevance occurred to me. "Someone has my forms and my signature in their possession. What is this about?"

"Don't you see? They can take you down professionally. People who never saw you can file charges against you for things you've never done. Sexual allegations, insurance fraud. It wouldn't take much to ruin your reputation or mess with your license. Even a false allegation could wipe out your referral base."

My powerlessness and the injustice of the threat produced a rage that was difficult to contain. Worse, I lost hope. What was the point of fighting powerful underworld people who could destroy my life? Or, God forbid, the life of a precious member of my family. CouldI ever forgive myself if they hurt or destroyed Laura? I turned toward Charles; I had nothing to say. I was readyto leave.

But Charles still wasn't done. "Do you remember the little girl I spoke about that I watched over from my window?"

I nodded and swallowed hard in anticipation of what was next.

"Yeah, Ruthie's her name. Well, I wasn't able to watch her round the clock." He paused before continuing. "They knew she meant something to me..." Reaching into his other pant pocket, he removed a small manila envelope fastened at the top. He inclined his head, a nonverbal go- ahead to open the package.

I wish I hadn't.

Onto the beach blanket spilled eight child-sized teeth, many still attached to bloodied gums. Clearly, they had been yanked from a child's mouth. I picked one up for closer inspection and steeled myself for another gruesome story. Before I could even return the baby tooth to the envelope, Charles presented me with a chunk of shiny blond hair, obviously once in a ponytail.

"Do you see what they did to this kid, Chris? They sent me a videotape of the torture fest along with a few selected body parts. Every day lately someone puts another small package of Ruthie in my mailbox. I tell ya, if I ever catch the fucker." He brought himself down from the brink of rage. "It was the worst video I've ever seen. She was screaming bloody murder as they yanked her teeth out with a pair of pliers. They did the same to the poor little girl's fingernails--one at a time. I have them, too. You see the hair? She had beautiful hair, Chris. They chopped it with their damn dagger. One of the assholes in the video--they all had their faces covered so they couldn't be identified--kept waving different body parts in front of the camera. He mouthed a couple of 'fuck you's' intended for me. If I ever find the asshole, I swear I'll do to him everything he did to Ruthie." His bottom lip began to quiver.

"I'm sorry Charles," I mumbled. "I know she was very special to you." If there was something more appropriate to say, I couldn't find it. How must it feel to watch such a video? I wondered and felt real compassion for him.

"No. No. You don't understand, It" he said in a broken voice. "It wasn't that *she* was so special to me. I didn't know her at all. But she was a child, you see. Children should never be hurt by adults. We are supposed to take care of them, protect them, nurture them, love them. Not torture them and never, ever kill them. What kind of a religion is that? What kind of sick people are they? You don't hurt children!"

Tears followed his emphatic speech. I was about to attempt to say something comforting--God knows what--when he spoke.

"You probably think I'm weak to be blubbering like this, but I know what it's like to be abused as a kid. I know what it's like to be forced to give a man a blow job. My uncle would say, "Charles, do you like coffee?" Then he'd dip his penis in some lukewarm coffee and make me perform on him. And my mother, she would sell me for nickel beers. Drunken bar people would take me outside into the station wagon and do whatever they wanted to me for a lousy nickel beer. Chris, do you know what it's like to hide in a closet, sometimes for hours, because you know your mother is having people over? Oh, and I knew they would get drunk and eventually someone would want to have sex with me. And they'd always find me. Always! I'd be in the closet with the shoes, hiding, smelling the leather. To this day I can't stand the smell of leather--and I'd pray to God, 'Once, just once, send someone in to save me, to get me out of here. Someone big enough to protect me.'"

"That someone never came. But you know what? I grew up. I became a man. And I know how to protect myself. So, no one will ever do that to me again. And you know what else? Money doesn't mean shit to me. Because I know how low people will stoop to get it. I'll never forget what my mother would do for it. So, I can't be bribed, and I won't be threatened--not by Alexander or any of the cultpeople. I'm not afraid of what they can do to me or my body. The only way they can hurt me is to hurt my children, or anybody's children for that matter. That's why I would do anything to help a kid.

I wanted to help Shirley when you told me she had a kid, but there wasn't a damn thing I could do. And that's why I intercepted some other children that they were going to butcher. I'll stop at nothing to save them, Chris. Because I know what it's like to be the child waitingalone for someone to come to the rescue. I swear to God, Chris, as long as I'm alive, I'm gonna try to be that someone."

And for the first time I knew at least two things:the Hanky Man, even with his capacity for violence, was one of the good guys; and if he wouldn't back down from doing what was right, how could I?

Chapter 31

Woofie's Island

After a couple of years of treading dangerously close to suicide, two visits to the psychiatric hospital, numerous desperation phone calls, and dancing with the devil, the end was at last in sight forDonna.

"Dr. C." she began proudly yet cautiously, "I am finally one--or I think I am." She smiled sheepishly, aware suddenly of how silly her statement sounded. "I knew I had an appointment with you today, so I made a concerted effort to integrate Lucy, along with the few remaining child alters. May I read my journal entry to you? I kept it short and sweet."

When last I was aware of them, Lucy and her dear stuffed pet were sailing steadily off to the peaceful world of Woofie's Island. It seemed to take forever to arrive, as probably the trip symbolized the healing Journey with you, Dr. C., through therapy.

The island possesses brea1thtaking beauty the likes of which Lucy has never known: lush vegetation forms a thick green forest, majestic coconut palm trees rise like skyscrapers, a calm crystal-clear sea surrounds the island like a protective armor. Cool white sand, soft to the touch, greets the foamingsurf at the shoreline.

I am there to welcome Lucy, Woofie, and the few nameless child alters. As I observe the latter, two boys and a girl, I gain more insight into their identity.

They are fragments of Lucy. That is, they were created by Lucinda herself when the terror became too great for even her to bear alone. Hence they do not exist apart from Lucy and dare not leave her side. I am struck by their innocence and moved by their courage. Oh, Dr. C., they are just precious little children.

I never catch their eye, for they never look up from the ground. Yet they are completely aware of their surroundings, like deer upon the initial scent of an intruding man.

The children are ill at ease, it is as if they sense danger! For upon the distant waters tread the steps of a man whom the children are at once drawn to and terrified by. That man continues toward them in a steady, confident gait, yet without hurry. He walks upon the water as though it were frozen solid. But the warm gentle sea carries a man who loves the frightened children and seeks them no harm.

He calls to them from the shallow water off the shore; they are mesmerized by his voice and so draw near to him. I, too, am drawn to the gentle stranger. I feel as if I have always known him. I tell myself I am mistaken.

Without words, he directs us to form a circle, each of us joining hands with two others. His touch is soothing and radiates throughout the children until every trace of fear melts away into the water and is carried out to sea.

His eyes are soft and loving as he calls the children even closer to him. At last, the man speaks:

"Do not fear my dear children, for I am with you.

You are brave and loyal and pleasing to God, who is your true father now. You have served Donna well and protected her from great pain and suffering. Now it is time for you to rest. Come to me and I will remove your sorrow. Come to me and I will dry your tears. Come to me, sweet children, and I will make you whole!"

As though choreographed, we fall as one into the shallow tide, baptized by the love of the kind stranger. I surface first. And before I could think to tend to the children, I knew that I need look no more for them. For they were within me! They were at last one with me, and I with them! I am whole at last!

The gentle stranger holds me and whispers that he will never leave nor forsake me. I know to trust him immediately. Smiling, I turn from him, preparing to head to the shore, with full knowledge that the stranger will return soon. But he calls after me and asks, "Donna, have you forgotten?"

Embarrassed but not sure why, I turn around and ask, "What have I forgotten?"

He removes a soaking wet Woofie from the water and suggests, "Lucy would want you to care for him." After all, this is his island!

At this point I hadn't yet realized the implications of being whole--my dear Lucy and I were one at last! And I know by now the first thing you'll ask me, Dr. C: "How do you feel about that, Donna?"

Well, I feel a variety of emotions to be sure, but they seem to fall into two basic categories-- triumph and fear. I am so relieved to finally find peace and to know, to really know that I am whole at last. No more lost time, no more embarrassing realizations about things I've done, no more nightmares to torment me in my sleep. I'm grateful to God for the strength to carry me through what has felt like a never-ending process. And I'm thankful to you, too, Dr. C., for your willingness to accompany me on my Journey.

In fact, I'm gonna stop reading from the journal long enough to give you something to expresses a small token of my appreciation for what you've done and meant to me.

*   *   *

Donna brought her typical matching purse on this day, but also had an additional tan bag with a variety of painted fruit upon it. She reached into the bag and presented me with a gift--a maroon Bible, with both the New International Version (NIV) and the King James Version (KJV) side by side. Inside the front cover read the following inscription:

> *When you came into my life, you touched me with your care, and healed me with your love.*
>
> *Through it all,*
>
> *I saw God's love in you--*
>
> *His compassion,*

His patience

and His faithfulness.

--Donna

I was very touched by the gift and the dedication. I was also pleased to note that it was written all in the same handwriting. I still use that Bible today.

But before I could return any sentiment of my own, Donna returned to the journal entry.

> *Dr. C., the second category of emotions to reckon with fear, seems as alive as ever. I feel foolish asking this, but where do I go from here? What do I do? How do former multiples act when they are frightened? Where do they take refuge? Do I really have the coping tools necessary to live a normal life from here? What is normal, anyway?*
>
> *I don't mean to be negative or sound ungrateful, I just feel a bit overwhelmed right now with the responsibility of being happy resting upon my own shoulders now. The past is over; I no longer have the luxury of blaming my parents or my childhood for any current misery. I can't even blame Peter. It's my job to be happy from here on, and Dr. C., I don't know if I'm up to it.*
>
> *You wouldn't be opposed to my creating a few new alters here and there if I needed to? Would you?*

She must have looked up long enough to witness my jaw drop to the floor. Again, before I could address her question, she smiled and confessed, "Kidding, but I had you, didn't I?"

"Yeah, you had me, all right. I must hand it to you. It's great to see you smile and laugh, even if it is atmy expense. But I gather the fear part is real, isn'tit?"

A nod and somber expression replaced the smile.

"Well, let me respond by first saying, congratulations! What you have accomplished over the past couple of years is extraordinary. It's a testament to your courage and your faith. I am so very proud of you."

Her round face gave way to an uncontrollable all-encompassing smile. She held that position silently for what appeared to be thirty seconds. She was at last triumphant and capable of absorbing my praise--sentiments, as Lucy expressed earlier, that she was unaccustomed to hearing in her disastrous childhood. And now she reveled in them like the child soaking up applause at a piano recital. I played the proud parent, rising to my feet andapplauding wildly!

That moment of victory was ours to share, if only for a while. For soon it passed, like celebrations invariably do, to fade into a here-and-now concern over reality.

"The fear is completely normal and understandable. Truthfully, I had never anticipated what comes after integration, either. You are my first client to get there. And now that you claim to be finished with your past, it's a matter of doing life like any other healthy person would--one day at a time. You deal with whatever comes your way by experiencing and expressing the appropriate feelings and without switching to someone else."

"More than that, you take with you the confidence that whatever lies in store, Donna, you have the capacity to face it. You are more than a survivor. You are the victor! And wherever you choose to aim your life from here, I expect that you'll be a success. God will always accompany you on your journey--do not lose sight of that."

"I won't, don't worry. I understand what you're saying, and I suppose you've told me all of it before, but it doesn't hurt to hear it again, I know. One more thing I have to ask. I hope you don't mind, but may I have a hug?"

I held Donna tightly, wanting to communicate not only pride and affection, but perhaps a deep sadness as we both knew that the end of our relationship might be drawing near.

That was not the last session with Donna (nor did I intend her to leave so soon after integrating), but we have had surprisingly few sessions over the past four or five years. Ironically, whenever she does return for treatment, she does so to gain a little more perspective and insight into her relationship issues--the very same reason she initiated therapy with me in the first place.

She crosses my mind often, and of course the telling of her story makes it come to life all over again for me: the horror of her childhood, the struggle with Lucinda, and the triumph of her spirit. In retrospect, I know the healing journey that Donna and I traversed together was as much a gift for the therapist as it was for the client.

And I thank God for the privilege of having taken that Journey.

Chapter 32

Shirley's Vision

While I wouldn't reveal to Shirley the particulars of my meeting with Charles the previous weekend, I reluctantly shared that he would be of no use to her. I was no longer willing to enlist the help of a man with such a propensity for violence. Predictably, the information proved devastating to her.

The cult, if one could trust all the information I had received so far, was having its way with both of us. And as predicted, therapy was useful for little more than attempting to uncover the latest in a series of abusive incidents directed at punishing and controlling Shirley.

She never wavered from her original style of presenting weird symptoms, which led invariably to the unveiling of yet another unresolved incident. Now, however, the reported incidents no longer involved her childhood; they were all from the past week or two. At least we could revel in the knowledge that she had made peace with her childhood. That accomplishment no longer seemed like much in the midst of our hopelessness, but it was all we had.

As gruesome as her decades-old memories, these new tales required little more than remembering and grieving. For example, she put pieces together while under hypnosis, of watching a nine-year-old boy's eye being gouged out by a hammer's claw. The justification? To teach all thechildren a lesson in obedience and especially secrecy. Naturally, a cult surgeon would do the repair work, and the outside world would hear only of some sort of unfortunateaccident.

Shirley related that they were now toying with her daughter, deliberately inducing posthypnoticsuggestions that the nine-year-old sleep soundly past her clock's morning alarm. Shirley cried in frustration, claimingto have to carry her daughter half-asleep into their car, shoes, and socks still in hand.

The cult messages often contained threats to Shirley's and my well-being. We were at the group's mercy, and I didn't want to treat her any longer. I was a whipped pup, tasting defeat in every session. But terminating her would be the worst move I could make and would likely result in her suicide. Self-destruction had always been Shirley's way out-- if things ever became unbearable, she could always die. Somewhere her belief system included the notion that no hell in the afterlife could ever compete with that of the life she had already endured. I could hardly dispute her contention.

Yet, Shirley continued to persevere in treatment, hoping that something would click and release her from the relentless pursuit of the cult. That epiphany occurred during a Friday morning session a full two and a half years after Shirley's and my first appointment. I honestly don't remember the exact conversation that led to the moment of truth. But as for the revelation itself, I'll never forget it.

We were discussing some absurd form of escape from the cult, like relocation to another area of the country or such. Neither one of us was buying the concept when abruptly if not casually, Shirley interrupted me with a quiet declaration: "God just spoke to me. He gave me a vision."

"A vision'?" I echoed.

"Yes. I'm lying on top of an altar, fastened by my hands and ankles. People are all around the altar, with my father standing at the opposite end, you know, where my feet are hanging off the edge."

"Are you a child or an adult?"

"Not a child. I'm me, just as I am now. Anyway, my father has a dagger in his right hand and is preparing to sacrifice me. It's a night of a full moon, and of course some type of sacrifice must be made. I am that sacrifice, bringing special pleasure to the group members."

"Why would your death bring special pleasure to them?"

"Because I am believed to be a traitor. I've never developed into what they had in mind for me. They worry that I'm trying to leave the group or else that I'm telling you things that I shouldn't. No one serves as a better sacrifice than a dissenter to the group. Anyway, the vision doesn't end there. My father is to sacrifice me, and for some reason, he doesn't do it. He tells the group to release me, and I walk away completely unharmed."

She paused and shrugged as if that was the entire story.

"Is that the whole vision?" I was immediately aware that Shirley's spontaneous 'vision' prompted reminders of a Biblical story, where Abraham was prevented from sacrificing his son, Isaac.

Looking back at me incredulously, Shirley answered, "Yep, that's it. I'm gonna get out after all." It seemed so simple to her. No joy, no excitement, no sense of awe.

I needed to inquire further, maybe because it wasn't all that simple to me. I summarized our interaction, then said, "You don't know why or what else happens; you only know that you're out. Out for good?" I asked, "or just for that episode?"

"No, I'm out. I will be out for good. Forever. That's it."

"When?"

"I don't know. That was the whole vision. That's all I got."

"I don't mean to discredit you or to sound skeptical, Shirley, but you're certain that the vision was from God? Has this ever happened to you before?" I was sounding more like a prosecuting attorney than a therapist, but this was far too important to dismiss. Maybe I was only protecting myself from believing in something that might disappoint me later.

"I never had anything like it before, Chris, so I have nothing to compare it to. But I know that it most certainly was from God. It's His way of promising me that I will be released safely from the group. As far as when."

"She shrugged, frowning, probably disappointed that I wasn't more enthusiastic.

For all intents and purposes, that was our session. The woman had endured forty-plus years of severe torture and domination of every aspect of her life, then suddenly God supposedly contacts her with a less-than-complete message of hope and escape from the cult. If the vision had really come from God, why hadn't Shirley's reaction been more extreme? Certainly, some type of emotion would be in order, in what could arguably be the most important moment of her life.

How could this be God's inspiration? Where was Moses' burning bush? Or St. Paul's bright light on the road to Damascus? Was this really some type of hallucination on Shirley's part, or just a fantasy that she embellished to escape the ravages of a clinical depression?

But this was Shirley, not an alter. And if I hadn't learned it by now, it was one more lesson in how she seemed to operate within a reality different from that of the rest of us. The rules that governed everybody else didn't seem to apply to Shirley. Time and again she had taught me to believe in her when her presentations appeared less than credible. In reviewing the journey we'd taken together to this point, I could only reaffirm that Shirley wasn't inclined to lie, exaggerate, or deliberately steer us down errant pathways. As far as I could detect, she wasn't psychotic or wrought with hallucinations or delusional beliefs. I didn't have an explanation for what had happened to her that morning. Not at that point.

I continued to take Shirley with me, as I often did, throughout the day in my thoughts. Another jigsaw puzzle with too few pieces. Somewhere in the course of the afternoon, I stumbled upon my own hypocrisy. Didn't I claim to have heard the voice of God in California in a less- than-dramatic fashion? Didn't I report a clear, convincing, and life-changing message from God prior to my abnormal psychology lab class? Wasn't that the reason I came to Florida in the first place? I had not witnessed parting seas, bright lights, or burning bushes in my experience, either--just a still, small voice!

I remembered the days of my extensive scripture memorization... how I had learned of *God's* majestic power and authority to direct the heavens and the earth with a single word. But the same almighty God is writtento speak at times in a still, small voice that can bedetected by those who belong to him.

How dare I limit God--or Shirley for that matter--with my skepticism? Why couldn't He deliver Shirley from the cult if He so willed?

As to the message, I had firsthand experience with patients as well as many in the Christian church who claimed to hear the voice of God--some while praying, others while sleeping, and still others while engaged in various and sundry activities in the secular realm. Were they all hallucinating--or merely deluding themselves--in believing that God spoke individually to the common man?

Of course, some individuals cite "God's will" to rationalize some behavior when they're really superimposing their own desires on the Almighty's. But was everyone who claimed to hear from God guilty of creating their own message and footnoting God to give it authority? Surely not, I concluded, well aware that this category of "delusional" people included yours truly.

No, it was possible for an individual to hear from God, and therefore even Shirley could potentially receive such a message. I would leave that option open as one possible explanation for her reported vision.

Besides, we would have the opportunity to assess the accuracy of her message in the coming days. If she had heard from God, we could expect her to be delivered at last from the hands of the enemy.

I had one doubt, though: The cult might hypnotize her into believing she had withdrawn, so she would once again be unaware of her participation. Wait a minute, I thought, couldn't I verify through Charles? Yes, that was it. Perhaps we could know after all.

And if the vision had not come from God, at least it had given her hope--something that had been missing for several months. And for now, that was a priceless treasure, one I would be happy to remind her of for weeks to come.

Wouldn't it be perfect justice if Shirley's deliverer from ıtan's grasp was not me, the therapist; nor Charles, the government; but God, the conqueror of evil? The thought of God's intervention filled me with excitement and anticipation.

Were my hopes dangerously high, or was I exercising the faith that I had been taught could move mountains? The answer took longer than either of us anticipated. But at last, we had the answer.

Chapter 33

The Deliverance

I sneaked into the nightclub and crouched behind the disk jockey's booth. I looked around the room for Lauraand dug into my pocket for her engagement ring. Clutching the small velvet box tightly, I gave the kid the go-ahead. As planned, he cleared the dance floor, and one of the waitresses set a wooden bistro chair in the center. I grinned, watching Laura's reaction when the DJ called out her name and asked her to comeforward.

Her hand flew to her mouth, and she reluctantly let herself be pushed by her girlfriends to the chair. As she sat down, a spotlight blinked on and the club's lights were dimmed more than they already were.

Time for my performance. I spoke into the DJ's microphone, and my plea for her hand in marriage filled the club. Laura sat in shock as I read a corny poem--one I had written myself--promising her a lifetime of bliss… or at least an opportunity to watch *Knot's Landing* on Thursdays. I rounded the disk jockey's booth and watched my beloved's jaw drop. Laura's friends, my co-conspirators, were laughing and shrieking as I dropped to one knee.

Virtually everyone who knew Laura was on hand to witness my proposal of marriage to her. We danced, accepted champagne and congratulations, then drove off in a limousine.

Several nights later, she called, still aglow from visions of matrimony dancing in her head. "Hi, Sweetie," she gushed.

"Been thinking about you all afternoon, especially after hearing about our engagement on the radio."

"What?" I must have depleted all my eloquence on my patients that day.

"Yeah. A disc jockey from a Youngstown radiostation was in the crowd the night you proposed. He told everyone about how romantic you were!"

"Yeah, that's me, Mr. Romance," I offered sarcastically, aware that my RQ (romance quotient)was normally on the same level as oatmeal.

"So, tell me about your day," she asked.

"It was fine. And yours?"

"No. Not 'fine.' Tell me about your day. I want to know about it. Share it with me, please!"

"Honey, I'm in therapy all day. That's my day. What do you want to know?"

"I don't know. Something! Anything! What kind of patients do you treat? How do you help them? What happens in your sessions?"

"You're serious, aren't you? Okay, let's see. Well, I had a woman accuse her husband of all kinds of weird things, which he denied. I didn't know whether he was a pathological liar or if she was delusional."

"Did you figure it out?"

"Yeah, when she accused him of breaking into her room, sneaking into the bathroom, and kidnapping her dentures.
Then he reportedly used a file to whittle them down sothey wouldn't fit her anymore."

Laura laughed. "Tell me more."

"All right, I had a ten-year-old who couldn't wait to

become an adult, so he could watch all the horror movies he wanted, play video games until he dropped, and of course, become a cop."

"That's cute," she cooed. "What did you tell him?" "Well, I told him that adults call those the Big Three. They're basically what all adults do after the kids go to bed."

"More."

"I had a woman with poor self-esteem whom I tested for depression. When I told her that her symptoms didn't qualify her for clinical depression, she said, 'That figures, I can't do anything right.'"

"Next was an elderly blind woman whom I've enjoyed a lot of success with. She thinks the world of me, but she's so proper, I couldn't resist teasing her."

"What did you do?"

"I told her, 'Mary, didn't you get the message I left for you? Today is naked Wednesday. Everyone in the waiting room, including myself, is totally naked except you!' She just smiled, blushed, and said, 'Oh, Doctor.' So… are you glad you asked?"

"Well, it beats 'Fine, how was your day?'"

"Wait," I said, remembering. "There *was* something significant in my day. I had a lady--a cult survivor--who claims I've been chosen to help a lot of people hurt by the cult. She told me never to lose my faith again and that a lot of temptation is ahead for me."

"Chosen? By whom?"

"I asked her the same thing. She said both sides--good and evil. The latter, she claims, wants me to join them. As much as it sounds like the ramblings of a crazy woman, I've heard a lot of it before from my contact." Suddenly I remembered Charles's no-talking-on-the-phone rule and froze over like Lake Erie in January. "It just struck me as weird, that's all."

Then speaking as if someone might be listening, I concluded, "It was probably nothing, really. So, what did your folks say about the engagement?"

The message on the office answering machine was typically Shirley. "Chris, hi. Please meet me at the courthouse for tomorrow's session, okay? Thanks."

The Sarasota County Courthouse has a small, pleasant courtyard where couples get married and where employees eat lunch at small tables. On this winter's day, Shirley sat alone, waiting, a small mound of her generic-cigarette butts piled on the ground near her feet. While this indicated anxiety, her eyes seemed vacant.

Barely acknowledging my presence, she stared past me and asked, "Can we get started? I've got a lot to tell you."
"Sure. Where do we begin?"

She shrugged, and I watched her face collapse into helplessness. I wouldn't allow her to fall any further. I decided to take charge of the session.

"Somewhere inside you is a place we need to go," I said. "Let me ask you to close your eyes, focus, and take us to that place. Relax. It's okay now."

The wind picked up, stirring the dirt about the courtyard and adding an ominous flavor to an already overcast morning. A pair of bespectacled young men sporting double-breasted suits and briefcases hustled noisily into the courthouse. Shirley never opened an eye, and I took that to mean that her concentration was already intact.

A moment later, her eyes flew open, as if she had been

rtled by an inner visualization. This time she appeared fully
esent and ready to talk.

"No need to ask who I am," she began. "We no longer
have separate identities. We need to sort out the pieces of an
experience from this past weekend. We have not givenany
thought to this since it happened."

She cleared her throat. "We met Saturday night, under
the full moon--a significant day in satanic worship. Tome, the
celebration had a different feel to it. They assigned my usual
tasks--preparation of the altar and sterilization of the dagger-
-to someone else. Everyone ignored me. I didn't know why,
but I knew it wasn't good. I felt very *anxious,* to use one of
your words.

"Then the psychiatrist we told you about took us aside
and spoke in that hypnotic drone of his. We fell into a trance
not nearly as deep as we usually go when hearing his voice.
Maybe because we fought it, I don't know. Yeah,that was why.
We were really on guard that night because we knew
something was terribly wrong. Terribly wrong," she repeated,
the way people do when drifting off into a sound sleep.

Shirley closed her eyes for barely a second, then warily
turned her head to the right and left. I was about to begin an
inquiry when she resumed her account.

"Yes, we have switched again. But don't worry. We are
nothing more than temporary. After we tell you the story, we
will no longer be separate. There will be no need to integrate
us." She looked around again and asked, "It is safe to talk here,
isn't it?"

I attempted to reassure her, but she cut me off and
returned to her story.

"We were to be the sacrifice. This was our special night.

The psychiatrist told us that after serving the master since birth, laying down our lives would be a wonderful and joyous final act of dedication to him. He wasn't asking me--he was letting me know what had been decided. I could do the noble thing and volunteer or disgrace myself and my father by resisting the sacrifice.

"We tried not to feel hopeless--or feel anything, for that matter. We knew we didn't have the strength to fight anymore. Still, as much as we hate our father we didn't want to see him exalted in our death. But we just kept our mouth shut and waited, prepared to comply reluctantly. Some part of us remembered how we felt as a child when we knew that we were to be raped by our father. We just wanted it to happen so we could get it over with. But we didn't want it to happen. Do you know what I mean? We never wanted him to touch us! We hated it!"

I knew this was not merely a rhetorical question. Shirley needed some input and reassurance. I echoed her sentiments with a twist: "For you, anticipating the abusive event, whether sexual as a child, or what was in store for you Saturday night, was about as bad as going through it."

"Yeah, if not worse." She didn't acknowledge whether or not she thought I understood, but the fact that she continued with her memory of Saturday night suggested that she felt heard. "I sat alone on a stone and stared at the blazing fire that some of the men were perfecting in the clearing. For the first time I felt a sense of relief because I knew it would be over soon."

That unnamed alter, like her predecessor, gave way to yet another one at this point. She lifted her head with a meek, apologetic look upon her weary face.

"A woman approached us," she continued. "Probably in her late seventies. She had never said or done anything mean to us, but we never felt like we had the right to talk to her because she is a woman of great means and influence. Before her husband died last year, he was very prominent in local politics as well as in the group. She's been coming to the meetings alone."

Some noticeable facial tics and presumably another switch. But again, she picked up where she had left off, although in a somewhat deeper, more assertive voice. "The woman put her hand on our shoulders and said, 'I am fully aware of what is planned for you. But I am not long for this world, and quite frankly I don't really care to be. I believe I am ready to meet my master tonight. Would you allow me to take your place?' We started to respond, but she didn't allow us to speak. 'I will see to it that you are released tonight from the group. I'm aware that this is what you really want. And with the power I wield here, no one can dishonor my dying wish to take your place as the sacrifice tonight. Nor can they interfere with your release from the group.

They are not to bother you or interfere with your life from this point. You are free to go now!"

Shirley reported being pulled aside one more time by the group shrink, who hooked her up to electrodes. I gathered his intent was to promote confusion and significant amnesia. I watched her face contort in painful recollection of the electric shock. She repeated a couple of warnings issued her by this man in case she should consider opening her mouth about the group.

She did not stick around for the sacrifice or have the opportunity to thank the woman. There was no final and official dismissal, nor a run-in with her father. According to Shirley and her legion of alter helpers, she was released. She ran through the woods until she located her car.

Her account finished; I returned Shirley to her hostess personality. As always, I accepted her accountand cautiously rejoiced with her. But had she truly been released by the cult family that had literally owned her since the late 1940s? I wanted very much to believe that she had walked away from the evil underworld, without a consequence to pay from this point on.

Shirley and I said farewell, then I made my way back to my office. I delivered a desperate prayer, pleading with God to make this dream a reality. Moments later, it hitme: Shirley's vision! That day in my office she said she had been promised deliverance. And while her vision never forecast a benevolent older woman as the savior, Shirley was to be sacrificed on the evening of her salvation. If all this was true, her prophecy had cometrue!

I wanted to believe this, but getting my hopes up to high about anything opened me to disappointment and defeat. I was more likely to choose a cautious wait-and-see approach to Shirley's supposed deliverance.

I turned my attention to the elderly widow. "The kind satanist" was an oxymoron. In John 15:13, Jesus claimed that "greater love had no man than this, that he lay down his life for his friends." Could such a woman be capable of love? And Shirley was no friend to the widow. She was a nobody in the group, unless a despised defector. Why would this woman intervene for her?

The psychologist in me concluded that she was a depressed widow, incapable of negotiating life without her late husband. Being sacrificed presented her with an easy way out. Meanwhile, the man of faith within me maintained another contention: God had promised Shirley deliverance. And the great Creator of the universe had His time, place, and person appointed to accomplish His purposes!

It wasn't military force, government intelligence, or psychological warfare that sprang Shirley from the jaws of evil. Rather, it was the manifestation of God's love and sacrifice through the most unlikely of heroines.

And wasn't her sacrifice a powerful metaphor for God's loving gift of Jesus? Oh, how I wanted this to be true. For Shirley's sake, for God's sake, and for mine.

Chapter 34

Keeping the Faith

It had been far too long since I'd seen Richard and considering all that I had to share with him, a one-hour lunch at Pizza Hut would hardly suffice. But we would do our best, as he was in town only for a one-dayconference at Sarasota Memorial Hospital.

"I finally found your diagnosis in the DSM-4,"he told me, making his way to the all-you-can-eatbuffet.

"Oh, yeah?" I asked, piling several slices of the "thin and crispy" variety (to maintain the illusion that I was not overeating) on my plate.

"Yeah, it's called *erotomania* or *de Clerembault's Syndrome--the* delusion that a celebrity is in love with you. I think you got the worst form of it."

"Are you telling me that the anonymous valentine I got in fourth grade wasn't really from Sharon Stone?"

"You're hopeless," he said, laughing.

We settled into a far corner booth. Because of the time constraints, we talked around mouthfuls of pizza and salad. First Richard gave me a rundown of his life. His eldest, Joshua, would be leaving for the University of Michigan. "I couldn't be more proud of him. The other two, well, I haven't seen them at all."

He quickly changed the subject. "I've been doing some dating. Well, actually not dating. I'm sleeping with three different women--Su is from Japan, Meta is South African,

Angelina is Mexican."

"Richard's World Tour? Why three?"

He grinned sheepishly. "I don't know. Maybe because I can."

"Mind if I take my turn at a diagnosis?" His nod afforded me the go-ahead. "Sounds to me like you are terribly wounded by the ugliness of the divorce and the custody battle. You may need to forgive me for this, but I think you're currently doing at least three things now, Romeo. First, you're afraid to be hurt, so you're avoiding intimacy, keeping all three women at arm's length. Second, you're also pumping up the wounded ego, damaged in the divorce. And worst of all, I think you're punishing these women for crimes committed by your ex-wife. Do you likeany of these women?"

"Yeah, well, Meta is almost too good to be true.But, uh, she is a woman and *so--* ""--you can't trust her?"

"Right. I'll never let another woman do to me whatmy ex-wife did. I'd rather settle for the carnal pleasures of boinking women I don't care about."

"I realize I'm overstepping my boundaries as your buddy and not your shrink, but 'settling' is what you're doing. You deserve better, and so do these women. Every woman is not your ex-wife, Richard. Every day you hold on to your hatred is another day that you have allowed herto steal a page off the calendar of your life."

"How the hell do you forgive someone who stealstwo precious children away from you," he snapped.

"I don't ever intend to make light of your suffering. I can't even fathom what it would be like to be cut off from my children. I'm sure it's devastating. My point is that letting go of the hatred lets *you* off the hook, not her. Forgiveness never condones the behavior that wounded you; it only sets you free to go forward and live again. Listen, sorry to be so pastoral. You know us Christians--if we don't preach forgiveness, we forfeit our membership cards."

"No need to apologize, I can handle a little preaching from time to time. Just don't pass around an offering plate."

My fondness for Richard rose a couple of notches. He was brave enough to expose some vulnerable areas to a male friend. But even more impressive, the man subjected himself to my unsolicited advice without blowing a gasket.

Moreover, he could have trumped me with his credentials: He had gone to better schools and was an oft-published academician. Yet he digested my words along with the carbohydrates. I admired him for that.

"Okay. I'm off the damned hot seat. You're up, Cortman."

"Fair enough. Pick a topic," said I to my worthy inquisitor.

"Ohio."

"We're getting married in October. I hope you will come to the ceremony."

"Congratulations! I'm speechless! I thought you'd never do it. Much happiness to you both!"

"Thanks, Richard. I appreciate the warm sentiments, especially from you. You're not exactly the poster boy for matrimonial well-wishes."

I motioned for him to hit the pizza bar for one more round of self-indulgence. As we filled our plates, I described Shirley's successful resolution of her childhood issues, her vision, and reported emergence from the cult.

"How do you know she's really out?" heasked, following

me back to our booth.

"I don't. I only know what she tells me."

"Where do you come up with this stuff, Cortman?"he inquired while scarfing down some deep-dish pepperoni.

"Don't use up your skepticism yet," I warned, then shared the Hanky Man's involvement in my life,including our meeting at McDonald's.

Richard's face paled, and he set down the wedge ofpie that was almost in his mouth. 'A tongue? Holy McShit! How did you know it was a woman's tongue? Wait, I know, it was still wagging, wasn't it?"

"Quit asking me how I know things are true," I said. "I don't know what's true. I never know. All I can tell you is what's happening in my life."

I was aware of how defensive and edgy I felt. Except for the few times I confided to Richard on the telephone, I had kept all the nightmarish experiences and gut-wrenching stories to myself for over two years. I needed him as my sounding board, a nonjudgmental confidant. His quizzing me wasn't helpful at all.

"Are you sure it's safe to bring her down here to marry?"

I'm not sure of anything," I said angrily. "But what am I supposed to do? Stop living my life?"

I swallowed hard and felt a surge of nausea overtake my stomach. The thought of Laura being hurt because of me...

I pushed my plate away and fought hard to contain my emotions. I felt as if the evil that had been snapping at me these months and years was about to tear me apart.

I'm sure Richard could see my upset; concern darkened his face, and for once, my brilliant friend was speechless. He pushed his plate to the side and leaned forward on his elbows.

"You know," he began softly, "our friendship has been as meaningful to me as it has to you. Although Jesus isn't part of my religious heritage, I have faith in God. I believe that the good Lord has His hand on us and will guide us through our dilemmas. Even so, if I were you, I'd get out of this mess quickly. Just let everyone knowyou're done dealing with the underworld. The first time someone starts to remember stuff about candles and black robes,you stop it right there." He moved his right hand in a chopping motion to emphasize his point.

"Tell your patients that they stay in the here-and-now, or you'll refer them to someone else who dealswith this shit." "And you'll take those referrals?" I interrupted.

Richard shrugged. "Sure, why not? I'm not afraid of the devil. I married her."

We laughed heartily, successfully completing ourtask of lightening the mood. But I needed to respond to his advice, even at the risk of reintroducing the tension to our conversation.

"Seriously, Richard, I can't walk away from this.I'll be doing this stuff for a while, I'm afraid. I may sound like I'm fostering some martyr complex, but I can't turn my back on my clients. What I'm doing to treat them feels like a calling. Why else would such a disproportionate number end up at my door?"

"Why indeed?" Richard asked mildly.

"No," I said, responding to his unasked question."I am not attempting to convince them that they underwent horrible experiences. I am not suggesting any of this to them. They are telling me."

Richard held up his hands. "I know that. And I'm sure

ninety-nine percent of your caseload do not tell you that they have been in cults or that they have demons in their refrigerators."

"True. Thank you for that. I just need to be faithful to my clients."

"But at any cost?"

"Don't push it," I wisecracked.

"Well, I admire your faith, stubbornness, or whatever the hell it is. And you know what I like best about my meetings with you?"

I shrugged, expecting something cute. "Hearing about amputated body parts, violent government agents, and satanic cults always puts my world in perspective. How can I help but be relieved to live my life? I'm so grateful to you for the new perspective, I'll even pick up the check."

He reached for the check, and I pushed it toward him. "I'm touched."

"Oh, no need for undue sentiment. It was my turn Anyway."

*   *   *

October 6 marked the ten-day countdown to the big wedding. That evening's air allowed me to take an evening beach run without wearing a shirt, and I hoped the unseasonably warm weather would continue through the month's end. I walked out on the sand and headed towardthe water through a thick fog that limited visibility to ten yards. I glanced at my watch--just after eight. On a whim, I decided to head south on the beach instead of my typical northern route.

With no moon to illuminate the night, I knew I was

opening myself to injury; sandcastles and craters created a jogger's minefield. But I needed the exercise, with all the stress in my life.

A figure loomed before me, and I slowed my pace. As I approached, it vanished. *Odd,* I thought, and assured myself it had been a light from the beachfront condos distortedin the fog. Or was it? Just as my anxiety lessened, I thought I saw it again, moving toward me... only to disappear again. *Is it real?* I wondered. It seemed like a ghost fading in and out of the fog.

I'm just spooked from all the horrible stories I'm hearing from my patients, I decided, and chuckled, remembering that Halloween was just around-the-corner and--- "Look out!" someone shouted.

I yelped and jumped aside, petrified. I turned to see a figure disappearing into the fog. My heart raced uncontrollably, and I thought I was having a heart attack. *Will I die here on the beach, just before my wedding?* What with the fog, no one would find me till the next morning. Or would I wash out to sea? God,no.

I turned around and headed home, picking up the pace, afraid I was being pursued. I tried to get a hold of myself, but I was coming undone. *To hell with the sandcastles, craters, and the cult, too, for that matter,* I thought. *I can't take this anymore.*

Mom and Dad's condominium was not a place I'd often sought advice, but that was where my car took me when I left the beach.

Dad answered the door wearing nothing but a sawed-off terrycloth bath towel and a smile. His belly--the result of retirement, not beer--greeted me before the rest of him did. "You don't look so good," he said, ushering me inside. "Are you okay?"

"Yeah, well, I guess. I just happened to be driving around and ended up here. Mom sleepin'?" We headed into the family room. Dad sank into his favorite chair, a power recliner that no one else is allowed to sit in. I took an overstuffed easy chair.

"You know your mother. By nine-thirty, she's comatose. Then around three-thirty in the morning she'll wake up worrying about you kids and praying for you till she falls back to sleep. Tomorrow night she'll do it all over again." He picked up the television remote and turned off an ESPN evening wrap up. "So, what's up?"

"I don't know. I'm not sure where to begin."

"What do you say when your patients tell you that?" His point well taken, I related the evening's events, reliving them in an attempt to validate my own feelings of terror and helplessness.

Maybe it was the act of sharing, or maybe it was the feeling of safety in my parents' home, but I could not hold back the emotion any longer. "I'm losing it, Dad! I think it's finally getting to me!"

Tears poured down my cheeks. I had not cried for many years, and I felt ashamed and embarrassed to be sobbing in front of the man I had worked all my life to impress. Part of me considered excusing myself to the bathroom or just getting up and leaving. But I didn't move an inch except to wave off the box of tissues Dad held out to me. The effective release of pent-up anxiety and terror felt good and necessary. For three years I had been storing a warehouse of secondhand trauma-- listening to the most gruesome stories imaginable, and they had worn me down like the soles of my running shoes.

Somewhere within, a little boy was content to empty years of weakness and vulnerabilities to his daddy, in a way he had never done before. That child didn't know how to label what he was feeling or how to define what he needed so much from his father. He only knew that it felt good to cry.

Daddies are supposed to make monsters go away. Daddies are the ones to reassure their little boys that everything will be all right, and daddies need to remind their sons of just how special they are. But my daddy didn't know how to do those things--maybe because his daddy died when he was just a kid himself.

But there was one thing my father didn't do that made a vast difference: He didn't leave--not when I was one of five children to feed and clothe, not when I needed a place to stay during my internship, and not now when I craved his comfort during my current crisis. My father's way to say "I love you" was by always beingthere.

And there he sat with me, without uttering a single word, offering tissues to the shrink. I think he knew somehow that I needed to vent and would recover myself if he just let the water flow. I'm sure he would have satup with me all night if that's what I needed.

But that wasn't necessary. My tears and his acceptance of them proved as cathartic to me as they appear to be to my clients. I regained my composure and excused myself to the kitchen for a glass of water.

As I returned to the living room, the man spoke. "Listen, Chris, I know I haven't heard even half of what you're experiencing, but I can see what this stuff is doing to you. Your mother and I are very concerned, andwe pray for you every day. I know what evil people are capable of, and truthfully,

I'm amazed you're holding up as well as you are.

"Anyway, I don't know why you have to treat cult refugees and involve the government and the underworld in your life. You have a fine practice and an excellent reputation. Whatever happened to treating people with normal problems, like wives who nag too much?"

I smiled for the first time that evening. Appreciating his efforts to lighten the mood, I concurred. "Yeah, those were the days."

But he hadn't fully made his point yet, so he reached for his intense look that always meant that he was readyto deliver an important message. "If I were in that situation, I'd get away from all those shady characters. But there is one catch." He punctuated his point with a raised index finger. "If the Lord has called you to do what you are doing--if you are in the center of His will--then you don't have to worry. He'll see you through."

"What if it's not that simple?" asked the once-prodigal son. "Remember Dan Saint's brother?", Nate Saint had gone as a missionary to Africa, where he was murdered by some locals. "Wasn't *he* doing what God called him to do?"

"Sure," my dad replied. "And after Nate died, more of his family went to live with the same people and impressed them with the love of God and led them all to the Lord. So, the first missionaries were doing God's will and were martyred for His cause."

"Somehow, Dad, that's not such a comforting story right now. But I understand what you're saying: I need to decide once and for all if this is what God has really called me to do. If it truly is, then I need to trust that and let go of my fear. If it isn't God's calling, then I need to simplify my life and close the door to all this cult stuff."

I felt my burden lighten. My father was exactlyright. The only way I was going to survive was to give the matter over to God.

At that moment my sleep-rumpled mother appeared in the family room. "Chris! I just woke up praying for you. Are you okay, honey?"

"Is it three-thirty already?" I joked. "Must be time to go home. I'm fine, Mom. Really. Go back to bed."

I hugged and kissed her before walking over to the sacred paternal throne. Reaching over to hug my father, I whispered in his ear. "Thanks Dad, for everything. You really helped me tonight. I love you."

"I love you, too, Son."

I'm not sure, but I may have seen tears forming in his eyes. And that expression somehow provided me with all the information I needed right then: My earthly father loved me. My heavenly father loved me. Everything was going to be all right.

Epilogue

Shirley's dream of accounting for her days without amnesia came true. As of this writing, years after the older woman's sacrifice to free Shirley, she has had no contact with or trouble from the cult members. This would seem like a happy ending, but this book is not fiction, and all is not well for my brave client.

Incredibly, she has been stricken with multiple sclerosis, an incurable, degenerative disease that attacks the nerve cells. Shirley never feels well and is often too weak to participate in the normal activities of daily living. Most difficult for her is coping with depression, a symptom that often accompanies the devastation of MS.

Admittedly, I am dumbfounded by the woman's misfortune. The accounts Shirley shared with me are as awful as any I have heard in my office. Needless to say, she and I find it most unfair that she championed the bizarre symptoms of Multiple Personality Disorder only to succumb to multiple sclerosis.

And yet, neither one of us has lost faith in the God that miraculously delivered her from the cult on the night she was to die. We can only humbly pray that the MS is also somehow a part of His plan for her.

I'd like to think that this book is also a part of God's purpose in bringing Shirley through all that she has suffered, that He may be glorified through the telling of her story.

Donna, as noted earlier, has all but disappeared from my life. My most recent contact with her--requesting permission to tell her story--revealed that she was still dating, crunching numbers, and functioning well.

Another person who underwent a profound transformation is my friend Dr. Richard Levine. He exchanged his bitterness for a South African bride and a new lease on life. Even after several years of marriage, Richard still describes her as "too good to be true." My mentor and buddy tired of the impact that managed care had on his private practice and, unfortunately for me, headed out west to return to academia. Though we maintain contact via phone calls and E-mail, it's never the same as hanging out with him. I don't know if he truly understands how his support, honesty, and wit helped to keep me grounded during the most difficult time of my life.

Charles Evans, the Hanky Man, has also disappeared from my life. He wisely decided that meeting with me was attracting too much attention and putting us both at risk. I often recall his warnings of government corruption, which remind me of the Biblical description of "spiritual wickedness in high places"(Ephesians 6:12).

But as far as Charles is concerned, there is no higher calling for him than to save an innocent child from being butchered by the cult. I gather that he will continue his efforts until the day he dies, which I hope and pray will come about as a result of natural causes. For better or worse no one contributed more to my comprehending the struggle between good and evil. Charles's external validation helped me immeasurably in understanding the clients who shared their horror stories with me.

I have now worked with twenty-three different clients who reported experiences in satanic cults. (Still, this represents only a small fraction of the number of clients I have treated in my thirteen years of private practice.) At least half of those twenty-three have been referred to me due to my reputation for working with people with dissociative disorders. The others appeared for reasons still unexplained. I'd like to think God has had a hand in that.

Shawn Fisher sent a postcard well over a year ago to proclaim that she has at last been 'healed' from Chronic Fatigue Syndrome. She felt well enough to deliver a baby girl last year and is happier than ever. Gregg has not yet fared as well, but he remains grateful and optimistic, possibly because he believes his daughter is a gift from God--maybe because she looks just like him.

After Laura and I were married, she had to enduresome unusual stressors for a young bride, from middle-of-the- night phone calls to conversing with1 me in the bathroom with the water running during the height of my paranoia, shortly after Charles found listening devices in myoffice. Through it all, she has decided that she'd prefer a life with these challenges to a life without me. I love her dearly for that decision.

As for Dad, I admit that while I've always loved him, I'm currently fonder of him than ever before. Lately he's far more supportive than critical and has proved to be a real go-to guy in a crunch. He even coached my softball team in the spring of 1997, leading us to a league championship. (Sadly, I've still never been contacted by the Yankees' organization.) At this stage in my life, I am delighted to be so close to my parents, both geographically and emotionally.

I am convinced My Heavenly Father is responsible for orchestrating the extraordinary events of this past decade of my life. I am in awe of His love, patience, and capacity for forgiving, despite my repeated shortcomings. More than ever,

I believe that God has a plan for my life (and everyone else's, for that matter) and I hope that sharing this story is a part of that plan.

I won't even try to imagine what He has in store for me next, but whatever it is I accede to His will.

* 9 7 8 4 9 0 2 8 3 7 3 8 4 *